KUDOS for the Original Edition

"*Logs, Wind and Sun* made us realize what is really possible. It opened up a whole new possibility of finding what we want in a piece of land. We thought that land with no power was out of the question. We can't thank you and your husband enough for writing the book! Our dream has gotten even better and is soon to become a reality!"   — THE LEVACKS

"I'm almost finished with the book now and had to email you to let you know that this book may be as close to the Bible as it gets…self-sufficiency, that is."
        — K. CRAWLEY

"Because this book is so much fun to read, you'll not notice how much you are learning about foundations, log settling, chinking, solar and wind power and so much more. The authors have liberally peppered the book with humorous stories about the adventures and experiences involved in building their home. I got a few odd looks from office-mates here when I laughed out loud at one of the escapades."
        — TRACY JOHNSTON, LOG HOME STORE

"Many people dream of getting back to nature and living self-sufficiently in a house built with their own hands. The Ewings show readers how to do just that in this account of how they built a log house and then powered it using sun and wind."
        — *LIBRARY JOURNAL*, DECEMBER 2002

"Whether you'd like to try your hand at building your own log home, or just want to get more in-depth information on the process of constructing a home from logs, this hands-on guide takes readers through every step of the process. From selecting land and purchasing logs to wiring and roofing, the authors draw on their own experience, and the challenges faced by others, when they built their log home in the Colorado Rockies."
        — *LOG HOMES ILLUSTRATED*, MARCH 2003

"This is just the type of how-to book would-be owners/builders are seeking. You'll want to hear how others have done it! Beautiful job and well-researched. This book will encourage others to consider building their own log home."
        — WILLIAM LASKO, LASKO SCHOOL OF LOG BUILDING

Crafting Log Homes
Solar Style

AN INSPIRING GUIDE TO SELF-SUFFICIENCY

Rex A. Ewing and LaVonne Ewing

PixyJack Press LLC

Crafting Log Homes Solar Style: An Inspiring Guide to Self-Sufficiency

Published by PixyJack Press, LLC PO Box 149, Masonville, CO 80541 USA

ISBN 13-digit: 978-0-9773724-4-7

9 8 7 6 5 4 3 2 1

Library of Congress Cataloging-in-Publication Data
Ewing, Rex A.
Crafting log homes solar style : an inspiring guide to self-sufficiency / Rex A. Ewing and LaVonne Ewing.
p. cm.
ISBN-13: 978-0-9773724-4-7
1. Log cabins--Design and construction. 2. Log cabins--Energy conservation. 3. Solar houses--Design and construction. 4. Wind power. I. Ewing, LaVonne. II. Ewing, Rex A. Logs wind and sun. III. Title.
TH4840.E93 2008
690'.8370472--dc22
2008003346

Printed in Canada on chlorine-free, 100% postconsumer recycled paper.

ENVIRONMENTAL BENEFITS: PixyJack Press saved the following resources by printing the pages of this book on chlorine-free paper made with 100% post-consumer waste: 36 trees, 25 million BTUs of energy, 3,164 pounds of greenhouse gases, 13,134 gallons of water, and 1,687 pounds of solid waste.

Main Front Cover photo: Scott & Tess Van Wagner's home. Small photo: Rex & LaVonne Ewing's home.
Back cover photos (top to bottom): Rex Ewing maneuvering a log; John Benshoof's home; and LaVonne Ewing peeling a log.
Design, photography and illustrations by LaVonne Ewing (unless noted otherwise).

DISCLAIMER: PixyJack Press, LLC and the authors assume no responsibility for personal injury, property damage, or loss from actions inspired by information in this book. Home construction and electrical wiring are inherently dangerous activities, and should be regarded as such. Always consult with your local building codes and the National Electric Code before building a dwelling, or installing and operating renewable energy systems. When in doubt, ask for advice; recommendations in this book are no substitute for the directives of equipment manufacturers and federal, state and local regulatory agencies.

To John and Gretchen,

and Roger and Glee

without whom neither this book—nor its authors—

would have been possible.

TABLE OF CONTENTS

continued

continued

FOREWORD

Fiction often reveals fact. Take the 1944 Sherlock Holmes movie *Pearl of Death*, where the detective declares: "Electricity. The high priest of false security." How prophetic that casual utterance seems more than 60 years later, for look at how we depend on this precious power. Plugged-in gadgets proliferate, most of them superfluous. We squander electricity as if it were generated magically inside the wall sockets that our appliances cling to like lampreys rather than many miles away at plants that burn exhaustible fuels. False security indeed!

A recent newspaper headline caught my eye: "High Winds Cause Power Failures." I'd seen similar stories for years and thought nothing of them, but this time, having just read about the spread of wind power, I wondered whether, if more people relied on it, the headline might have read: "High Winds Cause Power Surge." I imagined folks scurrying through their gust-rich homes, looking for every electrical appliance they own to see how many they could plug in at once, at no cost to them and no harm to the planet.

That playful thought never would have occurred to me before I met Rex and LaVonne Ewing at a log-home show in Denver. They were touting their new book, *Logs, Wind and Sun*, about building a handcrafted log home and using the sun and wind to generate electricity. It caught my eye more because of the log home aspect. Building your own log home is hard work, I reckoned, but electricity comes easy wherever it flows from.

Talking with Rex, I realized I had it backwards. Living off the grid is the real challenge. Log homes by now have moved well beyond slapdash cabins stacked by countercultural back-to-landers into today's housing mainstream. To many people, however, solar and wind power still seem one step up from gerbils scampering on a wheel in a cage.

What makes the two facets of this book so compatible is that many log-home owners build in rural, even remote locations, where electricity comes at a steep price. What's more, energy efficiency and conservation have become pillars of the Green Movement. Log homes seem suited for off-the-grid living because they are built of a natural, renewable resource and are proven energy efficient.

Some people regard log homes as trophies and status symbols, but they are the exception. Most log-home owners I've met over the past 20 years as the editor of two log-home magazines rarely go overboard because, first, they aren't the overboard kind and, second, log homes cost enough nowadays that the people buying them rarely can afford to indulge in extravagance.

For all the different sizes and styles of homes they choose, they share one trait: individualism. It's what drives some to want to build their log home themselves, a desire that Rex and LaVonne understand because it led them to build their own home and seek an alternative to the grasping grid. That attitude now underlies the Green Movement.

Plenty of people nowadays pay lip service to

going green, but Rex and LaVonne long ago put their money where their mouths are. They live green day in and day out, year after year. Doing so takes not only commitment, but also a great deal of learning about subjects the rest of us have little concern with. When Rex starts rhapsodizing about inverters, amps and photovoltaic thisses and thats, he sounds like television kid-show scientist Don "Mr. Wizard" Herbert.

Another TV show pops to mind, too: *Green Acres*. In the first-season episode "You Can't Plug In a 2 with a 6," Lisa tells Oliver "the fooz blew." He explains that for their generator to handle the power load, each electrical appliance has a rating from 1 (can opener) to 6 (washing machine). The total value of the items that Lisa plugs into the wall cannot exceed 7. Realizing she can't use the coffee pot (2) and refrigerator (6) at the same time, Lisa ends up melting the electric coffee pot on the stove while trying to make coffee.

It's an entertaining premise, but in a solar and wind home, you have to make these sort of calculations. You must be disciplined about turning off any electrical device you aren't actively using at the moment. Those who grew up with Depression-era parents remember their constant admonitions not to waste electricity. It isn't about sacrifice, though, so much as it is about adjusting to a new way of looking at appliances and seeing them for the energy hogs that many are.

If we had to chop down trees, haul home the wood and load it into a furnace to generate electricity to power our toys, we'd probably decide we could get along just as well without them, especially after we found ourselves brawling with neighbors as the local supply of trees dwindles.

What will work, ultimately, is what already works: sun and wind. All it takes is a change of attitude by people who consume energy. Forty gazil-lion solar panels might keep the Las Vegas strip aglow, but a more constructive attitude is questioning whether we should be generating electricity to light neon signs.

Renewability, sustainability, recyclability—these are all noble-sounding ideals, but they mask the greater problem: over-consumption. Ever since World War II, Americans have shown no restraint or ability to resist merchandisers of superfluous products and services. "If enough isn't enough," teacher Ram Dass observes, "then more won't be better." It's a lesson we all need to learn. Rex and LaVonne Ewing are happy to teach us.

The trial and error of establishing and maintaining their lifestyle taught the Ewings plenty. Recognizing that others might be more inclined to convert to alternative energy nowadays, they have updated their original book with recent advances in sun and wind power. Plus it recounts the true-life experiences of other off-gridders who live in log homes.

Not everyone who reads this book will wind up living in a log home. Those who do will benefit immeasurably from Rex and LaVonne's insights and inspiration. Those who don't can still benefit by becoming aware of what's involved in living self-sufficiently. However much you embrace this lifestyle, it requires very little sacrifice, mostly just forethought. Don't underestimate that quality, however. If preceding generations had looked ahead a little better, perhaps our predicament wouldn't be so critical. It isn't too late, fortunately. Homes powered by the sun and wind offer true security. That's a fact.

— *Roland Sweet*
MOUNT VERNON, VIRGINIA

PREFACE *to the* NEW EDITION

When *Logs, Wind and Sun* was first published in the fall of 2002, LaVonne and I had no way of knowing just how much it would change our lives. But the book, like the two-year log-home-building odyssey that spawned its creation, was a labor of love, and one should never be surprised if auspicious events spring from such impassioned endeavors. Looking back on it now it all seems like a logical chain of events. Of course we would go on to produce several more books on alternative and renewable energy (RE); certainly I would begin writing columns for *Log Homes Illustrated* and *Countryside* magazines; surely people would write to us from all around the world to let us know just how much our simple book touched their lives…

Like I said, we had no way of knowing.

And so we were more than a little sad to let *Logs, Wind and Sun* go out of print in early 2007, but it was something that had to be done. While the log home building section remains as timely (and as timeless) today as it was then, the renewable energy section had become dated by five years of technological advances from an industry that continues to grow at an exponential rate.

We could have simply updated the renewable energy section, of course, but since we had already produced two sperate books on solar and wind energy (*Power With Nature* and *Got Sun? Go Solar*) it seemed folly to cover the same ground again with the same exacting attention to detail.

Instead, we hit on a much better idea: we decided to cover the broad aspects of renewable energy in a succinct little primer designed to give any RE neophyte a tight handle on the subject without bogging him or her down in a quagmire of detail. The rest of the space we devoted to the real-life stories of others LaVonne and I have met who have, each in their own way, done what we have done. These stories are interesting because they're about real people, individuals who prove that there are as many ways to go about solar-and-wind log-home living as there are adventurous souls willing to give it a whirl. They're intriguing because every home comes with its own challenges and every future log-home dweller meets these challenges in a unique fashion—sometimes grandly, sometimes minimally, ofttimes ingeniously. But always in the way that works best for them.

The very words "log home" evoke a time-honored sense of freedom; they conjure up mental images of life in the bosom of nature beyond the reach of the tentacles of urbanization, where simplicity is demanded and being true to oneself is obligatory.

If that is what you are after, you're in good company.

— *Rex A. Ewing*
JANUARY 2008

PROLOGUE *to the* ORIGINAL EDITION:
LOGS, WIND & SUN
~ *the contagious dream* ~

Years ago, in a past that seems far more distant than it really is, I owned a small spread with a rich, verdant pasture, a hay field, and far more Thoroughbred horses than any man in his right mind ought to own. I was a rancher and a businessman—a manufacturer of nutritional supplements for horses. And I was a farmer.

My father, driven man that he was, took precious little delight in any of my childhood antics, but even after I was grown he enjoyed telling new acquaintances the dialog he and I used to have when I was four or five. "Rex," he'd say, way back when, "what're you gonna do when you grow up?"

I'd stand up straight as a rod (so he'd say), stick my lip out resolutely, and answer with a certainty that would make anyone believe I could fly if I so intended, "I'm gonna get $500 and be a mountain man."

Anyone who ever heard this story would laugh at the little boy in rolled-up Levis and red cowboy boots who seemed to know his mind so well. But not me. I was serious. I was serious then, and I was serious later, when I bought a small acreage and build an octagon log home and a small log guest house. It cost more than $500, but it was worth every penny. Then, as fate would have it, it was all whisked away to the four winds, and I returned again to the flat dusty plains of eastern Colorado.

There I raised horses, made supplements, wrote articles for horse magazines, and harvested hay. And fought back a yearning to return to the mountains. Finally, when I could fight it no longer, I bought more land than I ever thought I'd need in a place I rarely ever had the chance to go. But whenever I did get the chance, I'd head for the hills and enjoy a day or two of heaven. I built a small frame cabin that encouraged the faraway dreams I nurtured, and when I wasn't there I daydreamed of the wonderful things I would do if I were.

It wasn't until I met LaVonne, however, that I even dared to rekindle the long-held dream of a life far above the hay fields and horse pastures. There was so much to leave, it seemed, that I could never in a lifetime leave it all. But lifetimes, I've since learned, are far more expansive than the petty things that somehow seem to cling to the mind's coattails, demanding—though hardly deserving—constant attention.

Besides, the baler was getting moody, the hay swather was held together with good intentions and questionable welds, and the horse herd was in serious need of thinning.

And whenever LaVonne was alone, her eyes would drift to western mountains.

I knew what was going through her head.

She was dreaming about getting $500 and becoming a mountain woman…

Dreams; it always starts with dreams.

Every beautiful thing ever wrought by the hands of humankind began as a dream, growing of its own volition from formless and fluid places, where disparate things can exist without contradiction in impossible relationships to one another.

Dreaming is something we all do too little of in a tight-minded society where the rules simply must be followed, even though no one is quite certain why. Dreams are, after all, just intangible wisps of errant energy. How ironic, then, that dreams—most of which are never nurtured to fruition—are exactly what keeps the lid from blowing off the pressure cooker we call humanity. If we can entertain in our minds the possibility of better days and better places, then the rat race becomes a little less ratty, and the rays of tomorrow's sun can find a way through to brighten the gloomy environs we inhabit today.

If you are reading these words, it's because you are a dreamer. You dream of living where you don't, and doing things you've never done. Compelling as it is, it's a frightening thought. But so is life; it's a risky business. And yet you push on, regardless. You weren't born knowing how to run a chainsaw, set a log, or wire a solar module to a charge controller. But neither were you born knowing how to run a computer or thread your way through rush-hour traffic in a rolling steel cage at 100 feet per second. If you can do the one, you can do the other, as long as you hold tight to your dreams. The trick is in not letting your self-limiting notions hamstring your abilities.

This is a book for dreamers, it's true, but only those who are ready to cast their airy aspirations to the fertile earth and nurture the seeds with sweat and toil. You may end up doing all the work yourselves, or you may simply use this book as a guide for determining the best way for others to proceed. Whichever path you follow, once you make the commitment you're halfway there.

LaVonne and I created this book with one idea in mind: to write the book we wished we'd had before beginning our adventure into uncharted territory. And what an adventure it's been! I thought I knew a thing or two about this business before we set out on this latest foray into the unknown, but I was mistaken. If this book were a comprehensive personal memoir of the knowledge we've picked up in the past three years, it would not come close to fitting within these pages.

Though we unabashedly relate a number of personal experiences—the good, the bad, and the comical—throughout the book, *Logs, Wind and Sun* is certainly not a memoir. It's much better than that. It's a hands-on, dirt-under-your-fingernails guide to making your dreams a reality.

This won't be the only book you'll buy to help you through the journey ahead, but with enough common sense and practical knowledge it could be. It was written to be used by skilled people whose experience allows them to fill in the gaps, as well as those less steeped in the trades who want to know how it all goes together, and what to expect of the crews doing the actual work. We can't all be builders, plumbers, roofers, cement workers, solar and wind installers or electricians, but we can—and should—know enough about each of these facets of construction that we can direct those who are doing the work.

Logs, Wind and Sun was written and compiled in a logical, orderly fashion. For that reason, it can be used as a reference book. But it's more than that. I find writing to be too much fun to restrict myself to the same, plodding style used in all the boring text books I so despised in school. So, while this book was designed to be used, it was written to be read; to make learning a pleasure, and knowledge a joy.

This book covers all the major aspects of building a log home and making everything work together as a cohesive whole. By reading the sections on foundation and log work, you will know how to build a home log by log. You will also know what's hard and what's easy, and why. And, just in case you might feel left out in the woods all alone, you'll learn about many of the successes and foibles LaVonne and I have experienced, walking the same path you are about to set foot on.

Other areas are less comprehensive. Heating and water pumping are covered in a way that presents the systems you may want to consider—and those you definitely want to avoid—without actually telling you how to install any of them.

Plumbing is a can of worms we peek into from time to time, without giving any of the worms a chance to slither out. I know enough about plumbing to discourage anyone who isn't already a plumber from trying their hand at it. Just the same, plumbing issues unique to log homes are clearly addressed.

The point is, I don't drone on about things I know little or nothing about. It wouldn't be fair to you. No one knows everything about this business, and if they did, I'm sure they wouldn't be any fun at parties.

So take a breath and get ready for the adventure of a lifetime. By the time you finish your new home, you'll be satisfyingly amused at the person now reading these words because you will have grown in ways you never thought possible.

— *Rex A. Ewing*
SUMMER 2002

CHAPTER *1*

LOG HOME LIVING, SOLAR STYLE

Designing for Comfort and Energy Efficiency

Nobody packs up, heads for woods, and builds a log home far away from the nearest power line on a whim. We've all got some pretty good reasons. The nearly universal appeal of living in a handcrafted log home is easy enough to understand. There is something deeply and profoundly instinctual about the look and feel of natural logs; they hearken to the spirit in a way nothing else can. To gaze at a home solidly built with logs is to trigger within the psyche a sense of warmth and strength unrivaled by any other building material. The grain and texture and individuality of logs strikes within each of us a resonant chord of kinship with Nature; a kinship often restrained, but never defeated. A log home invites us, in whispered overtures, to seek the source of the natural rhythms that sough so melodically through our souls.

The desire to live off-the-grid, however, is not so universal in its urging. For some, it's an extension of our natural passion for self-reliance and simplicity; for others, it's simply the most cost-effective solution to a nagging problem. Most of us fall somewhere in the middle. We know people living within a stone's throw of a utility pole who nonetheless refuse to be hooked into the power grid. We admire their determination.

For LaVonne and I, it was probably cheaper to go with wind and solar than to tap into the neighbor's power line, 2,000 feet away. But we'll never know, because we never asked the power company what it would cost to run power to our new house. We figured we'd already given them enough money for one lifetime, and suffered through enough blackouts to last through eternity. It was time for something new.

In 1998 we didn't realize the serendipitous nature of our decision. We just thought it was a cool idea. We didn't know that log homes require far fewer natural resources to build than conventional homes, or that they are warmer in the winter and cooler in the summer. We only knew we wanted to build our own from the ground up, and live in it.

Nor did we know that every time a kilowatt hour of electricity is produced at the local (yet faraway) power plant, over 1.3 pounds of carbon dioxide is released into the atmosphere; or that, for every watt used in the home, over 3 watts are wasted getting it there. We just liked the idea of creating our own electricity.

We've both come a long way since then; this type of enterprise has a way of changing a person. We've learned a lot about the efficiency of logs, and the utter practicability of homegrown electricity. We've learned new skills and new ways to think about old problems. We've learned how to conserve when there is little, and how to better use whatever is in abundance. Best of all, we've learned that two people, working alone, can build a beautiful log home, power it with the wind and sun, and live in it as though it were a palace.

DESIGNING FOR COMFORT AND EFFICIENCY

Whenever I hear or read anything about the pyramids of Egypt, I marvel at the abilities of the people who created this planet's greatest monuments with crude copper tools, and techniques abandoned so long ago we can only guess at what they might have been. I find it especially ironic that we moderns, with all our fine steel and impressive horsepower, would be severely taken to task to reproduce what the ancients have already done.

I then look at the snugly interlaced walls of the log home LaVonne and I built, and I smile. It's good that some knowledge gets passed on.

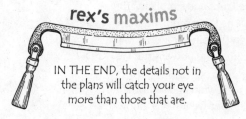

rex's maxims

IN THE END, the details not in the plans will catch your eye more than those that are.

I doubt that the first people who ever stacked logs together to build a house believed, in their wildest fits of fancy, that the building style they were initiating would prove more heat-efficient and less resource-depleting than the most prevalent building practices of their descendants thousands of years hence. But I'm sure they would have found the thought amusing.

Anyone who has ever had the pleasure of spending a winter living in a log home will tell you…log homes are warm and comfortable. The reason they are has very little to do with their intrinsic R-value; in fact, logs have a relatively low resistance to the passage of heat. But what logs *do* have is a tremendous amount of thermal mass. They soak up heat like a sponge, then radiate it back into the house as the inside temperature falls. (To learn more than you'll ever want to know about this subject, read *The Energy Performance of Log Homes*, prepared by the Log Home Council, and the Building Systems Council of the National Association of Home Builders; *www.loghomes.org*.)

This is very good news for people living back in the woods past the last utility pole, since it will take less energy to heat their log home than a similarly designed frame house in town. Since all central heating systems require *some* electricity to operate, the more heat-efficient the house, the more solar and wind energy will be left over for other things.

With proper design and placement of the house, the inherent resource-conserving properties of logs can be maximized to warm the house in winter and cool it in the summer. Although creating a comfortable living space is vitally important, it's not the only design issue that needs to be considered. You also want to protect your house from the elements, and provide for the extra non-living space you'll need for heating and electrical components. And, of course, you will want all the elements of your home to flow together into an aesthetically pleasing whole.

While most of these issues will resurface in pertinent places throughout the book, it will certainly be helpful to corral them all together now and examine each one in its turn.

PLACEMENT AND ORIENTATION OF THE HOUSE

For both warmth and solar exposure for your solar array, you will want to place your house in such a way that it has maximum access to midday sunshine. An east-west orientation of the long axis is best if you plan to roof-mount your solar array. Many people, however, prefer ground-mounted arrays.

Our solar array faces due south, with wind tower off to the east. *Photo: Ken Jessen*

Plan to put your house on high ground, rather than in a hollow or dip, if at all possible. Building on a hill, or a knoll, will greatly increase your chances of having usable wind energy, and it's much easier to plan for water drainage when the ground slopes away from your house in all directions. Besides, you'll have a better view.

You should also design your foundation so there is plenty of room between the ground and your first course of logs. The building inspector may let you get by with 6 inches, but plan for a bare minimum of 12 inches, and more if you live in a particularly rainy area. It's a thousand times easier to replace a piece of rotted lap siding than it is to replace a rotted log.

PASSIVE SOLAR: MAKING THE MOST OF THE SUN

Many of the old log homes you see back in the woods are little more than fortresses, with tight, economic floor plans, low-pitched roofs, and conspicuously few windows, all barely big enough to aim a rifle through. They were built back in the days when windows were considered to be a necessary—but barely tolerable—source of heat loss. These old homes were well designed to conserve any heat produced within the walls, but woefully deficient at allowing in heat from the outside.

The advent of efficient double- and triple-glazed windows has changed that myopic view of home design. Realizing the potential of free solar heat in the winter, most homes today—outside of those built in cheesy developments—take ample advantage of the sun's gifts. Log home builders have followed suit. Prow-

---

Window Ratings

Unlike the old days when windows consisted of one or two panes of untreated glass, there are now numerous glazing options, including windows coated with various metallic oxides, with the spaces between filled with sluggish, inert gases such as argon or krypton. These are all good developments, even if they can be a little confusing. Fortunately, when it comes to choosing the energy-conserving performance of various types of glazing, it all boils down to just two factors you need to consider: the U-factor, which is a measure of a window's heat emissivity (low-E, for instance, equals a low U-factor, which in turn means better heat retention inside the structure); and the solar heat gain, which is the amount of solar radiation permitted to pass through a window from the outside. Thus on the south side of a house in a cold or temperate climate you would want low-E windows with a high solar gain, while on the west side of the same house you should consider using low-E, low solar-gain windows, to block the incoming radiation during hot summer afternoons, while retaining heat through the winter night. For a wealth of information, visit Efficient Windows Collaborative at: *www.efficientwindows.org*.

---

like projections, with giant windows set between towering support posts, adorn the southern faces of many modern log homes.

This is all well and good, but like everything else, it's possible to get carried away. Too much glass will certainly keep a house warm on sunny winter days, but it will also allow an excess of heat leakage at night, or when the weather turns cloudy. You should strive for a balance. Design your house to allow ample sunshine on the south side, with as few doors and windows as possible on the north. Large windows, glass doors, and dormer (or gable end) windows that follow the contour of the roof all allow plenty of sunshine while enhancing the home's appearance.

If winter is a long, cold ordeal where you are planning to build, consider using triple-glazed, or super-insulated windows. They allow as much light to enter as conventional double-glazed window, but will retain appreciably more heat when the sun sets. Insulated window coverings are also helpful for nighttime heat retention.

You might want to consider tile floors for rooms with large south-facing windows. Tile floors—like log walls—can add to a home's comfort levels, by absorbing solar radiation during the day, and releasing it back at night. Nor is tile adversely affected by sunlight; it won't fade like wood or carpeting.

Big eaves are a must for log homes. They keep direct sunlight from hitting the windows in the warmer months as well as protecting the logs from rain and snow. Big eaves are especially important for keeping moisture off the log ends that stick out past the walls. As a general rule, the eaves should extend at least one foot past the log ends, for each 8 feet of vertical wall height.

> ## Light Tubes
>
> If you want natural lighting, but don't necessarily have a burning desire to see the sky overhead, light tubes are a great alternative to skylights. A transparent hemispherical dome collects and reflects light through a tube filled with highly reflective material that disperses light in all directions before it reaches the diffuser at the end of the tunnel. The result is an amazingly bright natural light, even on cloudy days. And unlike skylights that require a considerable amount of carpentry and finish work, light tubes are no more difficult to install than a roof vent. To learn more, check out *www.solatube.com*.

What about cooling? Standard air conditioning is far too power-hungry for a home powered by solar and wind-generated electricity. Fortunately, the same windows that heat your home in the winter can help cool it in the summer. The key is to provide adequate cross-ventilation, preferably of a type that allows air to enter near the floor and exit through the roof. Double-hung windows, or windows designed with built-in vents at the bottom are perfect for letting air into the house. To provide an exit for hot rising air, skylights—the ones that open—can't be beat; they are perfect for maximizing airflow through the house. Skylights also help to bring additional natural light into a house, something that is often needed in lofts with few windows. Just don't install too many of them, or you'll defeat their purpose. Unlike windows under big eaves, skylights are great for letting *in* summer sunlight and letting *out* hard-won winter heat. (Fortunately, this problem can be minimized by purchasing skylights with blinds.) For those living off-the-grid, ample natural light is a must. LaVonne put a small skylight in the loft walk-in closet, and very rarely needs to turn on the light.

Trombe Walls and Other Methods of Storing Heat

The amount of heat that enters a house through south-facing windows is considerable, and to ensure that this free heat is not squandered on furniture, carpets and dogs (none of which is all that good at storing heat), you want to place things in the path of the light that have appreciable thermal mass. What sorts of things? Well, the most obvious is ceramic floor tile. Tile can soak up a surprising amount of heat, and if it's laid over regular or gypsum concrete, as it would be for a highly efficient hydronic in-floor heating system (hint, hint), the heat gain is further enhanced.

Trombe walls are also terrific heat-storing design features. Consisting in principle of nothing more than a concrete wall, or wall segment, mounted within an inch or two of a south-facing window and sealed around the edges, Trombe walls are showing up in more and more homes these days, and for good reason: it takes the heat trapped between the wall and the glass 8 to 10 hours to pass through an eight-inch thick concrete Trombe wall into the interior of a building, so you'll just start feeling the heat of the noonday sun a little before bedtime. It's the stuff sweet dreams are made of.

Other indoor heat "sinks" that have been used effectively include rock and/or concrete planters, or even large water-filled metal columns coated with unreflective paint. You can let your imagination go wild on this one.

FLOOR PLAN CONSIDERATIONS

Log homes have great acoustics. Our neighbor, Dave, likes to play his flute in our great room, since the logs do such a splendid job of reflecting the instrument's melodious and eerie notes back to him. That's good; except that sound carries so well in our house that LaVonne, from the loft, can hear the crumpling of a cellophane wrapper in the downstairs pantry, every time I have a chocolate cupcake attack in the middle of the night. And that's bad.

Obviously, the best way to dampen sound is to build more interior walls, and insulate them. But, if you rely on a central wood stove for a good portion of your heat, you'll be leaving much of your house in the cold. So it's a trade-off. If you live in a noisy house, efficient zoned heating (such as radiant-floor heat) is the best solution to supply heat to your "quiet" rooms. But there's one little wrinkle to this solution you should bear in mind: floor coverings that best conduct heat also conduct sound. So, while carpeting may alleviate the noise problem, it will also make the boiler work harder. Tile and wood floors work great with radiant-floor heat, but they can make your house noisier.

Like I said, it's a trade-off. But, since radiant-floor heat is, by far, the best form of central heat for a log home on a PV/wind system, you'll be better off if you incorporate it into your house design, no matter what the acoustic price tag.

Whatever dwelling you currently inhabit, there are things you like about it and things you don't. Incorporate the good elements into the design of your new house, and do away with the bad. Consider the ease with which you can move from room to room, and floor to floor. Leave yourself plenty of room, and design the kitchen and bathrooms for efficient use.

LaVonne wanted (and got) a pantry; a large, roomy kitchen with a central island; more-than-ample cupboard space; and a window over the sink. I wanted (and got) a cozy, carpeted office; a small workshop in the basement; and an extra-wide log stair to facilitate the movement of furniture. Large walk-in closets, built-in bookshelves, and a handy-yet-hidden location for the washer and dryer are other considerations. Do you have a piano or a large roll-top desk that you're not likely to part with? Make sure you make space for them.

An open kitchen design with an island is handy and inviting. The pantry (behind the stove wall) stores the awkward appliances, vacuum cleaner, dog food...you name it.

WOOD, WOOD AND MORE WOOD

LaVonne and I see it all the time: someone builds a log home, then goes completely hog-wild finishing the non-log parts of the house with even more wood. Wood on the ceilings, wood on the gable ends, wood on the floor. Yes, it is possible to have too much wood.

While we'll be the first in line to extol the beauty of natural wood, there is a point at which it becomes excessive. The unique character of logs only becomes truly apparent when it is contrasted with other mediums. A tongue-&-groove wood ceiling may be a nice touch in the cathedral ceiling over the entryway or great room, but if it's used throughout the house you may find it to be too dark and "heavy." Drywall, when it's tastefully finished, greatly enhances the beauty of logs, while brightening the interior of the house. Stone or stucco on the inside and outside of your home will give it a rich, well-balanced appearance.

The same goes for floor coverings. Tile, wood and carpeting all have their places, as long as it's not *every* place. A wood floor works good in high-traffic areas; tile wherever water might be spilled. Carpeting is soft and comforting to the feet in bedrooms and on stairs. (But not log stairs!)

Even in familiar surroundings, the eyes like to explore. The more variety they find, the happier they'll be, so give them a lot to look at. Pick light and plumbing fixtures, and door and cabinet hardware, that will accentuate, without clashing. Every individual element of your home will say something about you—make sure it's the statement you want to convey.

NON-LIVING SPACES

Every house has a mechanical room where the furnace (or boiler) and the water heater are located. Since (in all likelihood) you'll be pumping your water from a well, you may also need to allow space for a cistern, and/or a pressure tank. Basements are great places to hide all the stuff you don't want to look at, but if you have a two-story house on top of it, you will have to plan a route for the vent stacks. In a log home, it's not always an easy matter, since flue chases are much easier to hide (or at least to obscure) when they run next to a frame wall.

We thought we had allowed adequate room for the boiler flue to pass on the east side of the office wall, thus missing the dormer upstairs. Then we realized that the eave on the loft dormer was so wide that the stack would have gone right through it. We resolved the problem by building a flue chase on the other side of the main floor office wall and extending it through the inside of dormer. We then adorned the corners of the drywall chases with decorative logs. In truth, it turned out better than we had originally planned, but it's still a good idea to think these things through, ahead of time—too many surprises have a way of turning your hair gray.

Plan on having at least one or two frame walls in your house. It will make life much easier for the electrician and plumber. Plumbing pipes en route to the second floor should be run through 2 x 6 frame walls (the larger studs are needed to accommodate the main waste pipe). The total number of walls you need will depend on how extensively the upstairs is plumbed.

Your house will also need to have an electrical room big enough to contain all the components of the biggest PV (photovoltaic)/wind system you will ever conceivably build. This includes—but may not be limited to—wall space for the inverter(s), DC disconnect(s), charge

LaVonne's Verities

You can never have enough storage space.

controller(s), a 120/240 volt AC transformer, and floor space for your battery bank. Here are few things to keep in mind:

- Your battery box cannot be located beneath any serviceable component, such as an inverter (according to the National Electric Code). And neither can anything else. It's really too bad, because that's the logical place to put the batteries, since you will want the large cables connecting the batteries to the inverter to be as short as possible. One clever way around this problem is to build the battery box on the *other* side of the frame wall, just *behind* the inverter, and running the heavy cables through conduit in the wall.

- Lead-acid batteries—the ones most used in off-grid PV/wind systems—need to be in a sealed box, vented to the outside. It only takes a one-inch PVC vent pipe, but the closer you can locate the batteries to an outside wall, the better.

- Inverters hum. Just how *much* they hum depends on how hard they're working. To keep your sanity, put the inverter in a room that can be sealed off from the rest of the house in general, and your bedroom, in particular.

- For the sake of efficiency, it's best to locate the main electrical panel in the same room with all the other electrical components. That way everything is in one handy place.

These ideas and suggestion should help you during the planning stage, and all throughout the construction process. By this point, you've probably begun to form a mental picture of what the house is going to look like, inside and out. Now it's time to figure out where to put it. ✎

rex's maxims

BUILDING A HOUSE is a surefire way to discover what you overlooked while planning it.

BUCKHORN CAMP'S SCHOOL-BUILT LOG HOME

While LaVonne and I were immersed in finish work on our log home, the directors at Buckhorn United Methodist Camp, a few miles to the north, were having their log home constructed by a log-home building school. Working from a design by B. Allan Mackie, Gregg and Donna Kernes harvested the trees—stout Ponderosa—from the camp property, then the Lasko School of Log Building came in and constructed the house on-site.

The Kernes used volunteer work groups from the camp to peel the enormous logs, which were then crane-set by students and instructor, Bill Lasko. Gregg and Donna closely monitored the construction, and pitched in to help whenever—and wherever—they could. In this way they ensured that their home was built to their specifications, and learned the valuable skills they needed to finish the house themselves.

Two volunteers work on a log purlin. *Photo: Bill Youngblood*

Scarfed notches look great with these large logs.
Photo: Jerry Svoboda

Framed gable ends support the log purlins and ridge beam. The 2 x 10 roof rafters are being set by a group of volunteers.
Photo: Bill Youngblood

Should You Decide to Build a Pre-Crafted Home...

Since handcrafting our own log home we've met quite a number of people who, unlike us, chose to go with either a custom builder or a kit-style home. It's understandable; many folks simply don't have the time or the inclination to peel, notch, and fit their own logs. Admittedly, it's a lot of work, especially if you have to make a living in the meantime, and a pre-crafted home provides a means to enjoy log home living without the wait—or, for that matter, the cuts and bruises, sweat and tears, and the sore, aching muscles.

CHOOSING YOUR HOME STYLE

So, while we sincerely hope that you will experience firsthand the pleasures and travails of log crafting, we fully understand that many of you will not. Fortunately, custom and kit homes have become so popular that there is an endless variety of log and corner styles to choose from: everything from small 'D' logs to full round milled, from custom hand-peeled logs to massive square timbers. And each with dozens of variations on the basic theme. The hardest part may be figuring out just which style you want and who you want to buy it from.

Once you've determined the log type that best suits your sense of aesthetics and your climate—the 6-inch logs that protect your Arkansas cousin from the elements may not suffice in frigid Minnesota where winter is more a way of life than a season—you'll be able to whittle down your list of manufacturers considerably. Log home shows are perfect places to meet with builders and manufactur-

ers, and to actually see and touch examples of their homes.

EVALUATE BID PROPOSALS CAREFULLY

From there it's a matter of homework. Get detailed lists of what's included in each manufacturer's package, bearing in mind that it's challenging to compare an item on one manufacturer's list to the same item on another's, since the quality of things like windows and doors can vary drastically. Compare lists and compare costs. Then ask what's been omitted; if this package were delivered to your site tomorrow, what else would you have to buy to finish the house? Every manufacturer will offer

several options for what they supply and what you will have to buy locally. The option you pick may depend largely on your timeframe for building, since it makes no sense to have things on site that will have to endure the whims of nature for several months before becoming part of your house.

GET REFERRALS, DO SITE VISITS

Referrals are an invaluable resource; nothing beats the candor of a homeowner who's already been through what you are only contemplating. Don't be shy. By this point you'll have a thousand questions. Ask them all, including how well the milled logs stand up to the elements (if it's a kit house), or how the custom builder addressed settling issues (if it's a handcrafted home). Did they deliver what they promised? Were there any big surprises?

Before you sign a contract, visit their yard and observe a house under construction. Ask them if you can watch a reset at a home site. It will give you a feel for how the crew works together, how careful they are, and how skilled.

Will they do follow-up? A good manufacturer will have a sincere interest in making sure you are happy with your purchase and will do everything in his or her power to answer your ongoing concerns and make sure the project proceeds smoothly.

- Before you sign a contract, visit their yard and observe a house under construction. Ask questions about issues raised in this book (such as how they address settling around doors and windows).
- Ask them if you can watch a reset at a home site. It will give you a feel for how the crew works together, how careful they are, and how skilled.
- Get references and talk to their previous customers.
- Carefully evaluate their lists of what is included and look for items not included. Also examine the quality of items (doors, windows, fixtures, etc.) specified in the bid.
- Do your homework and get a handle on the costs upfront. No one likes surprises.

A book to read for more information on this subject is *Log Homes Made Easy: Contracting and Building Your Own Log Home,* by Jim Cooper.

HOW INVOLVED DO YOU WANT TO BE?

How much of the work do you plan to do your-self? The options range from having your kit off-loaded at your site with a good-luck hand-shake, to hiring a builder for a turnkey house. We've met people at each end of the spectrum, but most fall somewhere in the middle: they have the shell erected by the log company or a professional builder, then do some or all of the remaining work themselves. Many serve as their own general contractor to avoid paying the additional 15 percent (or so) of the cost of the house a contractor takes for overseeing the work and lining up the various subcontractors.

It's a tough and frustrating job, certainly, but it can save you a lot of cash if you're up for the challenge and have the time for it.

MAKING THE MOST OF THIS BOOK

And that takes us to this book's "hidden" pur-pose. The way we see it, some of you adven-turous souls will be up to the challenge of tak-ing an odd assortment of dead trees and craft-ing them into a house. But most of you won't. You will instead purchase logs already notched, grooved or milled, and you may or may not erect the walls, beams and purlins yourself. But however you go about it, by reading this book you will have a much clearer understanding of the what is involved in creating a home, since we'll take you through the process of building a custom log home from bedrock to ridge cap. For our part, we hope this is all knowledge you take to the bank, for it should save you time and money each step along the way.

Foreman Stanley Johnson finishes up a 3-minute perfect notch.

After handcrafting a log cabin years ago, our neighbor, John Benshoof, decided this time around he'd contract a custom home from Log Knowledge of Fort Collins, Colorado. These photos were taken during his 3-day reset at his site.

My hope in sharing these logbooks is not only to tell "the other side of the story," but to reveal the path and timeline that we followed. After living in our home for over 7 years now, I'm pleased to say that chasing our dream was definitely worth it.

Having never built a home, I find myself questioning the amount of work it will take, especially a handcrafted log home. I ask Rex how this will all be possible...how *we* can do it ourselves? His ambiguous answer is not all that reassuring, but my dream is to live in the mountains, surrounded by wildflowers and pine trees. So I'm ready. I think it was Henry Ford who said, "Whether you think you can, or think you can't, you're right."

Summer 1998
We walk the home site and mark the corners with blue flags. With house plans not yet drawn, we are free to dream. It is truly difficult for me to imagine a house rising from the tall grass and bountiful wildflowers.

September 1998
The soil engineer examined the big inspection hole and smaller perc holes (that Rex dug by hand) for the leach field. It turns out our soil is fine. Check that off the list. Now Gary can push in the road. He walks the steep sloping meadow and says the road should go "here and up along there." A good route we had not thought of. Soon his big bulldozer inches up the road, pushing rock and brush out of the way. Wow...we are really going to do this!

Neighbor Curt fires up his old backhoe to dig the two culvert trenches, under the close supervision of Micky, our ever curious dog [1]. All Rex needs to do is jackhammer rocks along the edges for better drainage [2] and we'll be ready for log delivery and rain runoff.

Our grassy, wildflower-laden home site.

CHAPTER *2*

SITE SELECTION

Where O' Where Does This House Want To Be?

A high-mountain plateau, where a small brook filled with crystal clear water gently tumbles down a mild tree-lined slope into a two-acre lake where fish greedily jump for unsuspecting insects near the grassy island in the middle. On the high shore, a rolling meadow sprouting wildflowers of every conceivable hue gradually yields to a dense forest of tall, healthy conifers that hide your retreat from all but the birds gliding effortlessly overhead on invisible thermal currents. The sun rises over high mountains in the distant east, and similarly sets in the west. During the day your southern exposure is vast and unimpeded. Your sense of peace and solitude is perfect and complete.

If this is your land, then congratulations. You've just found the property we've all been looking for...the kind of place that, for most of us mere mortals, exists only in wistful dreams and—you guessed it—television commercials for log homes.

Most properties will fall a trifle short of the above-mentioned dream place. Realistically speaking, if you intend to build a log home and derive your electricity from the sun and wind, there are only two criteria that cannot be compromised: access and southern exposure.

rex's maxims

THE PERFECT BUILDING SITE
is the one place on earth where
instinct, logic and intuition
are all in agreement.

ACCESS

Like most things, access is a relative concept. If you plan to live off the grid, proximity to power lines is unimportant. In most areas, the same holds for phone lines, since cell phone service is getting cheaper and more far-reaching by the day. Television and internet service is readily available by satellite. That being said, you still have to be able to get to your place.

When I bought two 35-acres parcels back in the late '80s, I built a small, pole-frame weekender cabin on the piece farthest from the private road that snakes through the hills. With a stout (and temperamental) '72 Chevy flatbed 4x4, I bullied my way over rocks and bushes on the northern face to the top of a steep hill where I intended to build. The access there can more rightly be called two parallel game trails than a road. But I stubbornly persevered, hauling everything that went into that little cabin (including all the poles, one of which was 29 feet long) on the back of my cantankerous pickup. It was an accomplishment, certainly, but one fraught with limitations. Without a real road—one that rises gently, with no sharp turns, one which can be traversed by large, two-wheel-drive vehicles—the cabin will always remain without plumbing, central heat, or even a source of fresh water.

So, while it's true that with enough heavy equipment and dynamite you can build anywhere you can bludgeon your way to with a bulldozer, unless there is good access for cement trucks, well-drilling rigs, propane delivery trucks and lumber trucks (and—unless your land is laden with tall, straight trees nearby—logging trucks), building there is going to end up being more work than you'd probably care to ponder.

Ideally, your building site should be reasonably flat and several times the area of your proposed house. This will give you plenty of room to lay your logs out individually, as well as allowing space for big rigs to maneuver comfortably. If there's not already a good road to your site, *don't* hire the kid down the canyon who just picked up a bargain-basement bulldozer and is willing to christen it on the side of your hill for a smile and a handful of crisp greenbacks. As tempting as it may be to save a few bucks, you're invit-

After one of the wettest months on record, the well driller, loaded with water for drilling, must be pulled up our muddy new road by the excavator.

ing disaster unless your road is pushed in by a contractor with several years experience under his belt. Any seasoned cement truck driver can tell you horror stories about sinking into a new, poorly constructed road, and then sliding off the mountain. You don't want your road to be fodder for any new stories. Besides, if a truck gets stuck (or worse) because of *your* shoddily built road, you'll be held responsible for towing or repair costs.

SOUTHERN EXPOSURE

Our house is situated on a saddle, 500 feet above a creek, and surrounded on all sides by mountains. The sun rises here about an hour later than it does on the plains to the east, and sets an hour earlier. It's about as good a spot as you can hope for in this area. Since the solar wattage available from the early and late day sun is only a small fraction of what's available at midday, we lose practically nothing to the surrounding hills. At 40 degrees north latitude we have all the sunshine we need to power our house, even in late December when the days are so short that lunch is the only meal we can enjoy in daylight.

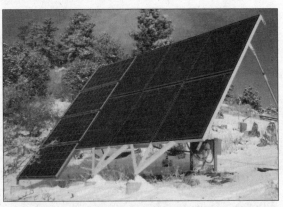
Our ground-mounted solar array makes for easy cleaning (pollen and dirt in the spring and summer; snow in winter), and it can be easily adjusted to best meet the angle of the sun.

Since your solar array will be a major investment, you'll want as much direct sunlight as you can get. If you plan on building in a valley, be absolutely sure that your winter sun isn't blocked by the hillside to the south. This can be deceptive. In July, when the sun burns high in the sky like a blast furnace ten feet overhead, it's hard to recall just how far south old sol retreats in winter. Several years ago I rented a little place in a deep valley one canyon north of where LaVonne and I now live. It

A Solar Pathfinder tells you if and when shading will be a problem for your PV array.

was bright and sunny in August when I moved in, but as fall approached I watched with dread as the sun crept ever south. Then, early in November, it just disappeared and didn't offer up a single yellow ray until the following February. The sun's arc was nearly identical to the topography of the mountain to the south; one day the sun was there and the next day it wasn't. Fortunately, I didn't own the place and it was wired into the grid, so I could at least see what I was doing as I shoved copious quantities of cordwood into the stove to keep from freezing to death during the three-month night.

Plan where you're going to put your solar array. The roof of the house is fine, but modules are much easier to clean and sweep the snow from if they are on the ground. Either way, you won't want them much more than 100 feet from your battery bank, because in low-voltage DC systems the size of wire required to carry the current without substantial line loss increases greatly with distance, and heavy wire can get pricey. It's not much fun to work with, either.

Drilling for water.

OTHER CONSIDERATIONS

WATER

Unless you get some bizarre satisfaction from driving a gas-guzzling pickup to town twice a week to fill up a big green water tank in the back, you're going to want a well. Talk to your nearest neighbors and the local well-drillers to see what you can rightly expect. In many areas the depth at which good water can be found is fairly predictable. In other areas (such as ours), it's anybody's guess. Our nearest neighbor, 200 vertical feet above us, got 3 gallons a minute at a depth of 340 feet. We drilled 540 feet, but lucked-out with a commendable recharge rate of 5 gallons per minute.

If your area is like ours, you'll just have to talk to everyone you can and take your chances. The two people we know with truly abysmal water wells (over 700 feet, 5 gallons per *hour*) both built on isolated knolls much higher than the surrounding terrain.

It's something to keep in mind.

WIND

The wind, of course, blows where it will. Some states are windier than others, and every point within each state is different from every other. Secluded valleys are generally not good places for wind generators; mountaintops are great. You could get a ton of expensive equipment and monitor the wind at your site over the course of a year to determine if it blows enough to justify the purchase of a wind generator, or you could follow my simple rule of thumb:

If the wind blows hard enough and often enough to annoy you,
you can probably make good use of a wind generator.

Placement of your wind tower is a little trickier than finding a spot for your solar array. Ideally, the generator should be mounted at least 30 feet higher than the highest point within a lateral radius of 300 feet. This isn't always possible, but it's a starting point.

DEPTH TO "THE ROCK"

In our neck of the woods, there are three categories of rock. First, there are the kind you can pick up or move aside with a bar or a bulldozer. Plain old rocks, in other words. Then there is what we simply call "rock," which is a variety of decomposed granite bedrock that is soft enough to chip through with the right equipment. Finally, there is "THE rock," a dense unyielding class of gneiss, firmly and stubbornly bound to the core of the planet. Attack it with a jackhammer— or even a backhoe with a hydraulic rock chipper—and it will laugh at you, defiantly. When we excavated for our basement we ran into a chunk of "the rock" the size of an RV. It took thirteen sticks of dynamite to convince it we weren't kidding around.

The point is, rock is troublesome, and "the rock" is downright recalcitrant. For your foundation you will, at minimum, have to dig below the frost line (30 inches in Colorado, up to 6 feet farther north). And don't forget the water pipes and electric lines that have to be trenched in. Or the leach field for your septic system; for good absorption, you will need a large, fairly flat area below your house (a minimum of 100 feet away from your well) where the bedrock is at least 8 feet down.

None of this is particularly easy if all you have is 18 inches of dirt over a ubiquitous expanse of "the rock." Of course, you don't really know how deep bedrock is until you start digging, but if the ground around your building site is studded with chunks of granite protruding from the earth like so many weathered teeth, it's a good indication that the process of digging may soon give way to the process of blasting.

AND FINALLY...

While every consideration mentioned above is important, there is one other criterion that should not be neglected, for even if you have

LaVonne's Verities

IF YOUR HUSBAND says he can do the impossible, don't try to talk him out of it. Just watch him closely.

good access to a beautiful, secluded spot with plenty of sunshine, an occasional stiff breeze, good well water and a deep cover of topsoil, the place has to *feel* right. Because if you are going to invest thousands of hours of your time—and gallons of your blood, sweat and tears—into the construction of a one-of-a-kind log home, it would behoove you to build it on the one piece of earth that feels truly kindred.

Cast reason to the wind for a moment; it won't help you. Walk the land and let it flow through you. Does the thicket of trees nearby hearken to your childhood fantasies of being alone in an enchanted forest? Does the rock outcropping on the hillside below resonate in your bones when you stand on it and gaze into the distance? Is the hawk overhead speaking to *you*?

Be happy. You're there. ∽

Log • ically   Solar

When it comes to cozy log-home living, anything more than just enough is too much. Neither Scott Van Wagner nor his wife, Tess, have ever told me as much, but it's evident by seeing their stylish 1,500-square-foot custom log cabin (see cover photo) near Telluride, Colorado that this is a philosophy to which they both heartily subscribe.

After several interviews to determine what would best suit Scott and Tess and their two sons, Max and Derek, local builder Ted Moews (see profile on page 116) meticulously designed and built the cabin. The heavy log construction features a well-glazed south side, including double glass doors opening onto both the upstairs balcony and first-floor porch. The classy Truman porch off the loft's guest bedroom affords visitors a view of the high Colorado Rockies in all their majesty. "It's a tight and efficient house that's as pleasing to look at as it is comfortable to live in," Scott says with evident pride. And "tight and efficient" are good qualities when it comes to staying warm at 10,000 feet.

The sheer mass of the large spruce logs ensures that most of the heat created

In this way, the only line leading to the house is a single 120-volt AC line, safely encased in conduit and buried underground. Neat.

There's a harmony that runs through every aspect of the Van Wagner place, and perhaps that's the way it should be. Scott, an amateur sax player, and Tess, a cellist and orchestra director for a Chicago north-shore school district, both sense it. "It's the sounds of silence," Tess says, "that make this place so special."

inside the cabin stays inside throughout the night. When it gets bone-chilling cold outside, the main floor can be heated by an in-floor hydronic system, while the loft has hot-water baseboard heat, both of which are driven by a propane-fired boiler. But mostly the natural-stone Rumford fireplace—a tall and shallow late 18th-century idea, designed to reflect heat back into the room while quickly removing smoke through the streamlined throat—is more than adequate. To heat the loft, the mason installed a damper near the top of the chimney to trap heat in the chimney's great thermal mass. "It's just good design, through and through," Scott has concluded.

Like the cabin, the photovoltaic system is well thought out and no bigger than it has to be. Because it's a vacation home, the 320 watts the solar array provides is plenty of power to keep a bank of twelve L16 batteries charged up in the Van Wagners' absence, and the Trace SW4024 inverter supplies all the power they need while they're in residence. The sum of the RE equipment, including the solar array and a Kohler propane-fired generator that gets its starting instructions from the inverter, is located in, and on, the generator shed, 50 feet west of the cabin.

House 1,500 square feet on 2 levels; hand-hewn, custom log

Heating Rumford fireplace; propane-fired boiler for in-floor hydronic heat on the main floor and baseboard heat in the loft

Water pumped by PV system from 185-foot well

Refrigeration propane

Solar array 320 watts

Wind turbine none

Inverter Trace SW4024

Batteries 12 Interstate L16s

Backup power 10-kilowatt, propane-fired Kohler generator, wired for automatic start

October 1998

We waited anxiously this crisp fall morning for the semi load of trees to be delivered. After a road inspection by the driver, I park myself up high on a rock and, with binoculars, watch his big truck rumble slowly past the first neighbor's drive. I lose sight of him for a moment and then see him stop on the steep, tight corner near the next neighbor's driveway. My heart sinks. Then, in utter disbelief, I watch him unload all sixty-four trees right there beside the road, and drive away! What a depressing sight. Our heavy house logs set in an ominous pile, over a mile from our property.

Never fear. My handy husband has a solution. He cuts, torches and welds steel and axles into two trailers [3]. The black spray paint is a nice touch, but I'm very dubious of this whole thing. The newly made log-moving transports are ready. Me?? That is questionable, but why lose sleep over it. If I know Rex, it's going to get done one way or another.

November 1998

Well, we did it! After many weekends of jacking up each log end [4]—chaining it to a trailer—driving slowly up the road—jacking up the logs to offload—rolling each log into a new pile—and going down for the next log...we are done. Every time I'd say how much work this was, Rex would laugh and say, "this is nothin', Honey." Lucky for him I don't have to touch those logs for 6 months.

February 1999

We apply for a building permit, house plans in hand. Only a few questions from the engineer to be answered and we can have the permit.

April 1999

Yea! We sold our house and 20 acres down in the flatlands. We (us, two dogs and a psycho but cute cat) will move to our small cabin (temporary living space of about 500 square feet, complete with an outhouse) in the mountains in May, providing we can pack, store, throw-out and haul decades of belongings. Hopefully the rain will slow down. Moving is exhausting, but the dream is getting closer.

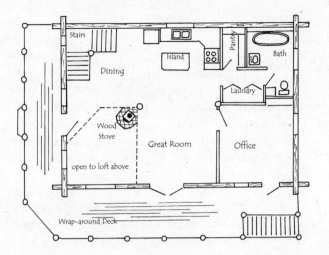

CHAPTER *3*

PLANS AND PERMITS

Paper Dreams and County Hoops

You've got the perfect piece of land, and there is a wide, firm road pushed into your building site. Long nights at the kitchen table have yielded a pile of pages roughing out a house you both agree is *the* house; the one you *will* build. Maybe you're not sure about the foundation specs, or just how beefy your joists, rafters, beams and purlins need to be, but no matter. The essence is there; all that's left is to wrestle with the devil in the details.

So what now?

LaVonne and I have very different ideas on how to proceed on a project. I like to make things up as I go along. I plan everything in my head and only resort to paper and pencil when the math exceeds my powers of rumination. LaVonne, on the other hand, is not happy until the minutest detail is addressed. While I was picking out viable prospects for the third course of wall logs, LaVonne was trying to decide what kind of tile design to use in the downstairs bathroom.

Even though it can get a little distracting at times, I have to admit that I admire her attention to detail. Much more so, I suspect, than she appreciates my cryptic spontaneity. And, while I still maintain that a formal blueprint is a waste of time for a garage, tool shed, hay barn or even a small cabin, I have to concede it's absolutely necessary on a project as complex as a log home.

FIRST STEPS

Where to go? Your first stop should be your county planning/building depart-ment. They can provide you with a list of their requirements for everything from road specifications to leach field types and sizes for different homes (usually, this is based on the number of bedrooms). They will tell you what they need to see in a blueprint before they can issue a permit.

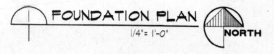

Armed with this information, you can then decide on how to go about obtaining your formal plans. If you have building expe-rience and managed to make it through high school drafting with a grade sufficient to keep your parents smiling, you might want to take a stab at it yourself. Mostly, the county just wants to make sure your roof won't collapse with 4 feet of snow on it, your floor won't sag under the weight of a bathtub or piano, or that your foundation isn't going crumble from the weight of your house. If something isn't up to specs they'll dutifully mark it in red to make sure the field inspector knows there's been a change.

Most of the extraneous lists you see on blueprints (window, electrical and plumbing schedules, for instance) are for the builder, not the county. While they will want to know where you intend to put your sinks and toilets and tubs—and if your egress windows are large enough to stuff yourself through—for the pur-pose of issuing a building permit they couldn't care less about your plumbing fixtures, the precise locations of your wall outlets, or if your windows are hung right or left. (Of course, you or your subcontractors *will* need to know these things at some point.)

Generally speaking, if you make a genuine attempt to show the county what your house is going to look like and how it's constructed, they will probably be willing to play ball with you.

Another option is to buy blueprints from one of any num-ber of vendors that sell them. The cost will be minimal com-pared to having custom plans prepared by an architect, but if it's not exactly the house you wanted, you will be limited to making only superficial changes in the course of construction, since the county will, by and large, expect your house to look like the plans. Providing you are able to find a plan that suits you, it's a cheap and easy way to go.

Should you end up hiring an architect, be prepared to spend some money. Many architects won't touch a log home, and those who do reckon it's worth a

> ### Permits Required
> We were required to get a per-mit from the county health department for the septic sys-tem; another permit from the county Building Department, and an electrical permit from the State of Colorado. Each per-mit required numerous inspec-tions before we could receive a Certificate of Occupancy.

premium. There are non-architect log home designers around, but they aren't much cheaper. Talk to the log home builders in your area and see who they recommend. Then talk to the county again and see what they'll let you slide by with. Like us, you might be able to find a drafting or architecture student or apprentice willing to draw up your plans for thousands of dollars less than a professional.

And remember: if you are in doubt about the structural integrity of any part of your house, a few hundred dollars spent to have an engineer review your concerns is money well spent.

CONCERNS UNIQUE TO LOG HOME BLUEPRINTS

Unless your county is even more persnickety than ours—which is hard to imagine—you shouldn't have to worry about details such as sliding jambs and floating walls on your blueprints. These things will all be examined by the field inspector and, unless they present a structural problem (if, for instance, you try to float a bearing wall), they should pass inspection with ease.

The county's biggest concern will be your structural log members. Unless there are a lot of log homes being built in your area, the folks in the Plan Check Division may not be all that familiar with the load bearing capabilities of logs of varying length and thickness. You can avoid this problem, of course, by presenting them with professionally prepared plans. Or you can talk to them beforehand and ask what they require. The book, *Log Span Tables*, (Mackie, Read & Hahney) may be helpful, both to you and the county, in determining how thick your beams and purlins should be.

> ### Blueprint Plans
> We submitted the following plans to the county building department.
> - Site
> - Foundation
> - Floor & roof framing
> - Floor plans for each level
> - Exterior elevations
> - Wall sections
>
> Upon approval of these plans, we were issued a permit. Each state and county will have different requirements, so check before starting.

Site-built log trusses will (rightly) be viewed with far more scrutiny than simple linear load-bearing members. Trusses present such a complex array of opposing stresses that they will probably require an engineer's stamp of approval.

Depending on the design of your house, there may be one more option available to you. In *most* log homes, *most* of the structural support members end up in the roof. And *most* of the time these members are overlaid with rafters of dimensional lumber. If this is the case with your house, you just may find that by either increasing the size of your rafters (from 8-inches to 10-inches, for instance) or placing them 16-inches OC (on-center), instead of 24-inches OC, that they, alone, will be sufficient to support the roof. If so, then your beams and purlins

Our two structural floor beams (shown above), plus two log support posts had to be graded by a certified log inspector.

become, from a structural standpoint, "decorative" and their size, grade and placement will no longer be of concern to the county.

PIER FOUNDATIONS FOR OFF-THE-GRID HOMES

If you're going to be building on rocky ground, you might be tempted to go with a pier foundation to save concrete and facilitate excavation. While it's true that pier foundations are often used successfully for log homes, they can be a problem if you plan to produce your electricity from the sun and wind.

Why? Unless you live in an area of the country where the mercury rarely dips below 30 degrees, you won't want to give up the energy it will take to keep the single water pipe entering your house from your well or cistern from freezing. In terms of raw wattage, the least efficient way to use electricity is to produce heat with it. Toasters, hair dryers, coffee makers, slow cookers—and heat tapes—are all notorious energy pigs. And since outside water lines in pier foundations are customarily wrapped in heat tape and then enclosed within an insulated chase, you will end up using electricity to heat a pipe that would not need to be heated with a conventional foundation.

But even if the heat tape takes a minimal amount of electricity, there will still be a lot of heat loss through the floor, especially if the floor is exposed to cold, winter winds. Don't get me wrong, here. I'm not saying it can't be done; only that it should be avoided, if possible. If, on the other hand, a pier foundation turns out to be the only practical way to go, you can minimize your energy loss by completely enclosing your foundation with rock or cinder block, then building a chase around your water (and sewage) pipes and insulating it to the nth degree.

SOLAR AND WIND POWER CONSIDERATIONS

In the house where you are now living, there is a single conduit with two heavy wires running into your main electrical panel. This conduit runs from the utility grid to the outside of the house, through a wall, to the panel. It's hidden in the wall and takes up no living space. If you plan to live off the grid or with a grid-tied system that has batteries, things will be much different. You will either have to plan for a separate room to hold your batteries and wind/solar components, or at least allow sufficient space within a storage or similar room. It's a good idea to design your solar and wind generating system before you design your house; that way you'll know how much space to allow.

To give you a rough idea of how much space everything takes, our electrical room is 9-feet by 4-feet, with a 7-foot, 4-inch ceiling. Our 24 L16 batteries fit nicely in 18 square feet of floor space. By squeezing components closer together, we

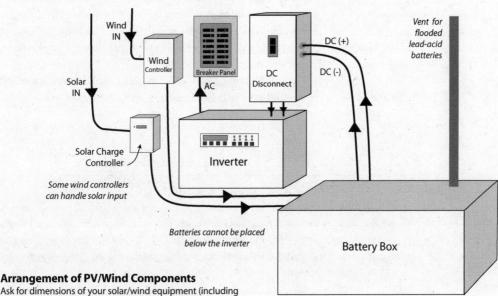

Arrangement of PV/Wind Components
Ask for dimensions of your solar/wind equipment (including batteries) to ensure you plan for adequate space.

probably could have gotten by with a little less space, but not much. If you can, leave yourself plenty of extra room. In particular, allow yourself space to expand the size of your battery bank, should you want to add more batteries later on.

Most wind and solar suppliers/consultants will be more than happy to help you design your system, and their catalogs give precise dimensions of every component you'll need in your electrical room, including the batteries. So, once you familiarize yourself with the essentials of a photovoltaic (solar) and wind system and understand what's what, it's a simple matter to draw a diagram detailing where everything will go.

<table>
<tr><td>

A Helpful Reminder

If you plan on using a propane refrigerator, be sure to run a gas pipe for it to your kitchen. We found, however, that our new Kenmore refrigerator uses under 400 kWh per year, and by not having to feed it propane, it has more than paid for the extra two solar panels it takes to run it.

</td><td>

HANG IN THERE!

It's easy to get dismayed with the seemingly endless list of requirements the county will hand you, even if you are familiar with the permit process. A lot of it may seem like no more than bureaucratic nitpicking. But if it is or isn't, there's really no way to get around it. (Ruffling their feathers, I learned long ago, only marks you for misery later.) So, give them whatever they want—most of it's just a lot of legwork, anyway. And once you pay your fees and get your permit, you can say goodbye to the desk jockeys and start dealing with the inspectors in the field. You will find that, for the most part, they're friendly, reasonable

</td></tr>
</table>

people who will cut you a little slack from time to time, providing you treat them right and don't try to sneak anything past them.

The best part is, you will then be officially cleared to break ground and get busy building with the logs you've been dreaming about all winter. ∽

Composting Toilets

In many areas, there is simply no place to put a large leach field. An indoor composting toilet is a viable alternative for such places. The newer, solar-operated models are quite efficient. You'll still need a small leach field for the "grey water," of course, but the restrictions will be far more relaxed. Besides, you'll save thousands of gallons of water per year.

The logging truck arrives with our load of trees.

CHAPTER **4**

LOGS

Dead Trees and Great Expectations

*I*t's a crisp, cool morning in early October. The hummingbirds have long since trekked south, and most of the songbirds have followed in their wake. Only the sparrows remain; the sparrows and the ever-present Steller's jays, ceaselessly announcing their coming and going with throaty squawks and disapproving glances.

A good morning to sit on the deck of our little pole-frame cabin, sipping coffee and warming slowly with the day as the sun inches over the mountain to our east. But not today. Though the winds are calm and the sky is clear, and it appears to all the world that utter peace has settled over the mountain like a calming vapor from a sorcerer's cauldron, we are both buzzing with nervous excitement.

Today is the day. Our logs are coming.

I check my watch. It's time. We load the dogs in the back of the pickup and head down the mountain to meet the logger at the county road. He's a little late, but not much. He sees our pickup and casually parks his truck in the middle of the paved road, as if it were his own private parking space. Tall and self-assured, he is completely unconcerned. Anyone who doesn't have the wherewithal to drive around him has no business being on a mountain road in the first place, he figures.

Before we take him on an inspection tour of our calamitous road, we take a walk around his truck. What we see is a little intimidating. Logs—or, more precisely, dead trees—all 50-footers ranging, we figure, from 500 to 1,600 pounds apiece. Some are straight with little taper, most fall short of that ideal by varying degrees. The butts range from 9 inches to 15 or better. The tips go from 10 inches to as little as 6. We try to imagine this disparate medley of logs somehow being transformed into a home. But we can't. Not yet.

Even though the road is dry, we keep our pickup locked into four-wheel low for good traction on the winding, washboard road that rises over 600 feet in a little under two miles. With a critical eye, the logger studies every pitfall along the way: the sharp switchback at the half-mile point; the narrow gap between the rocks near the top. The steep, snaking stretch to our building site. We breathe a sigh of relief when he finally says, mirthlessly, "Yeah, I can pull this road."

I drop LaVonne off at the building site and take him back to his rig. I then drive ahead of him to make sure no neighbors are coming down the hill as he's going up. The big truck lumbers up the first hill off the county road, then picks up a little speed on the mild incline approaching the switchback. I go past the switchback and disappear behind the mountain where I drive to the top of the hill and wait.

And wait. And wait.

After 10 minutes I can no longer convince myself that something isn't wrong. A drive back down the mountain confirms my fears....he's in the chair on the back of his rig, indelicately unloading our logs onto our neighbor's property with the hydraulic grappling arm of his loader. "Sorry, ol' son," he says. "This is the end of the road."

Apparently, the big, overloaded truck's rear differential was no match for the steep switchback a mile below our building site. I felt like I had driven into a brick wall on the way to my own birthday party. Later, LaVonne and I drove down the hill, and stared blankly at our mountain of logs as though it were a tomb for our dreams. We knew of no conceivable way to get them to our building site. We hadn't even broken ground yet, and already things seemed hopeless.

But, there's always a way if you want something bad enough and, boy howdy, we

Rex ponders how to move our logs over a mile to the building site.

did. After a few days of exploring a parade of increasingly desperate options—up to, and including, helicopters—I finally hit on a plan.

Sometimes LaVonne thinks I'm a little crazy, and sometimes she's right, but not this time. From some old I-beams and a couple of mobile home axles I had lying around our farm, I fashioned two small trailers. One rode on the ball of our Toyota pickup, the other rode just behind the balance point of the log. Using a high-lift mechanical bumper jack and chain, we proceeded to lift each individual log, one end at a time, and move the trailers under them. One by one, we wheeled our big 50-footers up the hill, where we jacked them up again, and then down, and rolled them onto old corral poles to keep them off the damp ground.

It took several weekends, from dawn till dusk, but in the end we had our logs where we wanted them with time to spare before the snows hit.

We popped a cork and celebrated; we had survived our first of many tests.

Our log-moving solution involved two homemade trailers. The top photo shows unloading the back end of a log. Then the front log end is lifted off the first trailer (left photo); the truck is moved forward; the log let down and rolled off to one side.

BUYING LOGS

I rest my case about the importance of access.

Assuming that your road is better than ours—and for your sake, I sincerely hope it is—you'll want to know where to get your logs and what to do with them, once they're delivered.

Unless you are fortunate enough to have a few acres of tall, straight, accessible trees growing on your land, you'll be buying your trees from a logger. As a rule, loggers don't advertise in the yellow pages, but log home builders do. Check with companies in your area that build log homes and find our where they get their house logs. Get as many names as you can; log prices and delivery can vary greater from one logger to another. Then visit their lots and see what they have; buying logs over the phone is a really bad idea.

If the plans for your house are completed, you will have a schedule of the lengths and thickness of the logs you need. You can meticulously try to pick out the individual logs you need or, like we did, you can buy a truckload of long, thick trees and cut them to length later. We found that our logger was willing to offer us a much sweeter deal on a full semi-load of long trees he didn't have to cut to length. In this way, we were able to take what we needed from each log and save the rest for deck supports, steps, benches or any of a thousand other things. (If all else fails, log ends are nice for heating your house.)

Either way, buy extra—you'll appreciate a selection when you get near the top and you're trying to keep your walls the same height. Besides, you'll always find a place to use them, even if they don't end up in your house. We bolted a 20-foot log between two leftover 50-footers, then set the whole contraption upright in the meadow below our house. Result? The most awesome rope swing in the canyon.

Species of trees vary from place to place. Our house is mostly lodgepole pine, with a few spruce and fir thrown in for spice. Unless you're willing to pay exorbitant trucking costs, you'll have to settle for whatever is native to your area. Straightness and uniformity are more important than what kind of tree it is. The less taper from end to end the better. For structural members, such as beams, purlins, or upright supports, straightness and lack of taper are critical, as is an absence of knots and twists (especially if the county requires your structural logs to be graded). Besides, endless days of running a drawknife over scores of kidney-jarring knotty logs can really dampen one's enthusiasm.

GREEN OR SEASONED LOGS?

There are pros and cons for building with either green or seasoned logs. Green trees are certain to be free of rot and insect

---

Log Twist

All types of conifer trees have a tendency to twist, giving them a spiral grain. Odd as it may sound, the direction of the twist is critical, since logs with a left-hand twist tend to become "unraveled" over time.

To determine if the twist is left- or right-handed, place your right hand on the log (pointing toward either end; it doesn't matter) with the middle finger running along the long axis. If the grain spirals in the direction your thumb is pointing, it's a left-hand twist.

Logs with a left-hand twist should not be used as support logs (purlins, beams, etc.) and should only be used as wall logs if the grain deviates less than one inch from the log's long axis, over a distance of 20 inches.

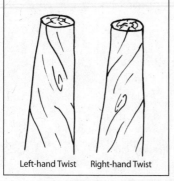

Left-hand Twist   Right-hand Twist

infestations, there is less cracking and checking (temporarily), they're more flexible, and they have a nice, pristine look about them when freshly peeled.

On the other hand, you will have to allow for several inches of shrinkage and—this is my biggest bugaboo—they're too heavy! No matter what kind of equipment you have to move your logs around, there's still going to be a great deal of manhandling involved. Why lift, pull, roll and spin 1,000 pounds when the same log dry weighs less than half that much?

So, as far as I'm concerned, it's a no-brainer: if you can get dry logs (but not too old), by all means do it. It will greatly facilitate construction, both from a tactical (moving logs from place to place) and a strategic standpoint (it's much easier to design, build and finish a house that isn't going to be 6 inches shorter in 2 or 3 years). In many states there are vast tracts of forest that have been killed by pine beetles. If you can find a logger working a contract in one of these areas you'll have all the seasoned trees you need.

No matter what state of dryness your logs are in when you build, if you can let the structure sit for a season after the log work is done, your finish work will be easier. Unless your logs are air-dried when you begin building, and you are able to let the house settle for a few months when the shell is completed, you should plan to put jack stands beneath your vertical supports, and leave ample settling gaps above doors, windows, and interior walls (see Chapters 13 and 14).

> **Wood Species Commonly Used In Log Homes**
>
> **East & Northeast** white pine, red pine, Eastern white cedar
> **Southeast** white pine, yellow pine, cypress
> **Central** white pine, yellow pine, Eastern white cedar
> **West & Northwest** Western red cedar, spruce, fir, ponderosa, hemlock, lodgepole pine
>
> Source: Fletcher Parsons, *Log Homes Illustrated*

Our logs were well-seasoned before we began construction, and we were able let the house settle over the winter after drying-in the roof. As a result, we were able to avoid a lot of the tedious procedures one normally has to take to allow for a spontaneously shrinking house.

CRIBBING YOUR LOGS

Green or seasoned, your logs may have to sit for some length of time before you get around to putting them in your house. They should be laid out individually, several inches above the ground, to allow for the movement of air under them. Old corral poles make good dunnage; culled trees or logs are even better. Longer dunnage poles are better than shorter; the reason will become obvious, once you begin rolling your logs with a bar and a peavey.

> Logs start shrinking in size when moisture content falls below 25%.
>
> Source: Fletcher Parsons, *Log Homes Illustrated*

Don't let the logs sag in the middle. Use enough dunnage to support each log every 8 to 10 feet. Even then, you will want to roll them every so often to keep them straight. And, since it's doubtful that you'll know which log you intend to use next until it's time to use it, lay them in such a way that they are all equally easy to get to.

Many books will tell you to peel your logs immediately. But unless it never rains where you live, I would strongly advise against it. Ma Nature put bark on trees for a reason, and it wasn't just to make them easier to climb. Leave it on until it's time to use the log! Any staining you get from the bark will be nothing compared to the discoloration you'll see on naked logs after a couple of hard rains. The only caveat to this would be if you live in an area where log-boring insects are so severe that you have to peel the logs to keep them from being destroyed by bugs. Most areas are not this bad. As long as your logs are above the ground and laid out loosely enough that they don't trap moisture, the few bugs you do get under the bark won't do enough damage to worry about.

Moisture Content of Logs

Green Logs above 30% moisture

Dry Logs generally means 25 – 28% moisture

Air-Dried refers to approximately 20 – 21% EMC (equilibrium moisture content)

Kiln-Dried logs that have had moisture removed quickly in a controlled environment; around 18 – 19% moisture content. Also sanitizes the logs, but does not eliminate all shrinkage.

Source: Fletcher Parsons, *Log Homes Illustrated*

GETTING TO KNOW YOUR LOGS

Okay. It sounds funny, but it really isn't. If you've never built a log house before, a vast field of rough, unpeeled logs can look pretty intimidating. Even though we had all of our logs laid out above our building site in late October, we didn't get around to building with them until the following September. Eleven months is a long time to convince yourself that what you are attempting is fundamentally impossible. *Can I really take all of these unwieldy trees and turn them into a home I'll be proud of?* You'll ask yourself this question more than once. The answer is: of course you can. But if you just lay them out and forget about them until it's time to start building, you'll be shocked at what your imagination has done to your logs after a long winter's hiatus.

No, I didn't talk to our logs (and I'm happy to say they didn't talk to me, either.) But I did spend a lot of time walking them, picking out which logs would be best to start with and which would be better for the top of the wall. I'd find artistic irregularities I wanted to be sure to place in highly visible interior walls, and others not so artistic I planned to cut out of door or window openings. Mostly I just dreamed

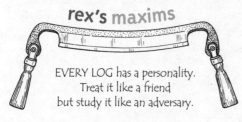

rex's maxims

EVERY LOG has a personality.
Treat it like a friend
but study it like an adversary.

about how good all those logs were going to looked peeled, notched and spiked into a wall.

However you do it is up to you, but believe me: the more time you spend with your logs on the ground, the friendlier they're going to be when it comes time to use them. And the less likely they'll be to sneak up on you in the middle of night and hiss in your ear that you're an idiot if you think they're going to agree to being part of your house. ∾

Log • ically　Solar

To see the potential lying dormant in Brookbank Canyon Ranch—a dilapidated 123-acre sheep ranch in Arizona's White Mountains—took the eye of an accomplished photographer and the imagination of a seasoned writer. And so it must have been fate when Jerry and Lois Jacka happened upon their future home in 1993 while returning home from an assignment for *Arizona Highways* magazine.

Restoring the original 30- by 30-foot ranch house (tree-ring dated to 1911) was the first order of business. Using a treasure trove of 6- by 12-inch timbers obtained from an old Navaho tribal sawmill building, the Jackas enlarged the main house from 900 to 4,000 square feet, painstakingly matching the look and feel of the original timbers right down to the dovetail notches. As a special touch, a giant standing-dead alligator-bark juniper was set into the great room before the walls were complete. A cache of weathered corrugated steel roofing—also from the Tribal sawmill—proved to be a perfect match for the original. The result is a stylish and sturdy solid-wood home that looks to all the world as though it has stood proud and stalwart against Nature's worst for the last 100 years.

But, difficult as it was, the restoration of the buildings (there was a bunkhouse, built in 1897, that also needed major work) was only part of the challenge facing Jerry and Lois, for there had never before been electrical grid power to the ranch. Nor would there be; the nearest power pole was $100,000, a utility easement, and an Environmental Impact Statement away—the latter two considerations resulting from the fact that Brookbank Canyon Ranch is totally surrounded by National Forest.

And the Jackas needed power. Besides the two restored buildings, there is also a shop building and two mobile homes used for the caretaker's and the guests' quarters. In all, there are three electric refrigerators, four televisions, microwaves, shop tools…need I continue?

For half the cost of grid power (and a fraction of the hassle), Jerry and Lois were able to have a solar-electric system expertly installed by Val-U Solar from Snowflake, Arizona. It meets all of their needs. Nine separate solar arrays, positioned on a south-facing hill 100 feet south of the house, combine for over 5,000 watts of solar capacity. In a nearby shed, the battery bank, comprising 32 Rolls-Surrette L16 batteries, is fed by five Xantrex C-60 charge controllers, and outputs its power to a single Xantrex SW4024 inverter. A 15-kilowatt Perkins diesel generator stands stoically by, awaiting rare backup duty.

You might call Brookbank Canyon Ranch a masterful blending of the old and the new; the timeless and the timely. Jerry and Lois just call it home.

House 4,000 square feet in main ranch house plus 3 other residences and a shop building; hand-hewn timbers

Heating wood and propane (forced air)

Water 600-foot well, pumped by generator and gravity fed from two large storage tanks

Refrigeration 3 electric refrigerators

Solar array 5,000-plus watts

Wind turbine Southwest Air 401

Inverter Xantrex SW4024

Batteries 32 Rolls-Surrette L16s

Backup power 15-kilowatt Perkins diesel generator, wired for automatic start; also controlled (along with the inverter) through a computer interface via a buried phone cable.

CHAPTER 5

TOOLS FOR CONSTRUCTION

Essential Tools for Pre-Log Construction and Logwork

T here is no substitute for good tools. The price paid for a durable, well-built tool will be paid back several times over the course of building a house by the countless hours of aggravation you'll avoid by not using bargain-box specials. This holds true for every type of tool, from expensive saws to relatively cheap hammers and tape measures. A tool that feels comfortable in your hands and stands up to the repeated punishment of daily use is an ally you cannot afford to be without.

Tools, like friends, should be chosen wisely.

PRE-LOG CONSTRUCTION TOOLS

GENERATOR

A generator will be a big ticket item, but if you're planning to live off the grid, it's no place to start cutting corners. You'll want a generator with at least twice the capacity needed to run your biggest load. This could be a welder, air compressor, or a well pump. A 1.5 hp submersible well pump draws around 11 amps at 240 volts, or a little over 2,600 watts. If that were your biggest load, you'd want at least a 5,000 watt generator to run it effectively. And most importantly, you'll want to be able to get that much power out of one individual circuit, which means you may need an even higher watt-rating.

Our generator is rated at 10,000 watts surge / 8,500 watts continuous power. However, since all generators lose 3 to 4 percent of their power for every 1,000 feet above sea level (and we live at 7,000 feet), the actual output is considerably less than that. Just the same, I have yet to find a tool that it can't run, and that's the way it should be. I can pump water from the well, and run an air compressor and a circular saw, all at the same time.

But beyond tools and well pumps, you will, on occasion, use your generator to charge your battery bank via the power inverter. This is the best reason among many for having a reliable, well-maintained, easy-to-start generator, since tinkering with a cantankerous generator in freezing weather when the battery bank is about drained isn't anyone's idea of a good time.

Most of the high-end sine wave AC power inverters (that will be in your off-grid home) have an auto-start feature built into their circuitry. If you choose to use it, the inverter can automatically start the generator whenever the battery voltage drops below a preset level. Some people—mostly those who are away from home for long periods of time, or who have inadequate wind and solar generating capacity—think it's the bees knees. Others, including us, use their generators so seldom they don't bother with it. If you choose to take advantage of this feature you should make certain that the generator you buy is wired for remote start. And, since gasoline engines, as a rule, need to be choked to start in cold weather, you will probably have to buy a generator than runs on either diesel or propane.

Look for a generator manufactured by a reputable company that stands behind its products. If it's a big generator (6,500 watts, or better) you'll want it to have an electric starter. If you plan to move it around, make sure it's mounted on a frame with pneumatic tires. And again, be certain it has multiple circuits, one of which is sufficient to power your biggest load.

SAWS

Circular Saws   I went through about a cubic yard of cheap circular saws until I broke down and bought a Sears Craftsman 7-inch worm-drive saw. That was over one garage, two barns, two decks, one workshop, one cabin and one house ago, and I still haven't had a lick of trouble with it. If it conked-out tomorrow I'd give it a proper burial with honors and go buy another one just like it. It's been that good of a saw.

Its only drawback is its unavoidable weightiness. It works fine for cutting lumber and plywood resting on sawhorses, but can be cumbersome for cutting things in awkward places, such as rafter tails. For that reason, I also have an 18-volt cordless trim saw with a 6-inch blade. It's gutless for long cuts in heavy lumber, but works good for everything else. The 24-volt models are even more powerful.

Make sure you have at least one heavy-duty circular saw you can depend on, because you'll be using it a lot. If you're inclined to shell-out the money for a good worm-drive saw, you won't regret the decision.

Compound Miter Saw A compound miter saw is extremely helpful for framing walls, floors, and roofs, and is absolutely essential for finish work, when exact angle cuts are a must. A heavy-duty 12-inch miter saw can easily handle 2 x 8's. For wider lumber, a model with a sliding blade can cut boards up to 12 inches wide.

Reciprocating Saw A reciprocating saw is one of those tools you don't use often, but when you need it, you really need it. One chore that comes immediately to mind was the time I had to cut two 6-inch diameter holes through $7^{1}/_{2}$-inch thick, nail-embedded rim joists to install fresh-air furnace vents. No other tool I know of could have performed that task.

I've also used a reciprocating saw for trimming floor joists in-place, cutting holes through the roof for vents and pipes, making rounded cuts on roof rafters where they meet the log wall, and cutting the holes for outlet boxes in log walls. Seldom used, but indispensable: don't build a home without one.

DRILLS

You'll want at least two drills; three is better. All of them should be variable speed and reversible. Here's what I suggest:

For screwing-down subfloor plywood, decking, etc., use a $^{3}/_{8}$-inch drill. Cordless drills work better for this because they turn slower, making them easier to handle consistently. LaVonne had trouble driving screws with our 120-volt drill, but found it quite easy with a 12-volt cordless model. The downside to using cordless drills is obvious: without enough spare batteries on hand, you

---

Construction Calculators

As much as I love working with feet and inches, it can be a bit maddening when it comes to squaring up a foundation or calculating rafter length using the Pythagorean theorem. To calculate the hypotenuse of a right triangle with sides of, say, 76' $3^{1}/_{4}$" x 32' $7^{5}/_{8}$", you have to convert the two measurements to their decimal equivalents (76.27083 feet x 32.63542 feet) before you can feed them into a calculator. And then the calculator spits back a decimal answer (82.95969 feet) that you will then have to convert back into feet and inches. That is, unless you have a calculator that understands feet and inches. And Pythagoras. After we had already finished the project, LaVonne bought me a pocket construction calculator she found at a lumber yard. You input the two dimensions in feet, inches, and fractions of an inch, press a single key, and it gives you back the hypotenuse (in our example, 82' $11^{1}/_{2}$") in the same units. Get one *before* you build; you'll be glad you did.

can work yourself out of a job in a hurry. That's why it's good to have both; when you start the generator to run the 120-volt drill, you can plug in the battery charger for the cordless model.

There are some jobs a $^3/8$-inch drill just can't handle easily; drilling deep holes in log walls for spikes is one of them, drilling large holes through thick rim joists is another. If it's in your budget, pick up a good $^1/2$-inch drill for the few times a $^3/8$-inch drill isn't up to the task at hand. I recommend a 120-volt model for the simple reason that you'll never run out of power, though admittedly there are some very impressive 24-volt cordless $^1/2$-inch drills on the market.

PNEUMATIC TOOLS

I'll admit it: I am now officially spoiled. I must have pounded about two million nails in my life before acquiring my first pneumatic staple gun. What had I put myself through all those years, and why? For fastening plywood to a roof deck or a gable end (or any of a hundred other things) a ¼-inch crown stapler can't be beat. I've since added a brad nailer and a finish nailer to my arsenal of air tools, and I wouldn't be without them.

The good thing is, staplers and nailers (unlike impact wrenches and spray guns) can do a lot of work before the compressor has to be recharged. This means you won't have to listen to the incessant blat! blat! blat! of a compressor (or the generator) while you're working.

BUILDER'S LEVEL

I'll refer to this tool in more detail in the next chapter. Often—and erroneously—referred to as a transit, a builder's level is a tool for establishing grade levels for foundations and floors, but lacks the sophistication of a surveying instrument. A little pricey, it nonetheless falls into the essential category.

LADDERS

You'll acquire several ladders before you're finished. We began with 16- and 20-foot extension ladders. By the time we were finished, we had added a 28-foot extension ladder, plus one 8-foot and two 6-foot step ladders to our collection. And this doesn't include the 32-foot

---

Odds and Ends

Following is a partial list of other tools you will need to complete the stages of construction prior to the log work:

Basic Carpentry
Tool belt
Framing hammer
Tape measures
Framing square
Combination square
Carpenter's pencils
Handsaws
Chalk box
Utility knives (brightly
　　colored so you can
　　find them)

**Excavation &
　　Foundation**
Men's leather gloves
Women's leather gloves
Plumb bob
Dry line
Flat bar
Crowbar
Straight bar
Spade
Flat shovel
Pickaxe

extension ladder we borrowed from a neighbor (and eventually took back, to demonstrate our good faith, when we needed to borrow his scaffolding).

Fiberglass ladders are sturdier and therefore safer, though they are a little heavier than aluminum. Look for ladders with good grips on the feet; it's no picnic when a ladder slides out from under you.

TOOLS FOR LOGWORK

Over the next few months you will personally get to know every one of the dozens of logs in the pile next to your foundation. Some you will like, others you won't. Some you will swear sprouted from the forest floor, years before you were born, for no other purpose than to cause you grief. Some you will threaten to reduce to cordwood and cast into the stove.

In the end, though, you will love them all. You will love them because each log will have found its special place in your home and—by virtue of that fact—will have become irreplaceable.

Log work is not difficult; at least not in the sense that writing complex software or rebuilding a car engine is difficult. But it is physically demanding. Just *how* demanding depends on two things: how much experience you have in working with logs, and how well you have chosen your tools. While the experience may take a little time, the tools we can address right now.

CHAINSAWS

Before we began our house, I had three chainsaws: two middle-aged Homelites and a geriatric McCulloch. They all ran well enough and any one of them was fine for felling and limbing the occasional tree or cutting up firewood. But none was the saw for building a log home. For that I needed a sleek and mean machine; a saw that was both light and powerful, rugged yet sophisticated. A saw that would start hot or cold, or warm, without my having to alternately curse and plead with it.

After spending a lot of time looking at different makes and models of chainsaws, I finally settled on a Stihl, model 036 Pro. At 12.5 pounds (minus the bar and chain) and 4.6 bhp with a 20-inch bar, it's the perfect saw for someone like me: medium height and build with good, but not extraordinary, upper body strength. Unless you're a bouncer at a

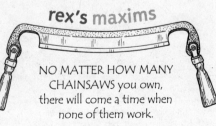

rex's maxims

NO MATTER HOW MANY CHAINSAWS you own, there will come a time when none of them work.

biker bar, building with 18-inch logs, you probably won't want anything much bigger.

Whatever you buy, don't scrimp. A cheap chainsaw is a world of misery waiting to happen. At the very least, make sure it starts easily and has good anti-vibration buffers. That way your elbows won't ache and your hands won't tingle at the end of the day.

POWER PLANER

Flat-based power planers are useful for everything from planing the treads of log stairs to giving a smooth, clean finish to cut log ends. Curved-base planers are great for smoothing down knots, knocking bumps off purlins and cleaning up scarf cuts. Though you may be able to get by without a power planer, there will certainly be times when you'll wish you had one. The heavy-duty power planers sold in log home supply catalogs are far better than the cheap models sold in lumber yards, though even they are better than nothing. Compare!—the deeper the cut, the better.

DRAWKNIVES

Next to a junky chainsaw, nothing will cause more needless exertion than a dull or poorly designed drawknife. It's not easy finding a good one, but once you do you'll think it's worth its weight in gold. Before beginning construction, we perused every flea market we could find, looking for drawknives. We bought three or four that ranged from worthless to passable. Three more knives borrowed from a friend were no better. Then LaVonne found a manufacturer on the internet, a log builder from Montana. He'd finally given up trying to buy a truly good drawknife so he designed and field tested his own. We ordered one, tried it, and quickly ordered another. Our average peeling time for a 50-foot log dropped from a grueling 2 hours, to a relatively smooth 30 to 45 minutes.

Get the heaviest knife you can handle easily, with a long enough blade that you're not constantly running your hands into the log. My knife has a 10-inch blade, LaVonne's an 8-inch. Even her short knife worked fine on 12-inch logs.

LaVonne's Verities

BUY THE BEST DRAWKNIFE you can, and then tell yourself that peeling logs builds character.

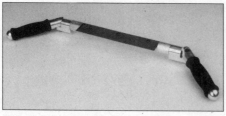

Bosworth Tools makes an excellent drawknife with adjustable handles. *Photo: Bosworth Tools*

CHISELS

A good chisel set is a worthwhile investment. Even if you don't use the whole set during log construction, you will later on when it come times to do the finish work. Get the kind with a steel shank in the handle so you can beat it with a hammer. I bought a set of Stanley chisels and mercilessly pounded the ends with a heavy framing hammer from the first log to the last, and never did any damage to any of them. Log home supply catalogs offer a variety of chisels. Most cost more than I'd care to pay without a compelling reason. So far, I haven't found one.

LOG DOGS AND LOG CLEATS

Log cleats are good for holding logs in the scribing position. Log dogs can be used for particularly stubborn logs that refuse to stay put, and they're more stable than cleats when working with a chainsaw. We made our own

Log cleat. *Photo: www.loghelp.com*

inexpensive log dogs from lengths of leftover rebar, and our log cleats with angle and flat iron. If you've got access to a welder and oxy/acetylene torch it's easy.

SCRIBERS

Scribers are used to transfer the shape of one log onto another. Used mainly for notches, you will find them useful for a number of operations. Many commercially available scribers are quite sophisticated and expensive. Most come with two spirit levels to ensure that the contour of the lower

A log dog on each end holds the log in place and prevents rolling when chainsawing the notch.

log is faithfully traced onto the upper log. I made my own with pencil rod and a few odds and ends, with a holder at the end for a pencil. To save some hassle next time around, I'll probably buy the real thing with a level or two.

Veritas Scriber. *Photo: www.loghelp.com*

PEAVEY AND STRAIGHT BARS

The peavey and the cant hook are used to roll logs; straight bars to slide, push and lift them. Any hardware store or lumber yard should have a selection of straight bars. Peaveys are a little harder to come by; probably you will have to get one by mail order from a log home supplier. I made my own by cutting a "V" out of a length of pipe, them bending it into a long cone and welding the seam. The hook was made from $3/4$-inch rebar.

Admittedly, the shovel handle I used is lighter than the thick handles on commercial peaveys, and as soon as mine breaks I'll probably bite the bullet and buy the real thing.

ELECTRIC WINCH

Logs are heavy, contrary, inertial creatures. Rolling logs is hard enough, but raising them without the right equipment is all but impossible. The mere thought of lifting the wooden beasts has culled many a poor soul who would *like* to build a log house from the ranks of those who actually do. But the fact is, it's done all the time and with a minimum expenditure of energy by those who know what they're doing. How? Well, you could lease a boom truck for a couple of months, or hire the Packers' defensive line during the off-season. Or you could invest in a good electric winch. (Of the three, this is definitely the cheapest.) The two manufacturers I know of that make 120-volt winches are Dutton-Lainson, and Dayton, though there are probably others. Find a model that is rated to *dead-lift* your heaviest logs, not just pull them. Spend a little extra for the remote. It will save you the trouble of having to climb a ladder every time you want to lift a log.

Peavey (left) and Cant Hook (right).
Photos: www.loghelp.com

Dayton electric winch.

A logger's tape is handy for measuring the long logs.
Photo: www.loghelp.com

There are dozens of tools I haven't mentioned here, primarily because I rarely—if ever—use them. Many log builders like to cut all, or part, of their notches with axes. I've personally never gotten the hang of using an axe for much of anything besides splitting firewood, so I can't recommend any particular style of axe.

Bark spuds are used to remove loose bark, thus making drawknife operations easier. On the right logs, a spud would be quite handy, but so seldom do I find a log with loose bark that I've never invested in one.

www.loghelp.com

The same goes for specially-shaped draw knives, adzes, and....well, the list
is a long one. I try to buy the tools I *need*, first, and *then* buy the ones that catch
my fancy. As long as I actually use the tools I buy, she-who-controls-the-purse-
strings lets me slide with a smirk and a sigh.

TOOL STORAGE

At this point, you're probably wondering where to put all of these new and
expensive tools. If you're worried about them walking away during your absence
(as tools often do) you may want to build a sturdy shed or invest in a tool trailer
to keep them from escaping. Otherwise, a portable garage (rubberized fabric over
a pipe frame) is inexpensive, easy to erect, and amazingly durable (and does not
require a building permit!). Ours has endured 90 mph winds and 1-inch hailstones without sustaining any damage. ❧

We erected a temporary
shed, with zippered
doors on each end, to
store tools and supplies.

June 1999

Gary is back, with a huge excavator [5]. Our dog, Newt, thinks such a piece of equipment would be perfect to get those pesky voles! It is a sunny, warm day for digging a foundation. The grass is unbelievably green, and it's a shame to dig up those wildflowers. The first scoop of dirt is huge. No turning back, I tell myself. Then Gary hits The Rock. What an awful sound! Just keep digging around it, says Rex. And so our hole in the ground takes shape, with The Rock in a corner. Thanks to a few sticks of dynamite, we have huge chunks of rock outside the hole (and a small spring in the middle of the foundation).

It's raining again, and the dogs [6] have fun in their newly formed lake. Slowly, in all this mud, we are making progress.

Where is that concrete contractor?? When work is plentiful, I've come to realize that subcontractors are not obligated to return phone calls. So we wait, while it rains some more.

Ingram Well Drilling can fit us into their busy schedule. This will be the big test. How deep will our water be? The drilling rig barely makes it up the muddy road and Larry sets up to drill. But the next truck loaded with water to lubricate the drill bit gets stuck. Call Gary. Maybe he and his excavator can help. Lucky for us, Gary is in town, and with lots of chain and teamwork, the truck is pulled to the top. This 'truck-not-making-it-up-the-hill' thing is getting hard to watch.

In between hail and rain, Larry drills and drills for water. I'm getting depressed. Nothing at 350 feet, 400 feet, 450 feet, 500 feet. Finally, water and lots of it at 540 feet. A hefty bill, but it could be worse. We are very relieved.

Excavation begins.

CHAPTER 6

EXCAVATION AND FOUNDATION WORK

The Indelicate Art of Replacing Rock and Dirt with "Mud"

THE EXCAVATION

Our land, beautiful though it is, has exactly one building site where the sun shines in abundance and the wind blows often enough to be useful. Before we broke ground, it was a mildly sloping meadow with an occasional granite outcropping rising from the ground near the perimeter. There were no rocks showing within 20 feet of where we intended to dig. Naively, we thought that excavating would be a simple matter; like scooping out quicksand with a spoon.

Then we were mugged by reality.

On the third stab at the soft earth, the excavator shuddered and the huge bucket made a sound like a freight train scraping against the side of a rock cliff. LaVonne looked at me as if to say, "Why does this sort of thing keep happening to us?" I looked back, thinking, *how should I know*? In any event, whatever was happening—and why—was immaterial. It wasn't like we could just move to another spot and try again; it was this site or nothing.

The man doing the excavating—Gary, a friend who knows a lot more about poking under the surface of these hard old hills than I'll ever know—suggested we keep digging. Maybe it was the only place within the perimeter stakes where the bedrock was so near the surface, he told us. Considering that he had just hit a granite wart on the back of Mother Earth less than 1/100th of the way through his task, we thought he was being a trifle optimistic, but thin on options, we told him to go ahead.

We watched each bucketful come out with anxious curiosity. After awhile we actually quit cringing every time the bucket cut into uncovered earth. A few hours later we discovered that, to our relieved amazement, Gary was right. The completed pit was 44-feet by 34-feet, 8 feet deep on the backside, 3 feet on the front. With one gigantic piece of bedrock in the southwest corner; right where we had planned to put a workshop.

Since there was no realistic prospect of removing the rock with a jackhammer (in my estimation it would have taken 10 days, two complete sets of lower lumbar discs and about seven kidneys), there was no choice but to blast.

Dynamite, we happily discovered, was cheap. The greatest cost associated with blasting was in hiring someone to drill the holes to put the dynamite in. Giddy with the prospect of having a completed excavation, I volunteered. (However much damage I inflicted on myself in drilling the holes, I reckoned, I was still body parts ahead of what I would have been.)

It went pretty fast, actually. I secured a pneumatic rock drill from a local equipment rental shop, complete with a V8-powered compressor, and attacked the rock that was covering my workshop. After 2 hours (and two carbide bits) I had 13 holes, each 2 inches wide by 2 feet deep.

The explosives expert Gary found for us—his name was Travis—was a mountain man who fit right in with every other guy holed up in these rocky hills. And his pickup was in even worse shape than mine. We hit it off right away.

One stick of dynamite, Travis told me, has the kinetic energy of a Cadillac hitting a brick wall at 90 mph. It sounded like it was going to be quite a show. After the dynamite and blasting caps were placed in the holes and all wired together, Gary covered the whole affair with a couple feet of dirt to keep the debris from flying out like shrapnel from a toolshed-sized hand grenade. Then we all hid behind a juniper tree and peered through the branches as thirteen speeding Caddies simultaneously converged on our troublesome rock.

Rex drills holes with a pneumatic rock drill for placing the dynamite.

I don't know what I expected—maybe something out of a Mel Gibson flick—but what we saw and heard wasn't it. The ground shook from 80 feet away, and a spray of dirt flew up like a dust spout from an earthbound whale, but the ear-splitting *Ka-Boom*! I was braced for was merely a loud, but muffled, *Whump*! Thirteen luxury cars smacking into a brick wall within a tunnel isn't nearly as impressive as on the streets of San Francisco.

The dirt blanket had done its job.

And so had the dynamite.

The rock was now in about a million pieces, ranging in size from sand pebble to dog house. Satisfied, Travis sat on his battered tailgate and wrote out the bill. He figured and re-figured, then shook his head and handed it to me, saying, "This is too cheap." We had to agree; it was under $200.

I can only hope that your excavation goes a little smoother. If not, maybe your explosives expert (or, more affectionately, "dynamite guy") will be as reasonable as ours. Here are a few things to keep in mind:

- ❧ Mark your footing perimeter before your excavator arrives. Make sure your corners are square, your stakes are exactly where you want your house to go, and you know at what depth you want the bottom of your footings. Allow for an extra few feet around the footing to facilitate the form work. The excavator should know the rest.

- ❧ Before the digging commences, stake out the location of your well, septic tank and leach field, per local regulations. You should also know where you intend to put your solar array and wind tower. Review your plan with the person doing the excavation. If he is experienced, he will be able to point out any problems you may have overlooked.

- ❧ You'll want to know—especially if you run into rock—where your water line is going to enter the house, and where your sewage line will leave it, since both will more than likely go under, or through, the footing or foundation wall. This means that the depth of the inlet for the septic tank will need to be determined before the foundation is poured. (Gas and electric lines, on the other hand, generally enter the house through the first floor rim joists.)

- ❧ For obvious reasons, it's a good idea to take care of any dynamite blasting *before* you drill a well.

FOUNDATION

Whether you hire a contractor or do it yourself, the cost of your foundation will probably be one of the biggest expenses of the entire house project, so make sure it's done right.

We had a concrete contractor lined out months before we broke ground, but once the excavation was complete and we were ready to begin the foundation walls, he kept putting us off. He always had one more big job to complete in town before he could move his crew up into the hills. Then, the day before he was scheduled to come up and look at our building site for the very first time, he hopped on a plane to Mexico for two weeks. So much for Pablo.

It was getting late in the season. We'd wasted over a month waiting for a guy who would never show. And every concrete contractor within 50 miles—at least those with the civility to return our phone calls—was booked solid for several months out. Within this dreary backdrop of betrayal and abandonment, I announced to LaVonne one night that we were going to do the foundation ourselves. The look she gave me was priceless; it was a *you've really*

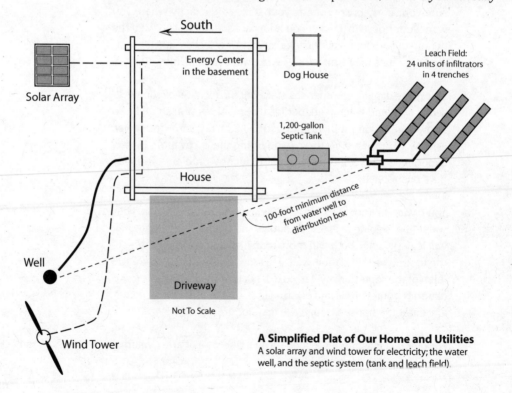

A Simplified Plat of Our Home and Utilities
A solar array and wind tower for electricity; the water well, and the septic system (tank and leach field).

lost it this time, Cowboy look, if ever I've seen one. Even though we were out of options—familiar ground, by this point—it was no easy matter to convince her that we could successfully complete a project as complex and labor intensive as forming and pouring a basement foundation. So, naturally I did what any man would do in my situation: I lied. I told her that forming a wall was really no harder than framing a wall; all we were really doing, I explained, was creating a vessel to hold liquid rock (I neglected to mention that the liquid weighed 80,000 pounds). It would probably be fun, I insisted. And, of course, I used the old catch-phrase that the experience would be "character building." She rolled her dazzling green eyes at the last part, and knew I was lying through my teeth about the rest of it, but they were lies she wanted to believe, so after I gave her an (honest) estimate of how much money we would save, she at last consented.

In the end—that mystical place in the unforeseeable future where all seeds at last bear fruit—everything worked out nicely. The thousands of dollars we saved by doing it ourselves was more than just compensation for our labor, and we were both brimming over with newly reconstituted character. Best of all, since we employed a new type of foundation system in which permanent polystyrene is used as the wall form (instead of traditional plywood or aluminum), our basement walls were insulated to R-28, not including interior gypsum board or exterior stone.

It is not within the scope of this book to give detailed instructions on the construction of every conceivable type of foundation. Other writers with far more foundation experience have already done that. There are, however, certain methods, techniques and tricks of the trade common to all foundations that bear elucidation here. Also, since many of you will elect to do your own foundation work, I'd like to elaborate (later in this chapter) on the polystyrene system we used for our walls. In our estimation, it's the answer to every do-it-yourselfer's dream.

WHERE IS NORTH?

If you plan to build your house along a true east-west axis for the purpose of placing your solar array on the roof, or if you just want your house to be square with the world, you'll need to know where true north is.

Those of us deficient in surveying experience generally rely on a compass and chart giving the magnetic declination for our particular area. With a bit of luck, you might be able to get within two or

LaVonne's Verities

IF YOU CAN DO IT
YOURSELF, DO IT.
At least you'll know when
you'll show up for work,
and that the job will be
done right.

three degrees by this method. If that is acceptable, great. Personally, I prefer another way. I own three compasses and a GPS, and I don't trust any of them enough to allow them to dictate the placement of my house. Besides, the magnetic declination for northern Colorado's Front Range tends to vary from publication to publication.

But why settle for an approximation when you can get a nearly perfect alignment with a couple of T-posts and the ability to locate two of the most conspicuous constellations (the Little Dipper and the Big Dipper) in the night sky? Polaris, the bright, terminal jewel in the handle of the Little Dipper (officially known as Ursa Minor) is the North Star. It is the pivot point around which every other star in the night sky revolves. The two bright stars delineating the outer bowl of the Big Dipper (Ursa Major) point to it from 30 degrees away. Once you know where Polaris is, all you need to do is to drive a post into the ground, either on your southwest or southeast corner. As you sight directly over the top of the first post, have someone to the north of you move a second post east and west until a sight line along both posts points directly to Polaris. You now have a true northsouth axis to work from, either for your excavation or foundation, or the alignment of your solar array.

North Star

Little Dipper

Big Dipper

Sight along 2 posts
to line up with
the North Star

Due to a phenomenon known as the **precession of the equinoxes**, the North Star changes every few thousand years. In the unlikely event that this book is still in print 12,000 years from now, some future editor will have to replace Polaris with the 0.1 magnitude star, Vega.

MAKING IT SQUARE

There are numerous ways to ensure that your foundation is square. Some are easier than others, some more accurate. Here's how I do it:

∾   Using the measurements for the outside of your foundation wall, drive a stake into the ground to mark one corner.

∾   Measure along one wall to find your next corner. Pound nails in the top of your stakes to ensure you have an exact point to work from.

At this point, we will defer to a clever Greek mystic of ancient times, and the theorem that bears his name. The Pythagorean Theorem, $a^2 + b^2 = c^2$, gives the formula for determining the length of a right triangle's hypotenuse when the length of the other two sides are known. (Unless you're a whiz at mental math, you will need a pocket calculator with a square root key.) Let's say your foundation is 28 feet by 36 feet. That's a and b. So what is c? It's the diagonal distance from, say, your northwest corner to your southeast corner. To find it, square a, then b, and add the squares together. In this example, $28^2 = 784$ and $36^2 = 1296$. Together they total 2080. Now, hit the square root key, and voilà! The answer, 45.60, is the exact diagonal distance in our hypothetical example.

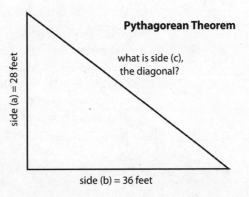

Pythagorean Theorem

side (a) = 28 feet

what is side (c), the diagonal?

side (b) = 36 feet

$a^2 + b^2 = c^2$
$28^2 + 36^2 = c^2$
784 feet + 1296 feet = c^2
$2080 = c^2$
square root of 2080 = 45.6 feet

c = 45.6 feet or 45' 7-3/16"

You'll need two long tape measures for this next part. Put one end of each tape on the nails in each end of your two stakes. Now, pull both tapes until the lengths you want bisect each other (at corner 3). In our example, it would be 36 feet for the long side, and 45.60 feet (45 feet, 7³/₈ inches) for the diagonal. Drive a stake.

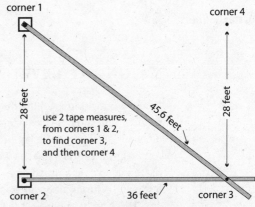

corner 1

corner 4

28 feet

use 2 tape measures, from corners 1 & 2, to find corner 3, and then corner 4

45.6 feet

28 feet

corner 2

36 feet

corner 3

Applying the Pythagorean Theorem to Your Foundation

Pull the tapes to the opposite corner (corner 4) in the same manner and drive your last stake. Now check and recheck all of your sides and diagonals. That's it.

Many books recommend the use of batter boards, once the corner stakes are in place. These are two boards, 4 to 6 feet in length, nailed to stakes set at right angles, a few feet outside the corners of your excavation. By placing nails along the top edge of the batter boards, you can then run bisecting string lines to determine the inner and outer perimeters of both your footings and your walls.

While I have found batter boards useful for pier foundations, where it's helpful to know if you've dug a hole just where it should have been, for full foundations they seem to be more work than necessary. Since the batter boards are at least a foot or two above the ground, and your completed excavation is at least 3 feet below it, you are forever dropping plumb bobs from string intersections to determine your corners.

In my estimation, it's easier just to re-square the footing stakes (via the Pythagorean method) once the excavation is complete.

corner of house

Batter Boards

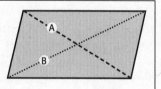

Out-of-square foundations can have opposite sides equal in length, but the diagonals will not be identical. Here, diagonal A is shorter than B.

MAKING IT LEVEL

If your excavation is a little out of square, it's no big deal, as long as you have room within the hole to make corrections when you lay out your footings. But if it's out of level, you've got problems. You want your footing to rest on undisturbed ground, and it doesn't work to backfill and tamp if you or your excavator dig too deep over a broad area. Eventually the dirt you put back in the hole will settle and your footing will crack, and then…Well, just don't do it.

There are many ways to level a foundation, ranging from clever to tedious. I'm going to tell you exactly one: a tripod-mounted builder's level. For under $300 you can set yourself up with a sight level (essentially, a low-power telescope with a spirit level on top), tripod and leveling rod. For a couple hundred more you can buy a laser level. It may sound like a lot of money, but by the time you finish your house, you will have used your level so often that you won't be able to imagine how you could have gotten by without it.

If your house is built into a hillside (as ours is) you'll need it determine the different elevations at each corner. That way you will know how deep to dig in the back of the hole. Once grade (the depth to the *bottom* of your footing) is established, you should take periodic sightings to make sure the hole is neither too deep nor too shallow. No hole is perfect; there will always be a few ups and downs, but try to keep them at a minimum. Remember: the *highest* point in your excavation will be the same grade as the *bottom* of your footing form, so start there.

As you form your footing, take sightings every few feet and then raise or lower the forms as needed. What holds true for your excavation is equally true for your footings: if the footing is a little out of square, you can offset the wall forms to bring the structure back into square. But if it's out of level you will either end up doing some fancy form work, or spending a lot of time shimming your sill plate. Neither is much fun.

Indispensible tools: a sight level and rod.

FOOTINGS

Most people who form their own footings use 2 x 10's or 2 x 12's (depending on the foundation specs) held in place with stakes and double-headed "duplex" nails. You can either use wooden stakes—which move from where you intended them to go as you drive them in the ground, and will then split as you drive a nail through them—or you can splurge a little and buy metal stakes, with predrilled holes, from a masonry supply. Either way, all you are really doing when forming the footing is building a continuous channel for concrete. If your footing happens to be the same thickness as your roof rafters, you can buy lumber of the appropriate length and use it later in your roof.

To keep the forms from spreading under the enormous weight of the concrete, you will need to nail 1 x 2 spacers every few feet along the top of your forms. The spacers will ensure that the finished footing is uniform in width, and will provide a bridge from which to suspend steel reinforcing rod (rebar).

If there will be water or sewer pipes going through your footing (or your foundation wall), wedge a PVC sleeve between the boards of your form where the pipe will enter the wall, keeping in mind that the inside diameter of your sleeve will need to be a little more than

Special framing of the footing is required around a remnant of "THE ROCK" in the southwest corner.

the outside diameter of your pipe. Once in place, drive a few nails through from the outside of the form to ensure it doesn't slip when the weight of the concrete pushes down on it. When the forms are later stripped, there will be a nice channel for running the pipe.

Some contractors like to install a keyway in the top of the footing. This a tapered depression made by pushing boards (with sides cut at 15-degree angles) into the wet concrete. It is meant to keep the vertical wall, soon to be poured on top of it, from sliding side to side. If it's in the plans, do it. But unless there are going to be unusual lateral stresses on your walls, you can accomplish the same thing by leaving the surface of your footing rough, and setting vertical lengths of rebar into the wet concrete every few feet. Again, refer to your plans.

When it comes time to pour, call in all the favors you can. There's no such thing as too much help at a concrete pour. At the very least, you will want two able-bodied men (sorry; the cement truck driver doesn't count) for an average footing. Twice as many is much better. Two men working the chute is ideal; that way, one will always be free to motion the driver to speed up the mud, slow it down, or drive ahead. Right in the thick of things should be another man with a shovel, tossing the wet mud forward whenever it piles up and threatens to spill over the side of the forms. If you're lucky enough to have a fourth man, he can tap the forms with a hammer to help the concrete settle out, then screed the tops of the forms with a board to level out the concrete before it begins to set up. However you do it, once the mud starts to flow, no one will be scratching their head wondering what to do.

LaVonne ties wire around the rebar to suspend it from the 1 x 2 spacers in the footing. The two piers in the center will support the steel support posts in the garage, and the log posts above them. Right: Joe screeds the mud to the top of the footing boards.

WALLS

With the completion of the footing there comes a profound sense of accomplishment. It is the first structure to rise from your ragged, unsightly excavation that is truly square and flat. Just imagine, then, how it's going to feel, seeing the completed concrete walls rising up out of the ground. For the first time, you will have a true feel for the size of your house, and an eye-level view of the height of your first floor.

Unless you are doing a pier foundation with tubular cardboard forms, you will find the walls several degrees trickier than the footings. No matter how square you have your walls marked out with chalk lines on the footings, they will find a way to twist out of square at the top. And the taller the walls, the more you will need to "rack" them back into square.

But first things first.

If you elect to form your foundation walls using plywood forms, I suggest that you rent them. Plywood concrete forms, though they are no thicker than regular $3/4$-inch plywood, are much stronger, since they are made of finer-grained wood, with thinner, tighter laminations, and they have a smooth, waxy surface that repels concrete and makes them much easier to remove than standard plywood. Besides, the only conceivable use you would have for that much $3/4$-inch plywood *after* the pour would be in your subfloors. But since flooring plywood is generally tongue-&-groove, you will find the forms extremely difficult to break down after the walls cure, because the concrete will "glue" many of the tongues to their respective grooves. To make matters worse, you will have done so much damage to your expensive boards—besides damage to the edges, large swatches of board will remain stuck to the concrete—that many of them will be unusable.

As I mentioned above, there is another way. Polystyrene concrete forms, though a little pricey, are easy for one or two people to work with, and the R-value they will add to a basement or crawl space will be more than worth the extra money in the long run, since your basement will cost much less to heat,

Longer lengths of vertical rebar have been wired to rebar stubs set in the concrete footing. Then the wall forms go up one row at a time. Horizontal rebar is added every few rows.

Wall forms are finished and ready for bracing.

and the pipes in your crawl space will be less likely to freeze.

There are several different manufacturers of polystyrene forms. Some make a better product than others. I suggest you make some inquiries before deciding on which one to use. While you will, of course, need to talk to the salespeople for the different brands of forms, you should also talk to a few concrete truck drivers, and concrete-pumping operators. These are the folks out in the field whose job it is to dump wet, heavy mud into these fragile-looking forms. They will be more than happy to regale you with stories about which types of forms have had disasters. Listen to them—they know what they're talking about.

The system we used is called Lite-Form®. The individual members are 8-feet long by 8-inches high by 2-inches thick, with slots cut every 8 inches to allow for the insertion of permanent plastic spacer ties. The local dealer delivered the forms herself, then spent

Pumping concrete into our foundation walls, with the help of friends.

over an hour with us on the job site demonstrating how everything went together. By the time she left, we were off and running.

It took us about a week—in a constant battle with heavy rain and sticky mud—to form a 28- x 38-foot basement with 8-foot walls, and then brace the forms and build scaffolding in preparation for the pour. LaVonne assembled the pieces while I cut, bent and wired the rebar in the walls and around door and window openings. It all went off without a hitch.

Whether you use conventional forms or one of the polystyrene systems, you will want to brace the walls before the pour. Considering that a 10-foot section of an 8-inch thick, 8-foot wall weighs in the neighborhood of 6,000 pounds when filled with wet concrete, you really can't use too much bracing. If you are pouring a basement foundation, you can run 2 x 4's up the side every 6 or 8 feet, then brace them in the middle and at the top with diagonal 2 x 4's, and anchor them to the ground with stakes. The vertical 2 x 4's are also handy to support the scaffolding you will need to work along the top of the wall during the pour. Brace your form walls inside and out, giving special attention to the corners, doors, windows and bulkheads, since these are the most likely areas for "blowouts" to occur.

As you install your bracing, use a level to make certain your walls remain perfectly vertical. Take multiple measurements across your walls and from corner to corner, then use the bracing to push or pull the walls back into alignment.

Before you pour the walls, you should determine if you need

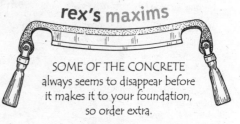

A pumper truck was the only method for us. Two men man-handled the nozzle and directed the mud into the walls; two men operated the vibrator; and one guy made sure there were no blow-outs. He also screed-ed the top edge and set the anchor bolts.

to use a concrete-pumping truck. If you are built into a hillside it's a good idea, since the walls on the low end will be higher than the truck's chute. With poly-styrene forms, the concrete needs to be poured in "lifts" (a maximum of 3 feet at a time, for our forms). At the very least, a pumper will save you the trouble of having to guide the driver on multiple trips around the foundation.

If you still have any friends left after pouring your footing, call them up when it comes time to pour the walls. Entice them with whatever it takes to get them to help, because you'll need them. During our wall pour, we had two men on the pumper nozzle, two trading off on the concrete vibrator, and another smoothing the tops of the walls with a trowel. We could have used more.

ANCHOR BOLTS AND BEAM POCKETS

The size and placement of the anchor bolts will be determined by local building codes, and should be specified in the plans. Examine your floor plan, then place the anchor bolts in such a way that the floor joists won't rest on top of them. It's a little trick that will save you a lot of work later.

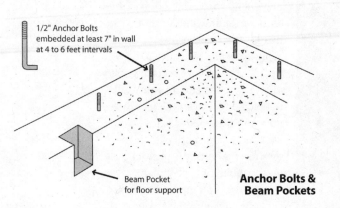

1/2" Anchor Bolts embedded at least 7" in wall at 4 to 6 feet intervals

Beam Pocket for floor support

Anchor Bolts & Beam Pockets

Beam pockets are simple to make. All you have to do is fashion blocks of dimensional lumber the same height and width of the beam, and screw (or nail) it to the inside of the form. Just be sure to leave yourself a little extra room—it's a lot easier to add metal shims later, than to chip out the sides of a beam pocket.

DAMP-PROOFING AND BACKFILLING

Damp-proofing is a good idea, whether or not your county requires it. The damp-proofing material is simply an emulsified asphalt applied to the foundation walls to keep ground water from seeping through the cracks that may eventually appear. A glance at the phone book should direct you to a professional applicator, or you can buy it at the lumber yard and apply it yourself with either a roller or a brush. Be sure and wear grungy clothes—the stuff will never wash out.

The amount of time the walls need to cure before backfilling the foundation is dependent upon several factors: the length and height of the wall, the wall thickness, the ambient temperature, and the nature of the soil. The longer you can wait to backfill, the better. Ten days for an average wall in normal conditions is usually acceptable. Two weeks is even better.

Rex damp-proofs the outside of our foundation walls with emulsified asphalt.

Ufer Grounding System

A Ufer grounding system uses the rebar and concrete in your foundation as an extra grounding system for over-current protection. Developed by Herbert G. Ufer during WWII to protect bomb storage vaults from lightning strikes, a Ufer grounding system is simple and inexpensive to install before the walls are poured. It is an especially good system to use in areas with dry (non-conductive) soil, and/or frequent lightning strikes. Any good electrician should know how to install a Ufer grounding system. If not, there is a wealth of information on the Internet.

CONCRETE FLOORS

Concrete flatwork is an art that takes months, if not years, to master. If you've never done it before, nothing I could possibly say here would make it any better for you. Flatwork is not the kind of thing you can learn by reading a book; it takes hands-on experience and lots of it. Besides, it would be hypocritical of me to try to tell you how to do something that I'm not particularly comfortable doing myself.

Whoever does your concrete floor, you'll need to decide how soon after finishing your foundation walls you intend to pour it. Of course, your below-ground plumbing will all have to be in place and inspected, and that will take some time. If you are planning radiant floor heat in your garage or basement, that will take a while to install, as well.

As much as you would like to have your floor poured as soon as possible, in many instances there is no technical reason it needs to be done right away (we waited almost a year after the completion of our foundation walls). So, before you get gung-ho to pour the floor, ask yourself how you intend to move your logs around as you build your log walls. If you don't have the luxury of using a boom-truck during your log wall construction, you may want to consider using a gin pole. This is a sturdy log that stands vertically. It will go through a hole left in the middle of your first floor, and rest in a hole dug in the dirt below. With a boom at the top from which you can suspend an electric winch, it will greatly facilitate the handling of wall logs. But it will be impossible to anchor into the ground if you've already poured your floor.

On the other hand, a concrete floor locks the foundation walls into place, and this is important with certain types of soil. If your foundation engineer insists that the floor be poured before the house goes up, you can still leave an area open for a gin pole, then fill it with concrete later. ∾

LaVonne's Verities

IF YOU WANT IT TO
RAIN, order a truck full
of concrete;
or better yet, order two.

July 1999

The concrete guy gets the boot and my darling husband says we can do it ourselves. I think he is crazy: we pick a corner in the muddy pit, and start forming the footing. I prefer graphic design, and Rex would prefer that I didn't ask so many questions. Our friend Joe shows up to help with the pour, and of course, it rains. We work in the freezing cold rain of the late day to smooth out the "mud," while getting the other mud up to our knees. Another day to remember (or not remember, which is it?).

Before you know it, we have huge piles of foam boards and plastics ties, waiting to be assembled into our basement walls. A simple demonstration from the dealer, and I'm on my way [7]. It's really pretty simple and enjoyable after the dirt-and-mud of the past few weeks... it's clean, dry and above ground. Reminds me of Lego toys. It is easier to work on the house when you can see measurable progress.

August 1999

It's a good day. We finished assembling the forms for our foundation...complete with two windows and a walk-in door. Two garage doors will fill the east side. The big pour is scheduled for Saturday when the neighbors can help. We are praying the rains stay away, just for a few days, so the trucks can make it up our road.

The pumper arrives early. What a sight to see that huge vehicle coming through the trees. The driver suggests we add more bracing to the walls, so everyone scrambles for the 2 x 4's, cordless drills and hammers. Then we wait and wait. Finally the mixer shows up and the pour gets underway. My job is to take pictures, and to keep the dogs out from under the wheels. A second load of concrete arrives too soon and it is getting way too crowded up here on top of the hill. (Actually, the second truck was to be the first truck...but he took a wrong turn. That flustered driver will probably refuse to drive in the mountains again.)

The pour took all morning, but we survived without any blowouts on the walls. The guys worked hard [8]. We couldn't have done it without them. Thanks—Errol, Dave, Joe and German!

Log • ically Solar

Sometimes things just seem destined to be. Soon after Dan and Ronnie Reisman decided to build a weekend cabin near Florissant, Colorado, they discovered that the log home company they'd chosen to work with (American Southwest Log Homes) had a model so close to Dan's design that it could be adapted with only minor modifications. It was an auspicious start that grew no less so as the project proceeded and the Reismans could see their modest-but-heartfelt dream grow to fruition. The end result, a 950-square-foot lodgepole pine cabin with an open floor plan and an eye-pleasing cathedral ceiling, was exactly what the couple wanted.

With one bedroom and 1½ baths, the RockinR, as they fondly call their spread, is mostly an open floor plan. This makes it both roomy and easy to heat, which is good, because Dan and Ronnie want to keep it simple.

The heating system, for instance, involves neither pipes, nor fans, nor ducts. It consists, rather, of a Jøtul woodstove and a pair of non-electric wall-mounted propane heaters. Domestic hot water comes (without a tank) from an on-demand propane heater. And the solar-electric system that supplies the cabin with electricity is small, simple, and neat as a pin.

Four roof-mounted, 125-watt BP modules provide the power; an OutBack MX60 charge controller conditions it; a bank of four Rolls-Surrette batteries store it; and a pair of OutBack inverters convert it to the 120/240 volt house current Dan and Ronnie need to run a select few appliances. And, of course, the 240-volt, 1.5-horsepower well pump they use to fill their cistern.

Aside from the solar array, all the components are sequestered in the "Genny House," along with the seldom-used 5,500-watt generator. The only electrical connection leading to the house is a single 120-volt line for the lights and outlets.

Ironically, Dan and Ronnie could've hooked up to the power grid for a little less than the $13,000 they spent on the PV system. In fact, as a draftsman for Xcel Energy's Electric Standards department, you might think Dan would feel compelled to. But he wasn't. Not only did he and Ronnie not want to look at denuded power corridor leading to the house, they didn't want the monthly electric bills. "This way is better," Ronnie explains. "Every time I turn on a light switch I smile!"

House 950 square feet on 2 levels; milled round logs

Heating woodstove; 2 propane wall-mounted heaters

Water pumped by PV system from a 500-foot well into cistern

Refrigeration propane

Solar array 500 watts

Wind turbine none

Inverter 2 Outback 3524

Batteries 4 Rolls-Surrette L16 style

Backup power 5.5-kilowatt, gasoline-fired Porter Cable generator

CHAPTER 7

THE FLOOR

Toward Building the Flattest Place on the Mountain

I t wasn't too long ago that building a log house or cabin meant building with logs throughout. Log beams under the floor, supporting log or heavy timber joists. If the nearest lumber yard was 50 miles away over invariably rough terrain—and your WWII vintage truck was liable to break down half the way there—it was a lot easier just to use the tall, straight trees obstructing your view of the distant, snowcapped peaks.

Today, with reliable vehicles, good roads and easy access to straight, strong, graded lumber, the only real reason to support the floor with logs is purely aesthetic: it's done to preserve the purer sense of the tradition. I can respect that. I sometimes dream that, if LaVonne and I were to sell this place and move 30 miles higher up the canyon into a densely forested high plateau, we might just go primitive, eschewing civilization and all modern conveniences. We would build an eminently non-code log house entirely from the land, just to prove to ourselves that we could do it. We would mill our own boards for the roof planks and floors, and split the roof shingles with a broadaxe. Make all our own doors and windows, and chink the walls with mud and ash. And, of course, our foundation would be massive piers of carefully stacked rock.

The pure, untainted, two-against-the-world romanticism of this notion, I'm sure, resonates deep in the heart of anyone who has ever considered building their own log house.

At the same time, however, I strongly suspect that you did not buy this book because you yearn to express, in its rugged entirety, the primal urge that growls from deep within your id. You want a home out of the city but not out of world. A grand log structure of rustic majesty that doesn't compromise, to any great degree, the habits of living you've honed since childhood or the comforts that make living more a pleasure than an ordeal. Beyond that, you want to finish your log house within your lifetime, and not spend any more time than necessary on matters that, in the long run, are unimportant.

All that being said, let me suggest—you knew I'd get around to it, sooner or later—that you support your floor with steel I-beams and engineered wood I-joists, rather than logs and timbers.

The reasons for doing this are numerous. I'll give you three.

Reason #1: The fact is, no one will see your fancy log work. If you are building on a pier foundation, or a wall for a crawlspace, the admirers of your craftsmanship will have to crawl under the house to see what you've done. And if you're building on a basement foundation, the only thing that will show when you are all done is the log beams which, since your basement is *not* built of logs, will probably clash, anyway.

Reason #2: Log beams are notched into the sill logs, and the joists that rest on them are notched into the course of logs above. That means you will use two full courses of logs before you arrive at the floor's surface. So by building a conventional floor and beginning your log construction on top if it, you will save yourself two entire courses of wall logs, a few notches and a whole lot of peeling.

Reason #3: If you're still not convinced, here comes the *coup de grace*. The modern floor is not simply a flat surface on which to set your chairs and tables; it's a well-planned highway of water, sewer and gas pipes; hundreds of yards of electrical wire (in and out of conduits); phone wires and low-voltage wires for thermostats, stereos, and computer systems. If you build your floor with logs, timbers, or even standard dimensional lumber, you will, at the very least, make more work for the plumber and electrician. And you may even run afoul with the county, since building inspectors take a dim view of the practice of drilling dozens of large holes through structural members that were not designed for such treatment.

Therein lies the beauty of engineered wood I-joists. (In our home we used a Weyerhauser product called Trus-Joist® or TJIs.) Consisting of a layer of wafer board set on edge between finely-laminated 2 x 2's, I-joists are designed to allow for the passage of pipes and conduits without loosing their structural integrity. Besides that, they are perfectly straight (which makes for a flat floor), have practically no vertical deflection, and can be ordered in any length that will fit on a lumber truck. For floors, they're a builder's dream.

SUPPORTING THE SUBFLOOR

If you are building a house and not a small cabin, I'll assume that your joists will have to span distances greater than 10 or 12 feet. That means you will need beams (usually steel I-beams) and posts between your walls to support the joists (and probably concrete piers beneath the posts, in the basement or crawl space). The I-beams should rest in beam pockets in the foundation walls, and the tops of the beams should be level with the top of foundation.

Once the beams are in place, it's time to install the sill plate, a continuous board of the same nominal width as your foundation walls. (So, if the wall is 8-inches thick, you will use 2 x 8 boards for your sill plate.)

Before you begin, measure the top of your foundation walls, corner to corner and side to side. If the walls are a little out of square, you can "rack" the sill plate to bring the structure back into square by marking the corners correctly and connecting these corner marks with chalklines.

To mark the sill plate for the hole locations for the anchor bolts poking out of your foundation walls, set straight boards on top of the bolts, making sure the edge of the board is even with your chalk line. Hit the board with a hammer over each bolt to mark the board, then drill your holes in the board. Since it's doubtful that the anchor bolts are perfectly vertical, or your board is perfectly plumb with your chalk line, drill the holes at least $1/8$-inch bigger than your bolts. This will be your "slop factor." (If your foundation walls are so out of square that you are not able to fix it by racking the sill plate, try instead to run the imperfections to one corner, then begin laying out the floor in the opposite (square) corner. This will make it much easier to lay the subflooring.)

Before bolting the sill plate into place, run a layer of thin, foam-like plastic insulation under it. The insulation will create a seal between the sill plate and top of the foundation. More importantly, it will keep the wood from coming into contact with the concrete, thereby preventing the rot that inevitably occurs when wood and concrete get together.

Now run boards along the tops of your steel I-beams, using the same type of insulation to bring them level with the sill plate. Secure them in place with

LaVonne bolts 2 x 6 boards to the top of steel I-beams.

^{1}/4-inch carriage bolts every few feet. Unless you're a glutton for punishment, I suggest you buy three or four high-quality drill bits for this operation. Cobalt bits are my favorite; high-speed steel bits, on the other hand, are next to worthless for drilling through I-beams. ***Note:*** *If you use structural laminated-wood beams for floor support, the wood must be separated from the concrete in the beam pocket.*

RIM JOISTS

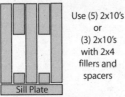

Rim Joists that Run **Parallel** with Floor Joists

Use (5) 2x10's or (3) 2x10's with 2x4 fillers and spacers

Sill Plate

Rim Joists that Run **Perpendicular** with Floor Joists

(2) 2x10's with 2x4 fillers and a spacer at the bottom

Sill Plate

With the foundation walls and I-beams plated, it's time to install your rim joists. These are the dimensional lumber counterpart of your I-joists (2 x 10's, for example) set on edge, even with the outside of your sill plate and toe-nailed in place with 16d framing nails. Since the weight of the logs will be so much greater than the weight of a normal frame house, it is advisable to use multiple rim joists along the walls that run parallel with your floor joists. Ideally, you should have solid wood the entire width of the sill plate. This will be expensive, however, so you may want to simply run 2 x 4 spacers between each course of 2 x 10, or 2 x 12, rim joists. Unless your log walls are unusually high, or your logs especially thick, two 2 x 4's sandwiched between three full-dimension rim joists should be more than adequate. (Some experienced log builders maintain that a single rim joist will support the walls, and build accordingly, using extra support only in the corners. Though it seems contrary to common sense, our county inspectors accept it.)

For the walls running perpendicular to the floor joists, run just a single rim joist, for now.

The wood I-joists are nailed in place through the outside rim joists.

LAYING-OUT THE FLOOR JOISTS

Starting at the most perfectly square corner, mark the tops of the rim joists for the placement of floor joists, according to the spacing noted on your blueprints. Repeat on the opposite wall and then chalk lines, from point to point, across the wood-plated I-beams. Lay out the joists and toe-nail them into the beams, then drive nails into the TJIs from the backside of the single rim joists. Wherever two joists break on a beam, you will need to put solid bridging perpendicularly between them. This is to keep them from "rolling" side to side.

After setting all the joists, you can install bridging between the ends. Since the joists will help support the log wall, you can get by with less support under the log walls running perpendicular with the joists. It's important, however, that it be solid across the sill plate, since you will be lagging the first logs through the floor and into the wood beneath it. (Again, some builders only add extra support at the corners.)

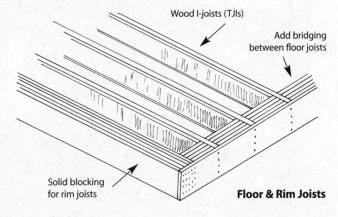

Wood I-joists (TJIs)

Add bridging between floor joists

Solid blocking for rim joists

Floor & Rim Joists

INSTALLING THE SUBFLOOR

To keep the finished floor from squeaking when you're headed on a clandestine mission to the refrigerator in the middle of night, the subfloor should be glued, and held into place with either screws or 8d ringshank nails. Epoxy-coated square-headed screws are the best since they strip out less than Phillips-head screws, saving you a ton of aggravation and at least a handful of screw bits. Do not use drywall screws; they're too brittle for flooring. There are several brands of flooring adhesive on the market. I have no particular preferences; they all do the job.

Starting from the squarest corner, chalk a line across the joists, 4 feet from the outer edge of the rim joist. The chalk line must be perfectly perpendicular to your joists, or you'll shortly run into trouble. Lay down a bead of adhesive on each joist and around the rim, then lay down a full sheet of $3/4$-inch tongue & groove plywood (T&G particle board is less expensive, but it won't stand up to rain and snow as well as plywood). Put in enough screws to hold it firmly in place, then move to the next sheet and complete the row. Start the second row with a half-sheet to avoid having two consecutive joints on a single joist.

Never hit a tongue or a groove with a hammer. If you do, you'll wish you hadn't. Instead, find a length of 2 x 4 long enough to lay across two joists and use it to drive the plywood home. After the first two rows are in place, go back and finish screwing down the plywood. Use seven screws on each edge and five screws in the field. Chalk lines are helpful for finding the joists below.

Finish the subfloor just as you did the first two rows. As long as your joists are square with the sill plates—and you didn't leave any gaps between sheets of plywood—the operation should go off without a hitch.

Subfloor

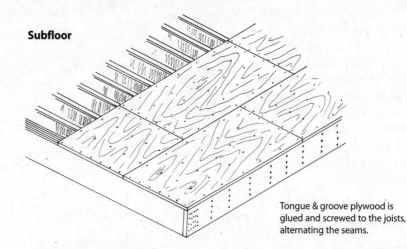

Tongue & groove plywood is glued and screwed to the joists, alternating the seams.

When you're all done, give yourself a pat on the back. Not only have you just saved eight or ten logs, you've made the plumber and electrician happy and will keep the building inspector from busting you for hacking-up your floor supports.

rex's maxims

Building a house is like ROLLING A ROCK UP A HILL that, mercifully, becomes just a little less steep with every step.

Walk around the floor and look into the distance. This will be the view you'll see from your first-floor windows. Enjoy the flat, clean expanse below your feet while you can. After today, it will be covered with bark, sawdust and tools, pencil marks, scratches and gouges. So, if you ever wanted to have a dance, now would be the time. ❧

August 1999

The steel beams and posts arrive. Rex maneuvers the old farm tractor into position so he can lift each beam onto the basement walls [9]. After a slip of the chain that almost costs Dave his pickup, Rex and Dave manage to lift and scoot each beam-end down the side foundation walls and into the beam pockets [10]. They are very glad the beams are not any bigger or longer!

Soon the sill plates are on the foundation walls and beams, and next up are the TJIs and rim joists. (Women...it will really impress your husbands if you learn these terms.) After some careful measuring, the joists are in place and the subfloor is glued and screwed down. I can't quite get the screws in far enough half the time, but I make a good attempt at it. What a nice flat floor! And it definitely looks out of place on this rocky, steep mountain.

Since the weather is good (and trucks can make it up our road), Rex orders the septic tank [11] and infiltrators for the leach field. Gary fires up the excavator (still parked in our trees) to backfill around the foundation, and then digs the trenches and the hole for the tank. The trenches must be level, so my job is to hold the leveling rod while Rex takes readings through the level and directs Gary with a thumbs up or thumbs down.

Log•ically   Solar

If you're lucky enough to own 25 acres in North Carolina's Blue Ridge Mountains, you owe it to yourself to do it right when it comes time to build your home. And so Michael and Dianne English did just that. For starters, Michael—a semi-retired process development chemist—took night classes at NC State University to learn the fundamentals of home design. Then he and Dianne drew up a set of preliminary plans which became the basis for the final blueprints prepared by Lincoln Logs, Ltd. for their 2,700-square-foot, two-level, custom log home.

Michael took on the task of general contractor, overseeing the setting of the house and most of the interior partition walls. Then he and Dianne completed most of the finish work, including the ceilings and interior woodwork, painting, ceramic tile, and the doors.

Since the property was two miles beyond the nearest power lines when they began building, solar energy was the only sensible option for the home's electricity. For this, too, Michael sought help from NC State, this time from the university's highly regarded Solar Energy Center. "They were very helpful," Michael recalls. "By the time we contacted Sundance Power Systems in Mars Hill to do the installation, we had a good idea what it would take to power our home."

Living at 4,120 feet in an alpine rain forest, it's best to make sure you have plenty of power to get you through a protracted spell of nasty weather, so Michael and Dianne made sure not to cut themselves short. The 48-volt PV system consists of 32 roof-mounted Kyocera 120-watt modules, feeding a pair of 2,500-pound Deka 48-volt batteries, capable of storing an enviable 76 kWh of electricity. All of the home's electrical loads go through a beefy Trace SW5548 inverter, with the exception of the 48-volt DC, helical-rotor well pump. Wired directly to the battery bank, it pulls water from 500 feet down and delivers it to a 500-gallon cistern at the somnolent rate of one gallon per minute.

It's a no-nonsense system so powerful Michael didn't see any need for a backup generator. He still doesn't, even after their Blue Ridge retreat was recently promoted from weekend getaway to fulltime residence. So, whatever Michael and Dianne ponder in the evenings, as they sit quietly in their rockers on the porch and listen to the sounds of nature all around them, you can bet they aren't worried about the integrity of their solar-electric system. And that's a nice thing not to think about.

House 2,700 square feet; milled 'D' logs, contractor set, owner finished
Heating wood stove; in-floor hydronic heating system with propane-fired boiler
Water pumped from a 500-foot well by a helical rotor, 48-volt DC pump into a cistern
Refrigeration electric
Solar array 3,840 watts
Wind turbine none
Inverter Trace SW5548
Batteries 2 Deka 48-volt
Backup power none

CHAPTER

PEELING AND LIFTING LOGS

*At Long Last, Let the **Real** Work Commence*

LaVonne peels log #45 for "the fort" on a sunny fall day.

PEELING THE LOGS

Ask anyone who has built their own log house what they thought was the hardest part, and chances are they will say "peeling the logs." That may be so—especially if the logs are well-seasoned—but it's a necessary step in the process: if you want to join the club you have to pay your dues. But more than that, peeling the logs yourself will help prepare your mind for the next step. You will come to know every knot and hollow in every log, and by doing so you will develop a kinship with your logs that will prove helpful in the near future.

When you remove the bark, you transform a lifeless tree into a unique element of your walls or roof, ready to take on new life in the grand organic gestalt that will one day be your home. Peeling logs, therefore, is a task that should be approached with resoluteness, rather than a sense of dread.

It does not take a great deal of strength to peel logs, though strength is certainly helpful. LaVonne, whose graceful, lithe stature belies her simmering endurance, peeled most of our logs as I notched and set them in the walls. Whenever she ran across a log that was particularly vexatious (of which there were more than a few), I would climb down from the walls and give her a hand. She never gave up on a log, but she certainly appreciated the help whenever she needed it.

I like to remove the knots before the log is elevated for peeling; it's easier on the shoulders and elbows. Some builders like to use an axe for "knot-bopping;" I prefer a small chainsaw or the Log Wizard. Cut the knots as close as possible to the body of the log to avoid elbow-jarring jolts when the drawknife catches on what you didn't cut off. If you use a chainsaw, wear eye and ear protection. If you don't, you'll soon wish you had.

The peeling environment should be as comfortable as possible. To avoid a chronic backache, elevate the logs to a comfortable height. I made a pair of 34-inch high, heavy-duty sawhorses to set the logs on for peeling. We'd hold the logs in place with cleats or log dogs and peel as much of the log as we could before rolling it. Most logs we could peel in four quarter-turns.

LaVonne's father, Roger, gets a short lesson before being turned loose with the drawknife.

Since our home site is on a gentle slope, we moved most of the logs onto the flat floor for peeling, with one end protruding through the door opening. The level surface kept the logs from sliding as we peeled, and gave us a surefooted surface to work on. After the loft floor beams were set, we had to peel the logs outside of the house.

By the virtue of their added inertia, big logs will slide a lot less than smaller ones as you peel them. To facilitate the peeling of smaller logs, I built another pair of sawhorses with sawbucks (a V-shaped wedge fashioned from 2 x 4's) on top. I ran a stout board between the sawhorses, then held them fast to the ground with stakes. For added grip, I affixed an arm to each sawbuck—with a 10-pound lead diving weight on the end—that would drop across the top of the log. This method worked great for purlins, railings, and spindles.

If you peel the logs as you need them, you'll avoid spending hours bleaching and sanding off the rained-on, weathered surface.

By the time you're finished peeling, you will have accumulated several cubic yards of peelings. And since you will have run your drawknives over several miles of log surface, they will be begging for a little R & R at the local sharpening shop.

LIFTING LOGS

We began our house with no concise plan of how to move our logs from the ground to the tops of our ever-growing walls. At first we used a pickup to drag the logs in front of a loader-equipped '60s-vintage farm tractor, which we then pressed into service to lift each log onto the wall. This worked well enough until the walls grew higher than the tractor could lift. Then we had to do some planning.

Log Wizard

I first saw the Log Wizard in use at the Log Home Expo in Denver and knew immediately I had found the perfect tool for knot bopping. No more complicated than a 3-inch planer attached to the bar of a chainsaw, it's designed to remove lots of material quickly. With a little practice it can also be handy for cleaning out the inside of saddle notches, or cutting small notches for pole fences or railings. The only catch is that you'll have to dedicate a separate chainsaw to its use, since it's a bit of work to take on and off.

Photo: www.loghelp.com

The boom is bolted onto the gin pole.

I'd used a gin pole before, in the small cabin I built in the 1980s. It was crude, at best: nothing more than a straight pole with a chainfall fastened to the top. But the logs were fairly short and right next to the foundation, so it was enough. (For my first log house, by contrast, I needed no equipment, since all the logs were short and I had full use of a whole crew of tough, labor-seasoned roofers.)

After a day's deliberation on the matter, we decided to place a gin pole through the center of the floor, like I had years before. The problem before us, however, was not a small one: how can one man and one woman raise a 30-foot pole, 8 inches in diameter, from the horizontal to the vertical? Deliberately, cautiously, and inch-by-inch.

I cut out a hole in the plywood between two joists and boxed the hole with 2 x 10's. I then dropped a plumb bob to the basement floor, marked the spot directly below the hole, and dug down a foot or so into the dirt. Next, I made a chute from three 2 x 4's fastened together at 45 degree angles, and ran it between the hole in the floor and to the one in dirt below.

We moved the gin pole into position on the main floor, then lifted the top of it as high as we could with the tractor, while the butt of the pole dutifully snuggled against the 2 x 4 chute I'd fashioned to guide its descent through the floor.

The electric winch, chained to the gin pole boom, pulls in a log to be peeled.

Next, I took six of the long 2 x 4's left over from bracing the foundation forms, and nailed them together in long, offset X's. I then nailed 2 x 4 cleats into the floor to keep the X braces from sliding back as we pushed the pole ever higher. By the time we pushed as far as we could with the third set of braces, the log grudgingly slid into the hole.

Admittedly, it wasn't the smoothest operation I've ever been a part of, but it worked. In the end, our gin pole rested in its earthen nest in the basement, and rose 20 feet through the hole I'd cut in the floor.

It worked, yes. But I really can't recommend this method to anyone, without a few modifications. Even though we got the job done, it was a little too risky for comfort. At the very least, two more people should have been placed at offset angles on the backside of the pole, working strong ropes secured to the top of the pole and dallied to trees or truck bumpers.

However much trouble the gin pole was to erect, it was worth it. Our crude contrivance worked perfectly for us. After adding a well-braced boom to the top of the pole—from which we hung a heavy-duty 120-volt winch—we could easily handle any log in our pile.

Here's how it worked: I used the loader tractor to lift one end of each log onto the wall. Then, by securing the cable from the winch to the elevated log end, we pulled the log a little past halfway into the house and set the end gently on the floor. At that point, we could hook the winch on the gravitational center of the log and lift it.

Once suspended, it was a simple matter to spin the log onto the wall and roll it into place. I should mention here that this takes a little bit a planning, since the log will have to go to one side of the gin pole or the other. Just *which* side depends on where you want the log to ultimately end up (right or left; butt end to the east, or to the west, etc.) It's often necessary to pull the log onto one side of the pole and spin it a full 180 degrees to the other side. If this isn't quite clear, don't worry—you'll only do it wrong once.

For those of you without access to aging farm machinery with whimsical hydraulics and questionable brakes, there are other methods to pull your logs onto the wall. One way is to erect a second gin pole near the wall where your logs are laid out, with the

rex's maxims

OPTIMISM and a little self-delusion are helpful from time to time.

A peeled log is lifted onto the house with the tractor.

Rex maneuvers a log suspended from the gin pole.

boom extending out over the wall. The only draw-back to this plan is that you will need two winches, or you'll need to move the winch from one gin pole to the other.

Alternately, if you have a door opening on a short wall facing your logs, you can drag each log through it and into the house. From there, simply lift one end onto the wall, then the other.

If all else fails, you can build a log ramp to roll your logs onto the wall. This is achieved by securing two strong logs at low angles to either end of a wall, then attaching a rope to either side of the inside wall. By hanging the rope over the wall and looping it around each end of the log you want to move, the log can be rolled up the ramp by pulling the ropes with a winch, or by hand. (The one drawback to this system is obvious: with each new course of logs you will have to reset your ramp.)

If you have stout trees on either side of your house, you may want to consider running a steel cable between them, then attaching a winch to a pulley that glides along it. Called a skyline, you can use this system to lift logs from the pile and safely pull each log over your wall with two ropes attached to the

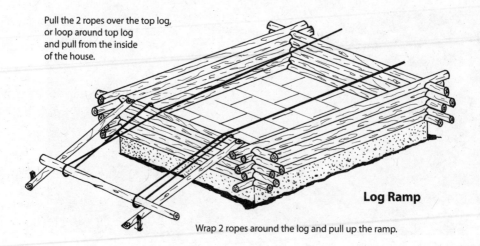

Pull the 2 ropes over the top log, or loop around top log and pull from the inside of the house.

Log Ramp

Wrap 2 ropes around the log and pull up the ramp.

pulley (one for pulling, the other for braking.) If there are no suitable trees nearby, the same thing can be accomplished with a pair of well-secured poles. I would not advise erecting this apparatus, however, without the use of a boom truck and lots of help from someone who truly knows how to do this sort of thing.

Whatever method you use to raise your logs, be careful! Chains break, ropes snap, cables slip and booms shatter under enough stress. Every system ever devised has its weakest point, and you *don't* want to be in harm's way when it fails. At every moment you should take stock of where you are in relation the log you're working with. What would happen if suddenly the chain broke, or the boom snapped off the gin pole? Never walk under a suspended log, and never stand on the downhill side of a log that's being moved; once a log starts rolling under gravity's tug, there's nothing you can do to stop it.

By way of illustration, in the course of building our house we had one log get away from us as we were fishing it out from between two others. One of our two dogs—the fastest and most agile, thankfully—was walking among the logs on the downhill side at the time. I yelled out, she looked up and saw the huge log barreling her way and—without a moment's hesitation—scurried to safety like a rabbit with its tail on fire. Knowing that neither LaVonne or I could have moved that fast, we were—from then on— humbly sobered into a more acute sense of caution whenever we were moving logs.

Though the process of moving logs may seem disconcertingly arduous at this point, once you settle on the system that's right for you and you set a few logs in place, you'll be amazed at how smooth the work proceeds. With every log, you'll discover a new trick or shortcut that will make this log easier than that one. And by the time you set the last log into place you'll wonder why you ever thought moving and lifting logs was so difficult. ∾

Josh French used a boom truck to lift and maneuver his logs.

August 1999

The last day of August and log work has begun, finally! Rex has been anxiously looking forward to this time; I just stare at the big pile of unpeeled logs and wonder, "How long will this take?" Rex cuts the first peeled log in half [12] and bolts each half to the floor. Then we peel and set logs #2 and #3 in position, scribe and cut the notches. Here we go!

13

12

drawknife. Thank goodness we found a good knife from Bosworth, a log home builder in Montana who happened to be on the Internet. The ones I bought at antique stores and flea markets can now decorate the walls.

Scribing and cutting notches are Rex's job. I'm worthless with a chisel after 10 minutes, so my job is peeling [14]. I've never been so weary in all my life.

September 1999

Log work begins in earnest. The first few logs are easy to maneuver and lift up on the house with the tractor [13]. Peeling logs is, well, work. It helps to have a beautiful fall day to work in...not too hot because you are burning lots of calories. Good music helps. The occasional easy-peeling log is a nice break, but I found that the most important item is a well-designed drawknife. My very own arrived in the mail after Rex got tired of me using his

14

A notch is scribed.

CHAPTER 9

BUILDING WITH LOGS: PART I

Scribing and Notching the First Course

There are two fundamentally different ways to build with full, round logs (as opposed to milled logs, or logs that have been flattened on two or more sides.) The full-scribe (or chinkless) method is preferred by some professional log builders, while the standard practice of simply stacking notched logs and later filling the gaps with chinking is almost universally done by do-it-yourselfers. While each method has its merits, in the end the method you choose will be based upon your level of expertise, the quality of your logs, the amount of time you have to complete the log work, or simply your own sense of aesthetics.

Not too many years ago, there was no truly durable material available for chinking a log cabin. Moss, mud mixed with straw, dirt and ashes, and masonry mortar were all used with varying degrees of success—or failure. The proponents of full-scribe construction had only to point to the hapless homeowner re-chinking his house every year to keep the cold arctic breezes out of his bedroom to prove that their method was superior.

The introduction of synthetic chinking changed all of that. Today's modern chinking materials are strong and pliable, seal tightly with the logs, and last

rex's maxims

THE SLOP FACTOR—
an undefined, immeasurable
quantity on which all builders
rely—takes on new meaning
when building with logs.

as long as the house. If properly applied, synthetic chinking has excellent insulative properties, and adds an undeniable measure of rustic charm to a log wall.

Our house is chinked. And it's the warmest house I've ever had the pleasure of spending a winter in. It's sealed up so tight we often open a window in December and January when the wood stove is blazing, just to get a little extra air. I can offer several reasons for our decision to build the way we did. Cutting grooves down the center of each log is time consuming. So is drilling holes in each log for pulling electrical wires throughout the house. Starting late in the season as we did, time was a distant luxury: I don't like shoveling snow out of the inside of a building, and I like roofing in January even less. Nor were our logs the straight, barely-tapered, archetypical logs one admires in million-dollar homes. Far from it. They were an odd assortment that ranged from beautiful to comical. Many had to be straightened with a chain and a come-along before they could be spiked into the wall. Not the sort of logs, in other words, that would ungrudgingly lend themselves to the full-scribe method.

Those are all good reasons for building the way we did, but the *real* reason is not among them. For us, it was a matter of taste, pure and simple. We concluded long ago that we prefer the looks of a chinked house over a chinkless house. The chinking nicely separates each course of logs, faithfully accentuating every subtle bump and curve, and thus setting each log in its own frame to be admired as a work of art in its own right.

Even if our logs had been as straight and uniform as utility poles and we'd had an eternity to build with them, we wouldn't have done anything differently. Except maybe that part about the chain and the come-along.

Chances are, if you're doing all the log work yourself, you will choose to build in the same way we did. I will not, therefore, take the time here to detail the full-scribe method of grooving logs. Not only is it hard to follow a narrative that skips back and forth between differing techniques, it would be dishonest of me to attempt to elucidate a method in which I am not adequately skilled. (For those of you who wish to build a chinkless log home, I refer you to B. Allan Mackie's excellent book, *The Owner-Built Log Home*. As far as I've been able to tell, the word "chinking" does not appear anywhere between the covers.)

MARKING THE FLOOR FOR WINDOWS, DOORS AND SQUARE CORNERS

Before getting to the logs, there are some preliminary details to address. For starters you'll need to know, within a couple of inches, where you intend to put all the windows and doors in the perimeter walls. That way, you won't run a chainsaw into any steel spikes when the wall is finished and it comes time to cut the openings.

Mark the rough openings for the doors and windows on the floor with an indelible marker or a grease pencil. Give yourself plenty of room on either side, being sure to allow for the thickness of the bucks you'll install in the openings to hold the doors and windows. Make bold heavy lines that will be visible to anyone straddling a wall several feet up, then connect the lines to clearly define the opening.

(You may not know with any degree of certainty where the windows are going until you've set a course or two of logs in place. That's fine. But you'll still need to know where the doors will be so you don't lag a section of log to the floor that will have to be removed later.)

Now, since you won't be able to measure to the outside corners of the floor once the walls start going up, you'll need new corner marks inside the log perimeter to use as reference points. To do this, measure perpendicularly in from the edge of floor. (Be sure that your marks will not later be covered with the first course of logs.) Make two intersecting marks in each corner, equal distance in from the edge of the floor. Measure along the floor side to side and corner to corner to make certain the new corner marks are square.

Using a tape measure and a spirit level, you will refer to these marks with each course of logs to keep your walls plumb and square.

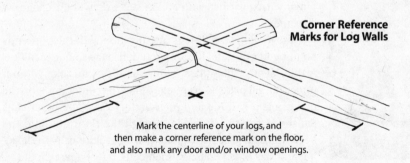

Corner Reference Marks for Log Walls

Mark the centerline of your logs, and then make a corner reference mark on the floor, and also mark any door and/or window openings.

THE FIRST LOG

"Log" is singular here because you'll be cutting it in half, right down the center of the long axis. Since this will be your first log, choose it carefully. Find a log that's straight with very little taper, and bigger than most.

Set each end of the log on blocks and roll it, looking down the length of it as you do. You'll be looking for straightness. Since you'll be cutting down through the top of this log, any curve that you see should rolled into the bottom position, rather than the side or the top.

When you are satisfied you've found the straightest axis, secure the log with cleats or log dogs, and chalk a line down the center of the log (measure to be sure). Using several passes with your chainsaw, cut the log down the center of the chalk line, never going more than a couple of inches deep on any one pass. This will take some time. Use a very sharp chain, and be certain the bar is in good condition, otherwise the cut will veer to one side or the other. Be very careful to maintain a consistent angle with the saw.

If you are not confident that you can do this, I suggest that you buy a bar guide to keep the bar at a consistent angle. Not only will you use it now for the first log, but also later for steps, purlins, benches, etc.

The first log is split in half.

Before your last two passes, cut the log all the way through in a couple of places on either side of center, and wire the log loosely together at these points. This will prevent the two halves from falling to either side—and breaking where you don't want them to—before you're finished cutting.

When the cut is complete, undo the wire, roll the two halves face-up, and study your work. The cut sides won't be perfectly flat, but they don't have to be; the weight of the house will take care of what the lag bolts don't. Just be sure to level out any irregularities with an axe, adze, drawknife, chainsaw or planer.

Move the two half-logs into position with the butt-ends pointing in opposite directions, and insulate under each one. A thin layer of fiberglass is fine; plastic foam (like you put under the sill plate) is ever better. Find the center point on the end of each half-log and measure across to the other side. Satisfied? Lag the half-logs through the floor and into the beefed-up rim joist below. (Your plans should specify the spacing and size of lag bolts; $3/8$-inch bolts, 4 feet apart should be adequate.)

SECOND AND THIRD LOGS, FIRST NOTCHES

Pick out two nice logs equal in size and quality to each other and to the log you've just halved. It's a good idea to mill the bottom side of each of these logs a little, to help them lie flat and to distribute their weight across the floor, though some builders don't bother with this step.

Position each log over the ends of the half-logs and stabilize them with cleats. **Remember: small ends should *always* go over butt-ends, and vice versa.** It is now time to scribe your first notch.

Without a single exception, every hand-hewn full-round log house I have seen built in the last 25 years has been constructed using the saddle notch—or a variation of it—for lacing the wall logs. There are several good reasons for this. First and foremost, the saddle notch is the simplest notch to scribe and cut. In addition, it sheds water as well, or better, than other notches because only the top log is notched. And, since it leaves the logs full-round, and therefore natural, on the ends that emerge from the wall, its proper execution is a treat to the modern eye that hungers for rustic beauty.

Scarf notches at the Buckhorn Camp home.

The common (round) saddle notch has two drawbacks, however, since there are two conditions that can cause it to open up at the bottom. The first is shrinkage of the lower log. The second occurs when the notch is cut past the widest point of the lower log, since the notch cannot hope to follow the log's curve as it begins to diminish.

For these reasons, some builders prefer to scarf their logs, especially if they're using very large or unseasoned logs. A scarf is simply a cut dished-out with an axe, planer or chainsaw on each side of a log. Incised at a 45-degree angle, it should extend a little below where the top log will rest on the bottom. The scarfs should not meet at the top: leave a couple of inches for the upper notch to settle on. The upper log is then positioned and scribed to match the scarf, taking out a little extra at the top of the notch to allow room for settling. As the log below shrinks, the notch above simply settles, without opening-up. And, with the curve now removed, the notch stays tight even when it falls below the bottom log's thickest point.

The method you choose will depend on the logs you

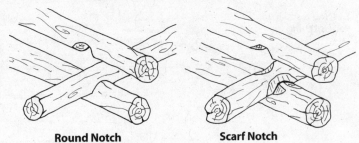

Round Notch   **Scarf Notch**

use, or simply your own personal tastes. If you plan to chink your house, it's easy and wise to chink the corners as well as the walls. In that case—since synthetic chinking materials expand to accommodate joint shrinkage—the reasons for scarfing the logs is not as compelling as it once was.

Either way, this is how the scribing and notching is performed: With the log you wish to scribe resting on the ends of the lower logs, sight along the bottom of it to ensure that it follows a straight line from one end to the other. If you milled it, it should. If not, reposition it so that the straightest side is on the bottom (or mill it).

Beginning at one end, adjust the scribers until the points *just barely* slide between the floor and the bottom of the log. Position yourself so the scribers are directly in front of you, and trace the shape of the half-log onto the full one, beginning and ending at the lowest points. Be certain to hold the scribers perfectly vertical as you do this, or your notch will not be true. When you're finished, scribe the outside of the notch, then move to the other end of the log—being certain to reset the scribers, since the space between the floor and the bottom of the log will doubtless be different—and repeat the process.

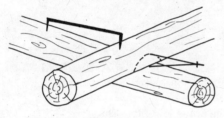

A log dog will prevent the log from rolling as you scribe the notch.

At this point you will need to decide if you want the ends of the half-log to stick out past the edge of the foundation wall. If there will be a deck directly beneath it, you may want to leave them; if so, cut the full notch. On the other hand, if the half-log end is just going to hang out there, you may consider hiding it for a cleaner look. For this option, cut the inside notch only to the middle of the log, and then lop off the end of the half-log below, to hide it in the half-notch.

Roll the log back 180 degrees (so the notch is facing up) and secure it so it doesn't roll off the end of the wall—and onto the napping dog below—when you

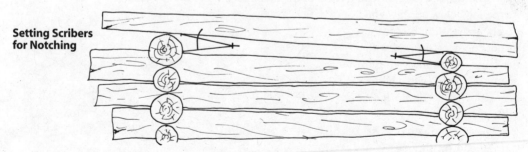

Setting Scribers for Notching

Measure the distance at each cross log to find the setting for the scribers.

start cutting. Before cutting the full notch, the scribe line should be legible all the way around the log. You will probably have to extrapolate on the bottom, where the lines disappear; just join the two line ends with a straight line and you've got it.

After scribing, the log is rolled over and kerfs are cut with the chainsaw.

Now the fun begins. Using a chainsaw, make a series of vertical cuts through the area enclosed by the line. Don't try to cut right to the line—you can't do it consistently, and it will make for a ragged-looking notch. Cut a series of parallel kerfs, leaving $1/2$ to $3/4$ inches of wood in between.

Next, take a hammer and knock out whatever wood readily breaks loose, then use a chisel (I prefer one with a $1^1/4$-inch bit) to cleanly incise around the line and an inch or so into the log.

There are several ways to proceed from this point. Sometimes I'll finish the notch with a chisel, other times I'll go back and clean it out with the tip of the chainsaw. It just depends on the log and how big of a hurry I'm in. However you do it, leave the notch a little dished-out in the center to allow some space for insulation and for irregularities in the log below. Bend down and, with one eye closed, sight along the edge of the notch. If all you see is the other side of the notch, then it's deep enough.

Repeat the process on the other end of the log. Lay a thin layer of fiberglass insulation on the log below, and roll the top log onto it. It will fall into place with a triumphant *whump*!

After knocking out the wood remnants, the inside of the notch can be cleaned with a chainsaw. Edges are best done with a chisel.

Check to see that the notches lie down snugly on top of the lower log. Modify the curves of the notches, if necessary, though you probably won't have to. If they ride a little high, find any high spots in the log between the notches, mark them, roll the log 180 degrees, and flatten them with a chainsaw or adze. Once it fits, cut your notches in the log at the opposite end of the floor. Don't lag down either log until they both fit snugly onto the logs below and you've made certain your corners are square.

MAKING IT SQUARE (AND KEEPING IT THAT WAY)

One of the reasons we love logs so much is the fact that they are never perfectly straight or perfectly round. This makes them beautiful. Technically speaking, it also makes them topologically unquantifiable. You can't locate the center of a log with the same accuracy as you can measure to the middle of a 2 x 4, but, by the same token, your eye cannot discern geometric irregularities nearly as easily. In other words, if your wall logs veer a *little*, here and there, the overall effect is neither unpleasing nor problematic.

The idea, however, is not to let the walls go willy-nilly but to keep them as square and plumb as you can, while at the same time understanding that perfection is fundamentally impossible.

Bearing this in mind, it's time to make the first course of logs as square as possible before lagging them down. Begin by marking the center of each log above the notch with a short line that runs with the long axis, and intersect it with another line representing the center of the half-log below it.

Keeping Your Corners Square

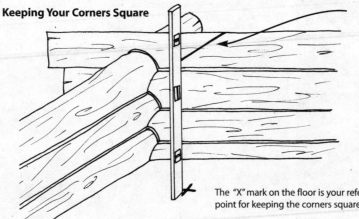

When each log is notched and set, stand a level on the floor at the X mark and then measure from center line of each log to the level. This measurement should stay the same as the wall rises.

The "X" mark on the floor is your reference point for keeping the corners square.

Measure from these marks along all four sides to make sure your distances are equal, then measure corner to corner to make it square. Remember the marks you made on the floor, earlier? You will want to position the logs so the center point of each is equidistant from those marks. When you're satisfied the first course of logs is as square as it's going to get, lag down the two end logs and pat yourself on the back; you're on your way! ∾

Log • ically Solar

Tom and Kathy Coseno's solid-wood home near La Veta, Colorado, was specifically designed to save countless thousands of British Thermal Units and kilowatt hours per year that would normally be consumed on heating and cooling. So far it's done exactly that, and has saved the couple a bundle in the bargain.

Conceived and designed by Michael Sykes of Enertia® Building Systems, the Coseno's 48-by-32-foot two-level house is made from milled and laminated Southern yellow pine. Grown on sustainable tree farms, this dense, resinous wood is highly regarded for it heat-storing properties.

But the wood alone does not account for the home's incredible ability to conserve energy. To understand that, you need to look at what an Enertia home has that other homes do not. For starters, a 6-foot-wide heavily glazed sunspace runs along the entire south side of the main level. You can think of the sunspace as the home's furnace. But for a furnace to work properly, it has to be able to distribute its heat throughout the house, and this is why the house also has two solid-wood north walls, with a 9-inch air space between them.

In winter, when the sun is low in the sky, solar energy is captured in the sunspace during the daylight hours. Vents opening into the attic then channel this warm air, through natural convection, over

the ceiling, down through the space between the inner and outer north walls, and finally into the walkout basement. From there it is again drawn back into the sunspace through vents in the floor, where it is reheated, and recycled. In this way there is always a flow of warm air around the outer surfaces of the interior of the house.

How effective is it? So effective that Tom and Kathy never bothered to install a central heating system, even though they live in a place where winter can be a very costly experience for most people. Instead, they have a small wood stove to take the chill off during spells of cloudy weather. "When others in the area were paying $400 – $500 per month for heating fuel," Kathy relates, "we spent $125 for wood for an entire winter." That's the price of a single cord of beetle-killed pine.

In summer, when the sunspace receives no direct sunlight, the basement, which is kept cool by the winter-shaded earth packed against the north side, provides the cooling effect. Air enters the house through north-side basement windows, runs up through the sunspace, and out through windows in the east and west side of the attic. With the constant movement of air through the earth-cooled basement, it's an effective way to rid a house of excess heat. According to Tom, who keeps meticulous records, the hottest it's ever been inside the house in summer is 76 degrees.

Tom and Kathy's home also uses energy— though precious little of it—from two active solar systems. The 1700-watt PV system is directly tied to the power grid in a battery-less configuration. The array, on average, produces 7-plus kWh/day, though the Cosenos use only 5 kWh per day. This miserly usage is made even more remarkable by the fact that theirs is an all-electric house.

The second system, for solar hot water, is a closed-loop glycol system, powered by a pair of Heliodyne solar collectors. The two panels transfer the heat they gather to a heat exchanger mounted on the side of an 80-gallon electric water heater that rarely draws a single watt of electrical power.

So let's sum a year's energy usage for heating—one cord of wood; for cooling—zero, zip, nada; electricity produced over and above their needs—over 800 kilowatt hours. I'd say the Cosenos are onto something with their Enertia home.

House 1,536 square feet on the main level plus a 1,410 square-foot walkout basement; milled and laminated solid wood walls above ICF basement walls
Heating small woodstove
Water public water
Refrigeration electric
Solar array 1,700 watts
Solar hot water 2 Heliodyne 4- x 8-foot panels, closed-loop glycol
Wind turbine none
Inverter Xantrex GT-series, direct-tie
Batteries none
Backup power utility grid

CHAPTER *10*

BUILDING WITH LOGS: PART II

Building the Walls and Tying-in Second-Floor Beams

If you don't feel like a bona fide log home builder after the first course, you will long before the walls are finished. Any hesitancy you feel toward choosing and notching logs will soon be replaced with focused confidence, especially after you've worked your way through a blunder or two. Just don't let the rarified air from the top of fifth course make you giddy; there's always planning to do, and the higher you go the more critical it becomes.

Laying the rest of the wall logs is not fundamentally different from setting the first course, but there are additional considerations and tricks of the trade that will be helpful as you work your way ever higher.

CHOOSE YOUR LOGS WELL

Picking out the logs for each course is a little like playing chess; you need to be able to think past the next move. A log that will solve a problem now may cause a bigger one later. This is especially true if your logs have a lot of taper, since you will always notch the small end over the big end (and vice versa), and big and small are often awkward bedfellows. At times it may seem that you've worked your way into a trap you can't get out of, but it isn't so. If it were, the backcountry landscape would be dotted with half-completed log homes and "4 Sale—Cheap!" signs, because everyone feels whipped at one point or another. In the course of building three log structures, I have yet to reject a log once it's been notched, though there were several I *wished* I hadn't notched. If asked today, however, to point out a single blunder on any of my log work, I'd be hard pressed to find it. In the end, it all works out.

On extremely rare occasions, it may be necessary to run a log in reverse order; that is, to put a big end on another big end, and small on small. Think the consequences through before doing this, however, since it's nothing you want to try unless there is no other way to level the wall.

Generally, you will want to begin with your biggest logs and finish with the smallest ones. That's not really a rule, however; it's more of a theme. Often a log will be of greater diameter than the one below it. Again—you'll do what you have to do to make it work.

The most important thing to consider when picking out logs is to avoid extremes—notches that are either too deep, or too shallow (a notch to the midpoint on the log is optimum)—because it will probably get even worse on the next course. If you have to bite the bullet and leave a bigger gap in the wall than you wanted, do it. It's better than the alternative. And when the chinking is all done, you won't even see it.

Whenever possible, hide large cracks (checks) on the downside of the wall. That way, they won't trap moisture, and you won't need to fill the crack with caulking or chinking.

Position large cracks (checks) on the down-side of the wall.

SCRIBING CONSIDERATIONS

You will always set the scribers for each notch by adjusting them to the space between the log you are going to scribe and the one below it. But exactly *how* you set them depends on what you hope to achieve. I try to get my logs to fit as close together as possible. If your logs fit so tight you have to climb the walls to see what your dog is barking at, you're doing fine.

Carefully observe the repose of each log as you roll it back and forth on the wall. Every log will have its optimum position, and it's your job to find it. If there is a bit of a curve in the log, roll it to the outside. You can pull all or most of it in after the notch is cut and the ends are spiked down by using a come-along secured to the gin pole or a lower log on the opposite wall.

Once the log is in viewing position, look for high and low spots along the gap. If you set your scribers for maximum depth on each end, how much chainsawing will have to be done in the middle? My usual self-delusional answer to that question is "not all *that* much." Then I spend the next half-hour running a chainsaw back and forth between logs until my notches finally lie down. You may not be as militant about tight-fitting logs as I am, and it's certainly not imperative that your logs fit so snugly. But

Knots and bumps can be removed with a chainsaw.

the better they lie down at this stage, the less settling (and chinking) there will be later on.

On the other hand, long, unsupported gaps (and there will be a few) should be shimmed every few feet to keep the wall from sagging later.

**Removing Bumps &
Knots for a Snug Fit**

For tight-fitting notches and logs, mark the bumps and knots to be removed with the chainsaw.

SPLICING LOGS

Long walls are often built with two carefully picked logs per row, spliced at the intersection of an interior log wall. The butt-joints are then hidden by the notches of the intersecting logs. To keep the joints from spreading you should spike each of the adjoining ends, then connect them together with a piece of steel banding held in place with 20-penny nails.

A long log wall is spliced in the center of a perpendicular log wall in Benshoof's home.

INTERIOR LOG WALLS

Interior log walls can add a nice touch to any home, and they're a slick way to hide the butt ends of spliced logs on the exterior wall. Curved openings are a particularly eye-catching use of interior logs.

SPIKING THE LOGS

Unlike the first course where the logs were lagged to the floor, the subsequent courses can be held together with spikes. The length of spike you'll need will vary, depending on the size of the logs, but $3/8$-inch x 12-inch spikes work well for most logs.

An interior arch in Benshoof's home.

Spiral or smooth spikes can be used for anchoring logs.

Some builders spike the corners and the walls near the corners, then drive heavy rebar into predrilled holes next to door and window openings, leaving long stretches without spikes. I, on the other hand, like my spikes 3 to 4 feet apart and staggered with each course. I place a spike near each corner and next to all window and door openings. Some builders advocate placing spikes through the notches, others don't. If there are enough spikes in the walls, it's doubtful the notches are going to shift.

Countersink the wall spikes so that half the spike is driven into the log below. Even if the spike is plenty long, countersinking is still a good idea, since it keeps the spike from pushing into the log above as the wall settles.

Drive spikes with a hand-sledge or a rigging axe; a framing hammer just doesn't command enough authority. Unless you're a glutton for punishment, pre-drill the holes (a little smaller than the spike—you don't want it to be *too* easy). Once you've hammered the head of a spike a little ways into the countersink hole, use a piece of rebar or a bolt to drive it home. And do yourself a favor— hold onto the rebar with locking pliers. There's nothing like hitting yourself in the back of the hand with a 4-pound sledge to muddy the rainbow accents of an otherwise beautiful day.

A come-along pulls in a log that curved slightly outward.

When you think you've built your wall high enough above a door or window opening that you can safely spike the logs, think again, just to be sure. Not only do you have to allow for the thickness of the door or window buck, but also for the distance the house will settle above it. If in doubt, wait until the next course to spike above the opening. A spike can ruin an expensive saw chain in a nanosecond.

DOOR AND WINDOW OPENINGS

It's common to use log ends and short pieces to build the wall segments between window and door openings, but it can also be exasperating if you're not careful. Differences in log thickness—from one side of the opening to the other—can add up by the time you reach the top and tie-in the two sides with a single log.

If you can, build with logs that run the full length of the wall and cut the holes later; otherwise choose your logs with care. Make sure the grain runs the same direction on both sides of the opening. If you do resort to piecing a wall together, you will have to find a way to elevate the log end at the opening and to keep it from rolling off the wall as you work with it. A pair of 2 x 4's nailed to either side of the wall with a spacer board in between is usually enough to hold the loose log end in place.

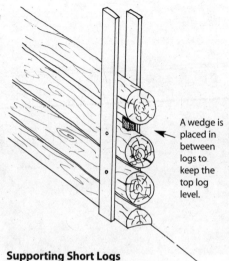

A wedge is placed in between logs to keep the top log level.

Supporting Short Logs
A cradle made from 2x4s, bolted/nailed to both sides of the lower logs will hold the loose ends of the shorter log lengths as you scribe and cut the corner notches.

Watching the walls grow higher every day is a constant source of pride and wonderment. Each night, as we walked wearily back to the cabin, we'd turn and admire what we'd done. The sense of accomplishment we felt was worth every sore muscle, every nick and scratch and bruise. And when the walls were at last complete we knew we had indeed scaled one very high hurdle on the long, arduous path to our dream.

KEEPING THE WALLS PLUMB, SQUARE AND EVEN

Every log should be set using the method described in the last chapter to keep the walls plumb and square. As the walls become higher than the level, simply wire the level to a long straight board. At that point, it will become a two-person operation to take accurate measurements. If the walls are exceptionally high or you don't trust a spirit level over such a distance, you can suspend a plumb bob from a stick with the proper distance marked along its length. It will take a little longer, but your measurement will be true.

It's also a good idea to monitor the height of the walls frequently—but not incessantly. It's easy to drive yourself buggy by taking constant measurements of the height of your walls, when it really isn't necessary. Even if you manage to do the impossible and get them perfect at some point, you won't be able to keep them that way; the next two courses will certainly undo all your hard work. That's just the way logs are.

Since logs are stacked big end to small, ideally only the even-numbered courses will be the same height on both ends. Measure the height on each end of every other course, and one or two places in the middle, by resting a level on the top of the log and measuring down to the floor. If you're an inch or two off, either from end to end or from one wall to the opposite wall, choose your next logs accordingly. As you approach the top, all measurements become more critical and your choice of logs needs to be even more exacting.

Before the final wall logs are spiked down, measure again along the sides, across the ends, and corner to corner. If you've been vigilant about keeping the walls square and plumb, little or no adjustment should be required at the top to bring the walls into alignment.

While you certainly want your height measurements to be equal all around, it is especially important that each wall be the same in height along its length. If two opposing walls are a little different in height, it will easier to adjust than if a wall varies in height from one end to the other. This is particularly true if you plan to construct your roof using conventional framing techniques, since you will need to shim the plate that the rafters rest on in ever diminishing degrees to make it level.

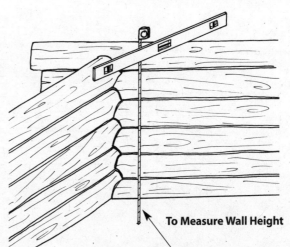

To Measure Wall Height

To monitor the wall height, place a level on the top log and measure to the floor. Repeat at the other end and in middle of the wall.

TYING-IN FLOOR BEAMS

When it comes time to tie-in the beams that support the second floor, you will need to willfully violate the rule that dictates only the upper log is ever notched, since these structural beams should never be cut more than one-third of the way through. You'll be much better off if you avoid cutting any of the structural beam; instead notch the logs above and below it.

With the second-floor log beam resting on the walls, measure from the top surface of the beam to the first floor on both ends *(see illustration on the next page)* and adjust the scribers to make it come out the same height once the notch is cut into the wall log. Measure again, after the notches are cut and the beam is rolled into place. If level, securely spike the floor beam into the lower log. Then scribe the upper logs around it, as if it were a corner notch. Simple.

What may not be so simple is deciding which course of wall logs to notch the beams into. There are two things to consider as you ponder this. First, the lower log notch that cradles the beam should never be cut more than halfway through, since there will be a tremendous amount of weight resting on just a few square inches of log. Also, you will need to factor in how much your house will settle after the beams are in place.

How much will your house settle? You can figure anywhere from as much as $^3/_4$-inch per foot for green logs, to as little as $^1/_8$-inch per foot for well-seasoned lumber.

rex's maxims

IF YOUR WIFE SAYS it is time
to quit for the day, dinner
will be much more pleasant
(and more than peanut butter
and jelly) if you agree.

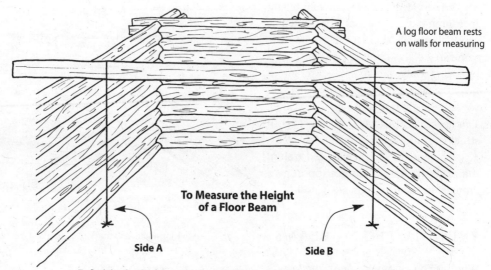

A log floor beam rests on walls for measuring

To Measure the Height of a Floor Beam

Side A

Side B

To find the depth of the notch for each side, measure from the top of the floor beam (where the upper floor will rest) to the floor below. Then adjust the notch depth accordingly so the top of the floor beam is perfectly level.

Example: If side A measures 105"; and side B is 106"; the notch will be 5" deep on side A for a finished height of 100"; and notch B will be 6" deep. Set the scribers accordingly.

Two floor beams are leveled and notched into place, and the next log (with four notches) is ready to be rolled over.

We set our floor beams at a little over 100 inches, allowing for 2 inches of settling (about $1/4$-inch per foot) and another $2^1/4$ inches for the finished floor ($3/4$-inch hardwood over $1^1/2$ inches of low-density concrete, in which our radiant-floor heating tubes were embedded). It worked out fine, though we were actually a bit surprised that our dry, tight-fitting logs settled the full 2 inches. The point is, a high ceiling is far preferable to a low one, so leave yourself plenty of latitude.

INSTALLING THE SECOND FLOOR

If the walls will continue a few feet above the floor beams, it's a good idea to take the time to install the second floor now. It has to be done sooner or later anyway, and it will make the remainder of the wall work easier and safer. As with the main floor, you will simplify things for the electrician and plumber if you elect to use wooden I-joists for the floor supports. Otherwise, careful planning will be needed to avoid cutting away the structural support the joists provide.

Square the joists and the plywood subfloor with the points marked on the first floor (the ones you used to keep the walls square and plumb). By dropping a plumb bob on both ends to the marks below, you can run a line to determine where the first joist should be set, then measure all the other joists from it. The plywood subfloor, in turn, can be laid out in the same way.

The butt-ends of the I-joists can either be notched into the wall—deep enough to allow adequate support—or a solid rim joist can be bolted to the wall and the joists connected to it with metal joist hangers. The rim joist method is the fastest, and it provides an extra support for attaching the ceiling below.

Exterior View of a Floor Beam
The logs below and above the structural floor beam are notched.

Second floor joists are set on log floor beams, with shims under any low spots. The ends of the joists are then trimmed even for the loft opening.

Staggered Ends

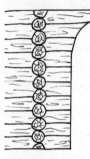

Arched Ends

Curved Ends

Angled Ends

The subfloor in the loft is glued and screwed down.

SECURING THE LAST WALL LOG

Wind passing over a roof tends to lift the whole structure, just like air passing over an airplane's wings. To make sure your roof stays where it is, you should use lag bolts to secure the top course of logs to the course of logs below. It may seem excessive, but the first time a 140-mile per hour gust hits your house, you'll be glad you did.

CUTTING THE LOG ENDS

One log wall is pretty much like another, but the log ends don't have to be. What you do with them will set the theme for the rest of the house. Is your home rustic or refined? Do you prefer randomness over order; straight lines over sweeping curves? It's purely a matter of aesthetics, since no one way is better than

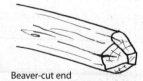

Beaver-cut end

any other. There are two rules to follow, however. First, the shortest log end should extend at least 9 inches past the notch and, secondly, all log ends should be protected by overhanging eaves.

Straight cuts can be marked with a chalk line or a straight board used as a guide; curved cuts can be marked (and kept uniform) with a long template made from plywood with the desired curve cut out of it. Random cuts depend on one's sense of randomness. I marked each log with a grease pencil per LaVonne's instructions, as she stood back and eyeballed the ends from a distance. ✆

September 1999

Now we need a gin pole. Sounds easy, but I'd rather not repeat this day. I've come to understand that Rex can deal with the concept of moving heavy things (a troublesome log, in this case) much better than I can. It is intimidating. Believe me...I was very happy to see that gin pole standing upright in the hole at the end of the day!

The electric winch on the gin pole's boom is quite easy to use. The tedious part is starting and stopping the generator to use it. A remote starting generator would've been handy. Now we are peeling logs set on saw bucks in the middle of the floor and lifting them with the winch. The pile of peelings is getting huge, and there is never a shortage of something to

sweep when the nieces and nephew show up for an afternoon [15].

Our first heavy, wet snow is hard to shovel out [16]...up and over the wall it must go.

October 1999

I keep peeling and Rex keeps notching. Our future home looks like a fort. And it will stay that way for many months, since the windows will be cut in after winter.

More logs arrive for the last few wall logs, floor beams, purlins and other roof beams. This log delivery made it closer... only a half mile from the house. Once again we use the homemade log transports for the large logs, and a 12-foot trailer for the purlin logs.

Log • ically Solar

Winter comes early and stays late where Ted and Katie Moews live; the road to their house is closed to conventional vehicles six or seven months of the year. They live so far off the beaten path that, were it not for the fact that they both enjoy broad reputations for their creative pursuits, you might think them hermits, or perhaps even old-time prospectors. But Ted and Katie are neither; with millions of acres of untouched wilderness just outside their back door,

they simply find life at 10,000 feet in Colorado's fabled San Juan Mountains agreeable to their perceptions of what life is all about.

It's not a new love affair with nature. The Moewses built their 1,550-square-foot, hand-hewn log home back in 1977 with trees they harvested from their own property and skidded to the building site with horses. Floor and ceiling planks were likewise milled from local trees, and stones for the fireplace and foundation were gathered from a nearby creek bed.

Cozy and rustic, the home boasts few mod-

ern conveniences, but that's the way Ted and Katie like it. Kerosene is used for lighting, wood for heat, and propane for cooking, water heating and refrigeration. Electricity is only needed to run a couple of reading lamps, a small television, a computer with satellite Internet, and various other small appliances and power tools. It is provided by a single 70-watt solar module, 8 Trojan L16 batteries, and a Trace U-series modified-sine wave inverter. To pump water from the well into the cistern, and to run larger power tools, Ted uses a 10-kW propane-fired Kohler generator, which is also handy to keep the batteries topped off.

Today, over 30 years later, Ted and Katie are still steadfastly resolved to their simple lifestyle, despite the fact that Ted has designed and built over 50 log homes for other people, some as large as 15,000 square feet. "I enjoy the creative challenge of designing and building a large range of projects," Ted told me, "but Katie and I are quite happy with what we have." No argument here.

House 1,550 square feet; hand hewn and owner built

Heating woodstove

Water pumped from well to cistern by the generator

Refrigeration propane

Solar array 70 watts

Wind turbine none

Inverter Trace U-series modified sine wave

Batteries 8 Trojan L16s

Backup power 10-kilowatt, propane-fired Kohler generator

CHAPTER 11

GABLES AND DORMERS

Design Ideas to Accent Your Roofline

Long before the walls are finished you'll be thinking about the roof. Having shoveled 3 feet of snow out of our house before managing to get it covered, we thought about the roof a lot. And when we weren't dreaming about the time when we no longer had to cover all of our tools and run for the shed every time a pregnant cloud passed overhead, we were thinking of ways to simplify the roof without sacrificing the rustic, hand-hewn look we'd worked so hard to achieve with the rest of the house.

The technique we used was not original, but it was clever and the result was even more than we'd hoped for. We did it for the simple reason that it served our needs at the time, since our blueprints called for heavy, trussed gable ends that would have had to be set with a boom truck; an unlikely prospect at the top of a steep, icy road in the dead of winter.

Invariably, every visitor to our home finds the loft ceiling to be the most impressive part of the house. Though LaVonne and I are a bit partial to the split-log stair, we have to agree that the overhead log work nicely amplifies the hand-crafted character of the rest of the house. It was an effect we achieved by taking a very simple roof design and adding embellishments later, after the structural members were covered and dry. I'll discuss our solution to a vexing problem over the next two chapters.

Rather than cloud a complex issue even more than necessary, this chapter is devoted solely to gable ends and dormers. While it is true that the roof members and the gable ends are woven together into a single structure, it is equally true that any roof system can be made to work with any gable end design, and vice versa. So, by first deciding on a gable end design, you will be able to proceed to the roof with half the problem solved.

A large gable end is set with a crane at Benshoof's home. This south-facing wall will be filled with windows between the vertical logs.

The gable ends are one of the first things a person notices when they see a house for the first time. They are, in my estimation, a defining feature of any log house. If they are done tastefully and in concert with the rest of the structure, the gable ends can add an extra dimension of beauty to an already striking house.

There are three basic styles of gable ends: full log, vertical log, and the standard frame type.

FULL LOG GABLE ENDS

Many consider full log gable ends to be a standard feature on any *real* log house. What, after all, could be more natural than continuing the walls right up to the peak of the roof? Nothing, obviously. It's a style that is often used today with very pleasing results.

Before you build with full log gable ends, however, there are a couple of things you need to ask yourself. First, how steep is the roof going to be? Since it is the nature of stacked logs to settle, the steeper the roof the more settling will become an issue. On a modern house, where plumbing vents, furnace stacks and stove pipes emerge through the roof from fixed points below, a roof that changes angle (pitch) appreciatively because of settling can cause a number of problems, all of which need to be addressed. With low-pitched roofs, where the gable ends are not so high, the problems are less severe, but still worthy of consideration.

The best way to deal with settling is to build the gable ends with dry logs and allow them to sit in place for several months before completing the roof.

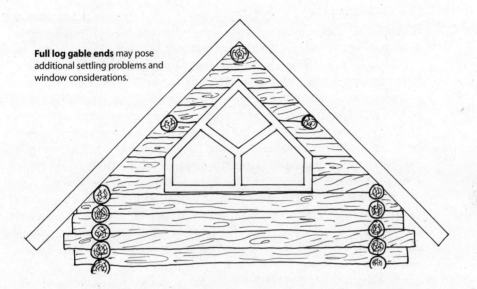

Full log gable ends may pose additional settling problems and window considerations.

Any settling that occurs after that should be slight. If this isn't feasible, then you may want to install "floating" rafters or roof beams, with slotted attachments to the purlins that allow them to slide up as the gable ends settle.

Heavy, permanently fixed window bucks, capable of supporting the roof, are often used with full log gable ends. They will stop all settling wherever the weight of the roof bears directly over them, but not on the unsupported log ends. So, again, they should only be used with well-seasoned logs.

VERTICAL LOG GABLE ENDS

When building the gable ends from vertical logs or heavy, milled timbers, you can avoid the headaches inherent in full log construction. Only the top members will bear any lateral load, so shrinkage and settling are no longer an issue. And with the enhanced support of the vertical members, windows can be of virtually any size. It is, in fact, quite common to build vertical log gable ends and fill every space in between with glass.

The amount of engineering required for the design and construction of vertical log gable ends depends entirely on how the roof will be constructed. If, for instance, you plan to use load-bearing purlins running the length of the roof, the load transferred to the gable ends will be substantial, and a considerable amount of engineering may be required. On the other hand, if you build the roof using dimensional lumber (or TJI) rafters of sufficient strength and spacing to support the roof without the purlins, the load transferred to the gable ends is insignificant. In this case, their design and execution is greatly simplified.

(It's been my experience that building departments are a bit reactionary when it comes to structural matters with logs. That is, they will either calculate that the purlins—and log beams, if you need them—will support *all* of the roof, or *none* of it. They don't care to assign percentages to any part of a roof system. So, if all you have to do is change the spacing or the size of your rafters to swing the pendulum from one extreme to the other, it's probably worth it. Though it may be a little insulting to see "decorative only" red-penciled next to your heavy beams and stout purlins on the blueprints, at least you're off the hook.)

There are two things to keep in mind if you plan to build your own vertical-log gable ends. First, all the log members of the gable end should be milled on two sides. Whether you plan to fill the spaces with windows, logs, or standard framing for stucco or siding—flat, straight sides are a must. You might be able to pull this off with a chainsaw and a chalk-line. (I did this on my first log house; it worked, to a degree.) But if you have a saw-guide or a chainsaw mill, or a friend at the local sawmill, you may be happier with the results.

Second, you will need to decide how to connect the members together. You can do this with any of a legion of complex notches (which the building department may or may not buy), long bolts or gusset plates, which are simply pieces of flat steel ($3/16$ or $1/4$-inch thick). Hidden gusset plates fit into slots cut into the

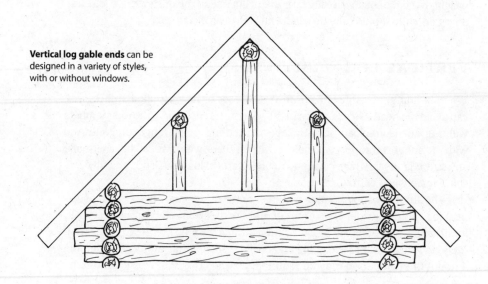

Vertical log gable ends can be designed in a variety of styles, with or without windows.

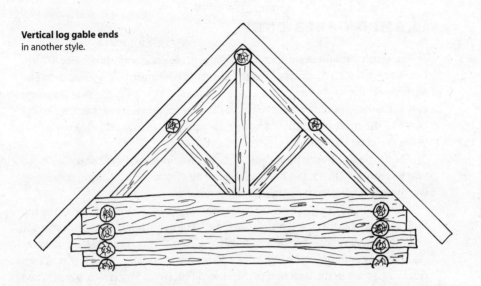

Vertical log gable ends
in another style.

truss members and held in place with countersunk bolts. For a nearly-seamless appearance, the countersink holes can be filled with dowel segments.

Setting vertical log gable ends will be tricky if they're being placed on walls several feet above the floor. Your best bet is to build them on the ground and set them with a boom truck. If that's not feasible, you may be able to slide them onto the wall using a log ramp, then raise them with ropes and a winch.

Whatever you do, have a plan before you start; you don't want to be forced to improvise as you go along.

Gusset Plates

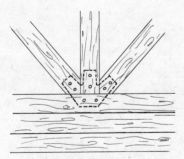

Use hidden gusset plates for a clean look.

Gusset plates can be a decorative element.

FRAMED GABLE ENDS

At first blush it might seem that framing the gable ends with dimensional lumber is a cop-out, so inconsistent with the rest of the house that you wouldn't be surprised if the log-home police came and hauled you away for even thinking about it. But it just ain't so. It's done all the time, often with spectacular results. Some of the most beautiful log homes ever built have framed gable ends, and yours could be one of them.

Some people frame their gable ends to save time and labor; some do it out of desperation. Others, I've been told, actually plan to do it all along. Whatever category you fall into, you have lots of company.

By building your gable ends in this seemingly pedestrian way, the sky is the limit as far as the effect you hope to achieve. (The same holds true, of course, for vertical log gable ends.) An exterior finish of stucco, or stucco with stone, can provide pleasing contrast to the logs below. To achieve the vertical log look, split logs can be attached to the wall before the stucco is applied. Wood siding and wood shingles are also widely used with pleasing results. Often vertical logs are inserted within the dimensional lumber walls to accent windows or serve as purlin supports. Some builders even attach horizontal split logs to framed gable ends to give a full-log appearance. The point is, wherever your imagination takes you, you can probably find a way to make it happen with framed gable ends; you'll certainly increase your window options by building the gable ends this way.

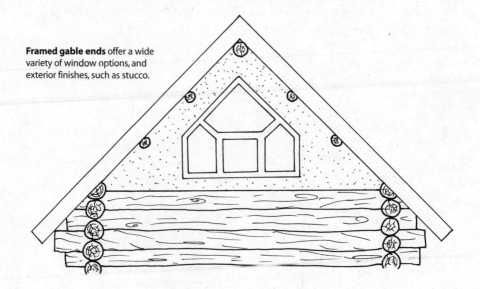

Framed gable ends offer a wide variety of window options, and exterior finishes, such as stucco.

What makes framed gable ends so versatile is the fact that all the support structure is hidden, leaving a flat, clean surface for whatever embellishments you might choose for the finishing touches. Be creative!

As mentioned above, we designed our roof so the entire load is carried by the rafters, subordinating the beams and purlins to "decorative" status. And, due to practical concerns (and, okay, maybe a little bit of desperation), we decided to forego the vertical log gable ends in favor of the more common framed variety. It was the right decision, and one we certainly don't regret. Not only did it allow us to cover our structure before the deep winter freeze, we were then free to add our beams and purlins whenever and wherever we chose, without any need to address structural concerns.

It was liberating.

In the end, you'll design the gable ends for your house based on the time you have to spend, the amount of work you believe the task is worthy of, and the appearance you want your house to have. No one way is better than any other, as long as you know beforehand the limitations of each. Play with different ideas for awhile, then be pleasantly surprised when you see the results.

DORMERS

Not only do dormers add a degree of charm and complexity to an otherwise boring roof, they also create extra living space in loft areas and are a pleasing source of extra light. In the winter, south-facing dormers with big windows can allow more warmth to enter a house than they permit to escape it. In summer, with the sun nearly right overhead, a dormer with big eaves will keep out the direct rays of the sun while providing an extra opening to enhance cross ventilation.

Our south-side dormer is filled with windows.

We originally planned to build a single dormer on the south side, then framed in another one on the north side just opposite the south dormer. The north dormer encloses an upstairs bathroom that wasn't in the plans. (The building inspector wasn't too thrilled about our deviation from the blueprints, but he finally decided to let it slide.)

So, by building two dormers, we added enough room that we could build a full bath under one and LaVonne's studio under the other. The extra time and material expense was insignificant compared to the beauty and practical use of space our two dormers provide. ∾

October 1999

We set the two log floor beams [17] for the loft, and with only a few more rounds of wall logs to go, we must get more creative on how to lift the logs onto the house. The winch can't be used to lift logs from the inside with the loft floor beams in the way, so we peel logs outside the fort and then lift them onto the wall, one end at a time, with the farm tractor...its questionable brakes make for a couple of dicey moments.

Thank goodness my clients are understanding about the wind whistling through the cell phone as I work on the house.

November 1999

A load of lumber is delivered for the loft floor, which we install before finishing the walls. It is much easier standing on a floor rather than perching ourselves on ladders. Rex always tips the delivery drivers, and it pays off in prompt delivery and careful service.

Yea! It's the end of November and I am done peeling logs (for a while). The last two logs were not easy-peelers...they were very green and full of sap. Or maybe they just seemed more difficult than the others because I knew they were the last two logs of the year. (It's the same idea that the last 100 miles of a big road trip are always the longest.)

A most unmemorable day was the Saturday afternoon when Rex gouged his knee with a chainsaw. "Why waste a perfectly good afternoon at the hospital?" he said. "I'll stitch it up myself." Good grief!! Cowboys.

The last two logs are on the house [18], and we are going to town to celebrate (if we don't fall asleep from exhaustion). The celebration continues the next day: we cut the gin pole in half and drag it out.

CHAPTER *12*

ROOF FRAMING

Taking It To The Top: Roof Beams, Purlins, Rafters & More

There are dozens of ways to design a roof for a log house, all working from but a handful of central themes. Of these, only a few variations are used to any extent in modern log homes. In this chapter I'll cover the basic details of the most practical roof designs in use today, and leave the embellishments up to your imagination.

OVERBUILT AND LOVING IT

It is the purpose of the roof to protect a house and its occupants from the ravages of nature. It is the purpose of the roof's support structure, in turn, to ensure that the roof stays over your head—rather than on it—through whatever adversity nature is able to dole out. Most of the time, for most houses, both systems do their jobs; other times one or both systems fail, sometimes dramatically and with dire consequences.

You can take heart, then, in the fact that the majority of log homes' roofs are greatly overbuilt. Generally, log beams (or trusses) are overlaid with purlins, creating a structure that alone is capable of holding up the roof. And then, dimensional lumber (or TJI) rafters—which provide a space for insulation and a framework on which to attach the sheathing—are installed at right angles to the purlins, adding an additional degree of support not found in conventionally framed houses. With such redundancy, the snow load—or the wind storm—that destroys a standard roof usually won't even stress the roof of a log home.

ROOF PITCH

How steep should you make your roof? It's a matter aesthetics as much as anything, though there are some practical issues to consider. Many of the old-time log builders regarded a low-pitched roof to be a thing of beauty. I won't argue that point one way or the other; the eye knows what it likes. But it has always been my belief that the faster water can be made to run off a roof, the less likely that roof will be to leak. This is especially true in cold, snowy mountainous regions where snow on the roof melts from the warmth of the house, then re-freezes when it runs down to the relatively colder eave, creating an ice dam behind which water can pool. And I'm not taking about a little water either. While doing repair work on a 3:12 pitch roof at a ski resort in the Colorado Rockies, I once unwittingly stepped over an ice-dam and sunk to my knees in cold, slushy water. (As I recall, it was the defining moment of a stupendously lousy day.) I decided then and there that deep snow and low-pitched roofs rate a little below ketchup and ice cream in the go-together department.

During that time in my life (when I wasn't vainly attempting to repair intractable leaks in ill-conceived high-mountain roofs) I did shingle repair in Boulder, a town that lies at the base of Boulder Canyon—a scenic, moody gorge that just happens to be one of the most efficient wind-tunnels ever devised by nature. Boulder is a place where—in the midst of one of its fabled windstorms—you might find an entire roof—rafters and all—lying in the middle of a highway a half mile away from the house it came from.

What I learned after examining hundreds of roofs in that windy place was that steeper roofs were far less likely to suffer wind damage than lower-pitched roofs. Moreover, roofs in the 9:12 to 14:12 range were practically impervious to the hurricane-like winds that roar down the canyon. Curiously, extremely steep roofs, such as mansards, fared no better than 3:12 and 4:12 pitched roofs. The only explanation I can offer is this: on roofs at (or near) 45 degrees, the wind works as hard to push the shingle against the roof as it does to tear it off.

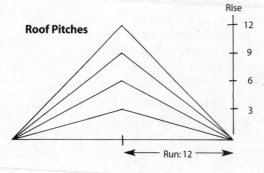

Roof Pitches

Rise

12

9

6

3

◄— Run: 12 —►

Whatever the physics may be, it's a fact that roofs within a certain range of pitch endure wind better than higher or lower pitches. It's something to consider if you're building on a mountaintop where gale-force winds are a fact of life.

If you happen to live in an area where it rarely snows or blows, of course, none of the above is of much interest. What difference does roof pitch matter then? In this case, it boils down to a matter of cost- and labor-effective living space. That is, you can increase your living area easier and cheaper by building 12-foot walls—with a floor at 8 feet—and constructing a steep roof over them, than you can by building 17- or 18-foot walls covered by a low pitched roof.

Roof pitch becomes a practical matter when you are adding a loft. Our loft inside is 26 feet side to side, with 3-foot knee walls. At first we considered making the roof a 12:12 pitch, since (as you may have guessed) I'm partial to steep roofs, and it's simple to build a roof and gable ends where all the angle cuts are at 45 degrees. But in our case it just wouldn't have worked. We would have gained a little more headroom near the

> ### Best Roof Pitch for Solar Energy
>
> If you plan to flush mount photovoltaic (PV) modules or solar hot-water panels to your roof, roof pitch suddenly becomes more than a matter aesthetics. For most applications you will want your roof pitch to be the same as, or steeper than, your home's latitude. In northern Colorado where we hang just above the 40th parallel, a roof pitch of 9:12 (36.86 degrees) to 12:12 (45 degrees) is considered optimal for most homes. The only caveat to this would be if you needed far more energy in winter than in summer—to run a solar hot-water heating system, for instance—in which case even steeper is better from an energy standpoint. In the end, of course, it will end up being a compromise between what the eye will accept and what efficiency demands.

walls, but the peak of the ceiling would have been 16 feet high. A 9:12 pitch was a good compromise: we still had plenty of headroom, and the peak of the ceiling came out at 13 feet, 9 inches.

A BASIC (STANDARD FRAME) ROOF

It's unlikely that you will construct your roof entirely by conventional framing methods without the addition of beams and purlins, but you could if you were so inclined. Consisting of nothing more than trusses, or rafters, over which plywood decking is then nailed, a standard frame roof is simplicity, itself.

However plain or uninspired this type of roof may be in its basic incarnation, it's a good point of departure for shedding light on the principles of roof construction, since many of the same methods and procedures will carry through into the construction of more complex roof systems. When discussing other roof types, therefore, I will refer back to this style of roof.

And just so you know, I'm assuming here that you have some knowledge of basic framing techniques, though you may never have laid out a roof before.

The Wall Plate

Note: If you are planning to install a tongue-&-groove ceiling over purlins, the roof design will differ from what is presented here, and you may not need to flatten the top of the wall logs or to install a plate. More on this later in the chapter.

The beginning point for a conventionally framed roof is the level of the top wall log, or the plate. With a builder's level, shoot both top wall logs (long walls) marking them every few feet at a height far enough below the top that you can create a flat area with a chainsaw, without cutting away too much of the log.

If you level the tops of the wall logs in place, be extremely careful, especially if the saw will be held below your waist! After 25 years of using a chainsaw without so much as a scratch, I finally drew first blood on this operation, and a lot of it. I was using the saw in the one position where the chain brake would not engage if the saw lurched toward me. And it did. It opened a 3-inch gash in my knee and made a tidy groove in my kneecap. The wound took a slew of stitches, and I hobbled with a cane for the next two weeks. I considered myself lucky.

Once both top wall logs are milled, you could notch and set the rafters directly on top of it, but I prefer to install (with lag bolts) a dimensional lumber plate on top of the logs, first. Not only does a wall plate give you a crisp edge to gauge the "bird's-mouth" notches cut in the rafters, the 1 1/2-inch edge also provides a solid, vertical surface for attaching the metal "hurricane clips" that help ensure the rafters remain attached to the wall in high winds. Additionally, if there is any disparity in height—either from one end of the wall to the other, or across the walls—shims can be placed under the plate to bring all the walls to the same level.

Finishing the Top Wall Logs

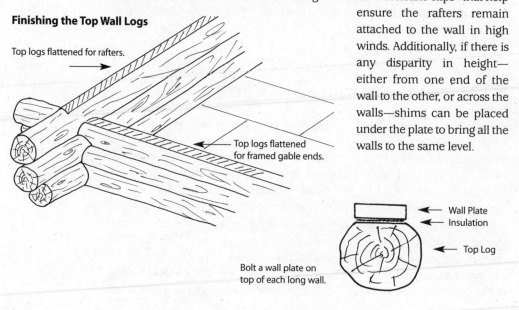

Top logs flattened for rafters.

Top logs flattened for framed gable ends.

Bolt a wall plate on top of each long wall.

Wall Plate
Insulation

Top Log

MEASURING FOR THE RAFTERS AND GABLE ENDS

Once the plate is lagged into place on the long walls, you can determine the two critical measurements you'll need to build the gable ends. *Remember that the top plate of the gable end will be on the same plane with the bottom sides of the rafters.* So, before you can build the gable ends, you'll need to determine the length (and therefore the angle) of the bottoms of the rafters. Here's how it's done:

- Measure the distance between the two wall plates, inside edge to inside edge. Then divide by 2. This measurement will be the actual run *("a" in illustration below).*

- Using the pitch ratio of the roof (9:12, for example, where 9 is the rise, and 12 is the run), multiply by the rise, and divide by the run. Let's say the distance from wall to wall is 28 feet. The actual run, to the center, would be 14 feet (or 168 inches). If the roof pitch is 9:12, we multiply: 168 x 9 = 1512; then divide 1512 by 12 = 126 inches. This is the vertical rise from the top of the wall plate to the inside peak of the ceiling *("b" in illustration below).*

- We now have the two sides of the right triangle: 126 inches of rise, to 168 inches of run. Using the Pythagorean Theorem, $a^2 + b^2 = c^2$, we see that the exact length of the bottom of the rafters is 210 inches. This is also the exact length of the top surface of the gable end's top plate *("c" in illustration below).*

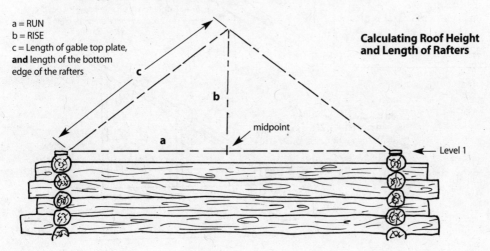

a = RUN
b = RISE
c = Length of gable top plate, **and** length of the bottom edge of the rafters

Calculating Roof Height and Length of Rafters

c

b

midpoint

a

Level 1

The framed gable end was assembled on the floor and is being tilted up, anchored securely in case of high winds.

For making bevel cuts on the framing members of the gable ends you will need to know how to calculate the angle of the roof. To do this, find the angle that corresponds to the tangent (rise/run). In a 9:12 pitch roof, for instance, the tangent is $9 \div 12$, or .75. The corresponding angle is 36.87 degrees. The quickest and most accurate way to find the angle is to use the arc tangent key on a scientific calculator. (If you don't already own one, here's the excuse you've been looking for.) Below is a table giving the angles for the most common roof pitches.

If a ridge board is to run the length of the roof, half its thickness must be subtracted from the length of the rafter before cutting. For a $1^1/2$-inch ridge board, this measurement would be $^3/4$ inches.

Build and brace the gable ends and install the ridge board (if one is used), then lay out the rafters. Unlike the floor joists, begin the layout measurements for the rafters in the middle of

Roof Pitch	Tangent	Roof Angle (degrees)
3:12	.250	14.04
4:12	.333	18.43
5:12	.417	22.62
6:12	.500	26.57
7:12	.583	30.26
8:12	.667	33.69
9:12	.750	36.87
10:12	.833	39.81
11:12	.917	42.51
12:12	1.00	45.00

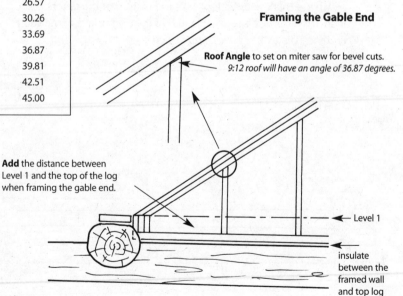

Framing the Gable End

Roof Angle to set on miter saw for bevel cuts.
9:12 roof will have an angle of 36.87 degrees.

Add the distance between Level 1 and the top of the log when framing the gable end.

← Level 1

← insulate between the framed wall and top log

the roof rather than on one end. This will ensure that the end rafters are equal distance from the gable ends, and will simplify the installation of the lookout rafters you'll use to support the eaves.

CUTTING RAFTER ENDS AND BIRD'S-MOUTHS

The easiest way to mark the cut angle for the top end of a rafter is by using a framing square. Lay it flat on the rafter with the long end perpendicular to the angle you wish to cut. Reading the inside inch marks, set the long end on 12 inches (the run) and the short end on 9 inches (the rise), for a 9:12 pitch roof. This will be the angle where the rafters will meet at the top of the roof.

The angle for the bird's-mouth (where the rafter rests on the wall plate) will be laid out in exactly that same way, only in this case we want the run, not the rise, so make a line along the long edge of the square *("Cut Y" below)*.

To complete the bird's-mouth, measure along the seat cut line from the bottom of the rafter to a point equal to the width of the plate. Then, using a square, make a right angle. A scriber can be used to mark the rafter if additional cutting is needed to fit around the outside of the top wall log. To save the time of setting

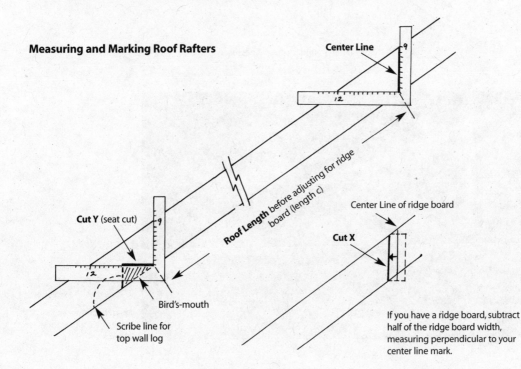

Measuring and Marking Roof Rafters

Center Line

9

12

Center Line

Roof Length *before adjusting for ridge board (length c)*

Cut Y (seat cut)

9

12

Bird's-mouth

Scribe line for top wall log

Center Line of ridge board

Cut X

If you have a ridge board, subtract half of the ridge board width, measuring perpendicular to your center line mark.

each rafter in place, scribing it and then cutting it, we bent a length of rigid copper house wire over the log and then traced the shape onto the rafter.

Rather than using a framing square for every cut, it's much easier to make a template, using a short board with the rafter angle cut on one end and the bird's-mouth on the other.

Cutting Rafter Ends and Bird's-Mouths

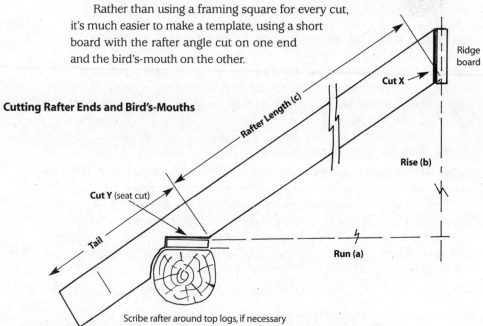

Ridge board

Cut X

Rafter Length (c)

Rise (b)

Cut Y (seat cut)

Tail

Run (a)

Scribe rafter around top logs, if necessary

Main roof rafters are in place; the south dormer is framed next.

Ridge boards are set in place on dormers.

PUTTING IN THE DORMERS

If you plan to install dormers, you should leave an opening in the rafters equal to the width of each dormer, then double-up the rafters on each side for added support. You can then go ahead and finish the main roof and complete the dormer roofs later. In this way, you can concentrate all of your efforts on building the dormers, which is good, because dormers—especially gabled dormers—are just a trifle complicated.

The most sensible way to proceed is to build each dormer in discreet steps. Begin with the gable end, followed by the side walls (if there are to be any) that rest atop the double rafters. With the walls in place, you will know the height of the ridge board and the double header on the main roof that supports it, so go ahead and install both.

The valley rafters are next. They begin in the corners of the intersection of the ridge board and the header, and end against the double rafters just before they meet the side wall. A compound angle will be cut on both ends.

The angle cuts on the valley rafter ends can be determined with a framing square, using the roof rise over 17 (instead of 12). Example, for a 9:12 pitched roof, mark the compound angle at 9 and 17, and bevel it at 45 degrees. There are complex procedures for determining the length of valley rafters, but they never seem to work on *my* valleys. Consequently, I just take careful measurements and cut the first rafter long, cutting and testing until it fits. With one valley rafter cut, the others are easy.

After the valley rafters, only the jack rafters remain. They, too, are easier to cut by empirical—as opposed to mathematical—methods.

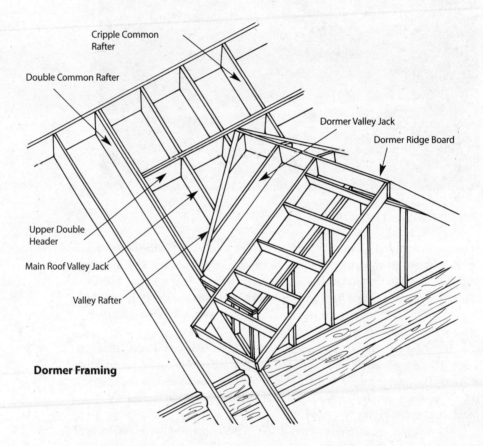

Dormer Framing

Cripple Common Rafter

Double Common Rafter

Dormer Valley Jack

Dormer Ridge Board

Upper Double Header

Main Roof Valley Jack

Valley Rafter

Constructing the Eaves

With the gable ends and common rafters in place on the main roof, all that remains is to build the overhanging eaves. Like so many things in construction, building the eaves is utterly simple in principle but rather tricky in practice, since precise measurements are hard to come by.

Your final common rafter should be farther from the gable end than the gable end will be from the edge of the eave. (The rule is 2:1 for cantilevers—2 feet inside the structure, for every foot outside—though this rule is rarely followed when building eaves, since the plywood sheathing provides extra tensile strength. If in doubt, ask your building inspector.) To save plywood, the distance between the *center* of the last common rafter, and the *outside edge* of the fly rafter should be a multiple of the spacing used for the common rafters. (For instance, if the rafters are spaced 24 inches on-center [OC] then the above distance should be calculated at 48 inches, 72 inches, etc.)

Lookout rafters run across the gable ends, perpendicular to the common rafters, and are joined on the outside of the eave with a fly rafter. They are generally spaced 24-inches OC, measuring from the bottom of the common rafters. Be sure to add the thickness of the sub-fascia, if sub-fascia is to be used.

Cut the lookout rafters, nail them into the last common rafter, and anchor each one to the top of the gable end. When all the lookout rafters are in place, trim the ridge board and add the outside fly rafter. Not too bad, huh?

All I can add are two simple tips. Deflection in the last common rafter may cause the lookout rafters to hang over the gable end unevenly, so be sure to push or pull the rafter straight

Lookout rafters and fly rafters are complete.

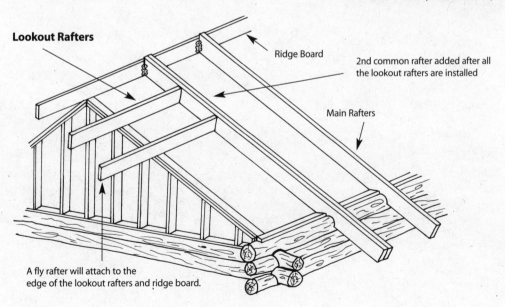

Lookout Rafters

Ridge Board

2nd common rafter added after all the lookout rafters are installed

Main Rafters

A fly rafter will attach to the edge of the lookout rafters and ridge board.

before nailing each lookout rafter to the top of the gable wall. Otherwise, the outside edge of the overhang will follow the deflection, looking at it will cause stomach upset, and thoughts of sheathing the roof will give you bad dreams. Also, you'll want to double-up the last common rafter *after* the lookout rafters are nailed in place (16d nails won't reach otherwise).

A ROOF USING LOG OR TIMBER RAFTERS

Logs or heavy timbers can be used in the place of dimensional lumber or TJIs for the roof rafters. Though the general lie of the roof is the same as with standard dimensional lumber roof framing, there are some important differences. Since the log rafters will be exposed, the ceiling (usually heavy tongue-&-groove planking) is attached to the top side of the rafters rather than the bottom. After the ceiling planks are in place, dimensional lumber sleepers are then installed on top of the planking. This will allow a space for insulation and a surface for nailing on

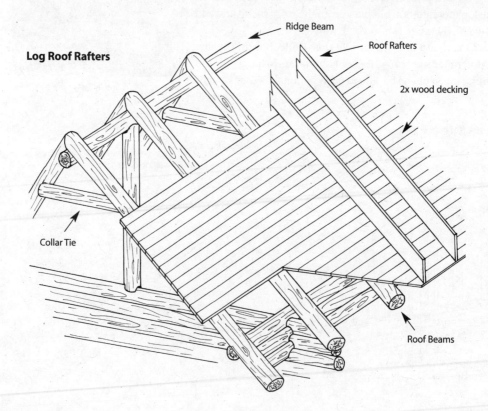

Log Roof Rafters

Ridge Beam

Roof Rafters

2x wood decking

Collar Tie

Roof Beams

the roof decking, since log rafters are generally spaced farther apart than standard $^1/_2$-inch plywood is designed to span.

A ROOF WITH STRUCTURAL PURLINS

If your roof plan calls for structural log purlins and a structural log ridge beam, they will have to be installed before the rafters. The placement of the rafters, however, depends on what type of ceiling you intend to install.

When installing a conventional gyp board ceiling—or some other material that will be installed *after* the roof is in place—the placement of the rafters in relation to the wall plate and the gable ends will remain unchanged from the basic roof style discussed earlier. This means simply that the tops of the purlins and ridge beam should all lie on the theoretical plane defined by the bottom side of the rafters (as yet uninstalled).

On the other hand, if you plan to install 2-inch tongue-&-groove ceiling planks over the purlins and ridge beam, the purlins should be placed on a plane

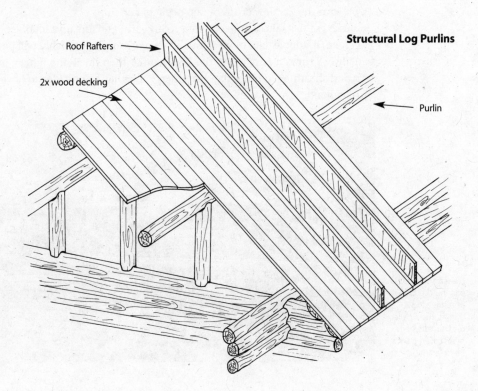

Roof Rafters

Structural Log Purlins

2x wood decking

Purlin

defined by the *outside edge* of the top wall log, since it is customary to extend the planks beyond the wall to serve as the soffit for the overhanging eave. (In this instance, the top wall logs are neither flattened nor plated.)

This type of roof calls for a great deal of planning—and a stretch of nice weather from beginning to end. Once the planks are in place and the rafters are attached with metal clips into the purlins below, any electrical wires for lights, smoke alarms, or ceiling fans must be run, followed by insulation.

This is usually the point where towering thunderheads crest the horizon, and the gentle breeze you've been enjoying becomes a stiff wind. This distressing change in weather has been mystically conjured up by the building inspector who wants to bust you for wet wires and soggy insulation. But there's no time to worry about it because you can't quit until the roof is sheathed with plywood and felt paper is nailed into place. So everyone descends on the roof like a swarm of mosquitoes, with the guys installing the felt paper yelling at the guys nailing down the plywood to hurry up and get in gear, which causes the plywood guys—who now, more than anything, just want to aggravate the felt paper guys—to slow it down a notch. And there you stand, trying to smooth over the disputes as the first few drops of rain begin to fall.

Like I said, it takes some planning. Start early, and line up a lot of (compatible) help. If it looks like more than a day's work (and it probably will be), you can always run felt paper over the T&G planks, then finish the rafters, insulation and sheathing another day. For emergencies, it's a good idea to have a big tarp on hand.

French and crew nail the T&G boards onto their log purlins. The smaller roof has already been covered with black felt paper.

PURLINS WITH FRAMED GABLE ENDS

Framed gable ends can either be built with beam pockets (and extra framing support under them) in which the purlins and ridge beam can rest, or they can be built smaller so that the purlins and ridge beam rest directly on the top plate. In this latter case, additional framing will be needed to fill in the space between the purlins and the ceiling planks.

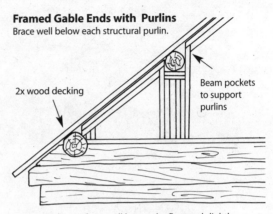

Framed Gable Ends with Purlins
Brace well below each structural purlin.

2x wood decking

Beam pockets to support purlins

Purlins and top wall log can be flattened slightly, at an angle, for a level surface.

The log home at Buckhorn Camp uses framed gable ends with large purlins, each adequately supported with dimensional lumber. Also showing in this photo is an arched truss.

The crew from Log Knowledge sets purlins on the vertical log gable end, an interior log truss, and a full log gable end.

PURLINS WITH VERTICAL LOG GABLE ENDS

Vertical log gable ends must be built to the height of the bottom of the purlins, since there is no practical way to build beam pockets into them. The spaces between the purlins can then be filled in with log segments or standard dimensional lumber framing.

PURLINS WITH FULL LOG GABLE ENDS

If you choose to use full log gable ends, it may take a bit more planning if you allow for settling. While the rafters (and ceiling planks) should be firmly attached to the outside wall (or wall plate), they must be allowed to slide against the purlins and ridge beam as the gable end settles. This can be accomplished by making slots in the planks and rafter straps so the heads of the fasteners are afforded some

movement. And since a shrinking gable end essentially makes the roof shorter from eave to peak, a few inches of extra space should be allowed at the top of the ridge beam to keep the ceiling planks and rafters from buckling as the shrinking progresses.

Benshoof's roof under construction: the purlins are set on the full log gable end (lower left side of photo) and the vertical log gable end (upper right side of photo).

INTERIOR PURLIN SUPPORT

ROOF TRUSSES

Long roofs often need additional support for the purlins and ridge beam one or two places along the roof's length. Beams are used if there is to be a living area directly below the roof. These are stout logs running directly beneath—and perpendicular to—the purlins, and held together near the top with horizontal log segments, or collar ties.

Trusses, on the other hand, are often used to support the roof beneath high ceilings where there is no living space below for the truss members (chords) to conflict with. Since a single truss can easily weigh in excess of a ton, they are almost always built on the ground and hoisted into place with a boom truck or some other suitable conveyance for lifting.

A truss can be held together in several different ways. Most common, perhaps, is the use of gusset plates—either internal or external—to connect the inner chords to the outer chords. Long bolts running diagonally through the outside corners are often used to secure the outer chords to one another.

Trusses can take on many interesting forms, with numerous eye-pleasing variations possible. Any issue of any log home magazine is likely to show pictures of several different truss designs. Coffee-table log home books are another good source for ideas. If you elect to use trusses, they will almost certainly need to be designed (or at least approved) by an engineer in order to meet code requirements.

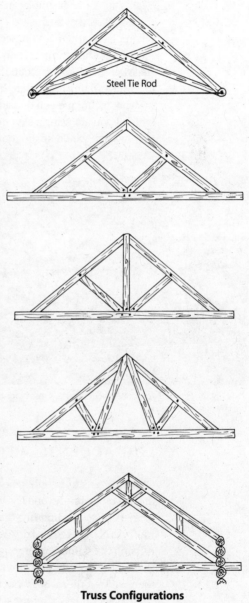

Steel Tie Rod

Truss Configurations

ROOF BEAMS TO SUPPORT PURLINS

Beams are a much simpler matter, as there is nothing particularly vexing about the installation of beams except that great care and forethought should be used when placing them. In particular, if the ridge beam is of greater diameter than the purlins, then the roof beams will be notched around it. Should you install the ridge beam before the roof beams, or should you erect the opposing roof beams together as a unit and notch the ridge beam into them? This will depend largely on what technique you're using to raise the logs. The latter method is probably better if you are using a skyline or a boom truck (or a very tall gin pole); the former method would be the more logical choice if you have to roll the logs up on the roof with ramps.

A view of the large log truss at Benshoof's house. Cross-bracing holds it in place until the log purlins are set.

I should point out here that care should be taken when using beams or trusses with full log gable ends, since it is the nature of such structures to be rigid and stationary and therefore not conducive to roof shrinkage. Unless the logs for the gable end are bone dry and tightly fitted—or some other measures are taken to retard settling—you might end up with a bowed roof.

LOG ACCENTS WITH A SIMPLE ROOF

Of the dozens of people who have toured our home—many of them accomplished builders—no one has yet guessed that our beams and purlins are not the primary system supporting the roof, or that they were installed months after the roof was completed and dry. You can call it a ruse if you like, but that would be missing the point. For although the lion's share of the support is, indeed, carried by the 2 x 10 rafters, our roof is far stronger with the beams and purlins than without them. So, what the building department calls "decorative logs," I call a "secondary support system."

But enough hair-splitting. It's a method that works well for anyone who needs to cover their structure quickly, since "accent" purlins and beams can be of smaller diameter than structural ones, which makes them much easier to move into place. Best of all, the roof overhead can serve as an A-frame for lifting.

Inside the house our roof line is 36 feet long, broken into three sections by two pairs of roof beams that run from the knee walls to the ridge log. Three rows of purlins adorn each side of the steeply-pitched ceiling. The ridge log and purlins were raised in 12-foot sections by running ropes through holes drilled in the dimensional ridge board and rafters. In this way, all the joints are hidden behind roof beams. We then countersunk lag bolts into the rafters and filled the holes with dowel sections. To discourage rolling as they were being bolted into place, we lightly milled one side of all the purlins before installing.

To ensure the roof beams would lie flat against the ceiling, we scribed and notched them into the top wall log and the ridge log, and around the purlins, then bolted them to the double rafters running along either side of the dormers.

Collar ties were then added every 4 feet. Ironically, they *are* considered structural, since they prevent the rafters from spreading and pushing out the sides of the wall. For ties between the rafters, we used logs the same size as the purlins. And between each pair of roof beams we used horizontal logs the same thickness as the beams.

The final touch came after the exterior soffit was installed: we bolted-up leftover pieces of purlins and ridge beams under the eaves, to make it look as though they extended through the framed gable.

The result of our shortcut method is really quite stunning; even after years of living beneath our "decorative" log work, LaVonne and I still proudly admire the rustic, hand-hewn view overhead.

The middle section of the ridge beam is lifted into place with ropes.

A finished look at the non-structural purlins, beams and collar ties in our loft ceiling.

EAVES

There is something about a log house that demands big eaves; they just *look* like they belong. Eaves that would overwhelm a frame house in town seem perfectly natural on a log home in the forest. That's good, because eaves serve the dual purpose of keeping rain off your logs and summer's harsh sunlight out of your house and off your logs.

LaVonne, with her unerring sense of proportion, determined that 32 and 24 were the magic numbers for our eaves (32 inches at the bottom of the roof, 24 inches on the gable ends). As usual, she was right; they're neither an inch too short nor an inch too long.

RAIN GUTTERS AND RAFTER TAILS

Should you leave the rafter tails at right angles with the roof or cut them vertical so you can easily install rain gutters? It depends on the width of your rafters, the pitch of your roof, and your sense of aesthetics. With wide rafters and a steep pitch, a vertical cut on the tails can make for a ridiculously showy fascia board.

On our roof I left the tails perpendicular to the angle of the roof, then used a table saw to rip redwood posts into wedge-shaped strips to rest the rain gutters against. If you need more that a 12-inch fascia board to cover vertical rafter tails, you'd probably be better off to leave them perpendicular.

For winter, OSB sheathing and 90# rolled roofing is nailed on the roof. We covered the gable and dormer walls with OSB and the windows with plastic.

MAKING IT DRY

To attach the plywood (or OSB) sheathing, begin at a bottom corner and follow a chalkline across the entire roof. Then start the second row with a partial sheet. Once the roof sheathing is on, you'll need to apply some kind of underlayment to keep things dry until it's time to install the finished roof. The type of underlayment you use will depend entirely on how long it will be before the roofing commences. If it will be but a matter of days, 15# felt paper should suffice; if two weeks to a month, you can get by with 30# felt. But if it will be an extended period of time, I suggest you dry-in the roof with 90# rolled roofing. All of these products come in 36-inch rolls. One roll of 15# felt will cover 400 square feet of roof; the 30# covers 200 square feet, and the 90# covers 100 square feet.

Overlap the seams 2 inches, then use roofing nails to hold it down. Space the nails 2 inches apart on the seams in high-wind areas (less in calmer environs) and make diamond patterns in-between the seams. A hammer-tacker stapler can be used to hold paper in place prior to nailing, and a few rolls of plastic wind strip from the lumber yard can save you some time nailing.

When should you install the finished roof? For starters, all the flashing and fascia should be in place. If you are using composition shingles and know what you're doing, this should be enough, since it is not too difficult to come back later and install the jacks around stove pipes and plumbing vents. If, on the other hand, you plan on a tile roof or a roof with metal panels, you had better wait for all the pipes to be pushed through the roof before beginning.

Soffits can be installed any time after the roof is dried in.

ROOFING MATERIAL OPTIONS

The roofing material you choose is truly the icing on the cake. From a distance, the roof is as noticeable as your impressive log work. Besides keeping the rain and snow out of your house, the roof will say something about who you are, what your sense of beauty is, and how practical you might be. So what do you use to give that perfect crowning touch to your beautiful home?

Until the middle of the 20th century, the thought of covering a log house with anything other than sod or wood bordered on blasphemy. These materials are, after all, as much a part of the land as the logs from which the house was built. And they were right at hand; sod is everywhere trees aren't, and a roof's share of shingles can be split with a broadaxe in a couple of days.

But times change. The engineering required to slide a sod roof past the county building department is formidable, but nothing compared to the labor and material costs incurred in making certain the roof neither leaks nor collapses under its own weight. And wood shingle roofs—the fact that they come from dwindling, old-growth forests notwithstanding—have a short life expectancy and a fire rating that falls somewhere between old newspaper and gunpowder.

So what's left? I'll briefly cover the three most popular options, though there are certainly more. I will not, however, try to conduct a short course in roofing techniques. I've done enough roofing to know that it's nothing that can be explained in one or two short chapters, much less in a few paragraphs. So I won't even try. If you've done some roofing before, or if you know a roofer or two, you may want to go ahead and do it yourself; otherwise, find a reputable roofer—not some scruffy kid in a beat-up Vega with out-of-state plates and fluffy dice hanging from the rearview mirror.

METAL ROOFS

Metal roofs are gaining in popularity by leaps and bounds, and for good reason. They are practically impervious to wind, fire and hail, and they come with warranties of 25 years or better. Snow slides right off a metal roof on the first warm day following a storm, and the new, baked finishes are minimally affected by ultraviolet radiation. Moreover, installation is fairly quick and easy, as most panels simply snap together and are held to the roof deck with hidden clips. And, since metal roofing is lightweight, there are no special structural considerations involved.

There are several manufacturers of metal roofing panels, offering dozens of styles, colors and finishes. You shouldn't have any trouble finding a dealer for any of them, though you should be prepared to pay a pretty penny—high-quality metal roofing doesn't come cheap.

CONCRETE TILE ROOFS

Concrete tiles are also quite popular, with a mind-dizzying array of styles and colors to accentuate your log work. Though resistant to wind, fire, rain, snow, sunlight and small hailstones, they can crack and break under the force of unusually large hailstones.

Because of the weight of concrete tiles, most building departments will expect to see beefed-up roof specifications, but it shouldn't amount to anything more than changing the size and spacing of your rafters.

Concrete tiles are not nailed directly to the roof, but are elevated by—and nailed to—1 x 2 bats attached to the decking through the felt paper underlayment. Hips and valleys require a lot of laborious cutting with a concrete saw, so be prepared to spend some time and money with this type of roof. If you've got an abundance of both, it's a classy way to go.

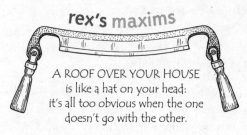

rex's maxims

A ROOF OVER YOUR HOUSE
is like a hat on your head:
it's all too obvious when the one
doesn't go with the other.

ASPHALT COMPOSITION SHINGLES

This may be a misnomer, since most shingles today contain little asphalt. Instead, they are made from fiberglass impregnated with either asphalt, rubber, or both. These improvements make for a durable shingle with superior resistance to fire, water and sunlight.

Considering what you get for the money, composition shingles can't be beat. The shingles we put on our house were manufactured by Malarkey Roofing Company. They are textured shingles that give the roof a rustic (almost mossy) look; something you would expect to see on an old wood-cutter's cottage deep in the enchanted forest. Our particular shingles boast a 35-year warranty and—best of all—a proven resistance to hail that many insurance companies (ours included) are so impressed with that they are willing to offer a 10 percent discount on homeowner's insurance.

I'm partial to composition shingles for the simple reason they come in small flexible units. I can put them down quickly with just a handful of tools, and if the roof sustains any damage from wind, raccoons, falling tree limbs or errant micro-meteorites, repairs are simple and easy. Likewise, it's not a major headache to retrofit plumbing or furnace stacks, or to later install lightning rods or satellite dishes.

Besides, they're beautiful.

> ### *UNI-SOLAR®*
> ### Roofing Products
>
> If you're planning on either a standing-seam metal roof or an asphalt shingle roof, you may want to consider incorporating *UNI-SOLAR®* roofing products into your design. These innovative products serve as both the roof itself and state-of-the-art amorphous silicon solar cells. The standing-seam panels can be blended into most other metal roofing products, and the shingles can be used for as much, or as little, of the roof as desired.
> *See Chapter 17 for more details.*

OPTIONS, OPTIONS, OPTIONS

Without actually taking the time to do the calculations, I feel I can safely say that if every person on the planet built exactly the same style of house, it would be possible for everyone to have a unique roof. The roofs and roofing systems I've offered here are the most practical and the most widely used in North America, but they hardly encompass the totality of what's out there. It would take volumes to do that. In the end, you'll do what works best for you. ∾

December 1999

No rest for the weary, at least not yet. Winter is coming and we need to get that roof on. First we frame the gable ends, and thanks to a my complicated window design, it takes a while. It will be worth it, I keep telling Rex.

Thankfully, Joe shows up to help with the roof framing, and nice weather holds for a time [19]. But one morning, the freezing winds arrive and the clouds drop. Men are relentless. They keep working. Me...I stand next to the propane heater whenever possible. The next morning another 8 inches of snow to shovel out. Phew!!

20

Now we can hibernate with the bears for a few months.

19

True to Colorado, the days get sunny and warm again while we put on the plywood sheathing [20] and temporary rolled roofing. Next up, heavy plastic over the framed window openings in the loft, and then plywood on the gable and dormer walls. We also pop in a temporary door on the west side to keep out the snow.

January 2000

I realize that I don't hibernate very well, and I can only do graphic design for so many hours in a day. For a change of pace, I gather up piles of moss rocks for the rock veneer that will go on the basement walls. And if I'm *really* motivated and if the weather is *extremely* beautiful, I'll peel a purlin. I take my time at peeling these purlins, roof beams, ridge beam and collar ties. But when Rex is done writing that novel, we'll be ready to 'decorate' our ceiling.

On the list of things to do: order windows, pick out tile and wood flooring, and shop for light fixtures and plumbing fixtures, especially that clawfoot bathtub I've always wanted.

April 2000

Spring is here, the novel is complete, and Rex is ready to abandon the computer for the tool belt. The purlins and roof beams are peeled and ready to be hoisted to the ceiling. Without soffit boards on the eaves, the drafty morning wind is chilly.

First we install the ridge log in three sections, pulling each section up with ropes run through holes drilled in the ridge board. Lag bolts firmly hold all the logs to the joists. Next to be raised are the purlins,

and then the very tricky roof beams that run diagonally from the top wall log to the ridge log. We must scribe each one to fit over three purlins, so there is no room for big errors. Chinking will hide the small stuff. The log collar ties add the finishing touch, and give dimension to a high ceiling. Looks great!

After asking around, we finally find a crew to do the garage floor flatwork. They level the dirt, getting the slope just right. Rex and I lay down 2-inch insulation boards so our radiant heat goes up and not down. Then comes wire mesh so the plumber can tie down the radiant heat tubing [21]. Dick and crew from Action Plumbing put the garage area on one thermostat and the workshop/battery room on a separate thermostat. (They did the underground plumbing last fall.)

The spring snows and rains arrive just in time to pour concrete. And as luck would have it, the first truck gets stuck about 40 feet from the house. Oh, it is maddening to see the truck, full of concrete, tilted precariously off our road while we wait for the tow truck.

Four hours later the truck is pulled to the top [22] and the contractors start pushing around the mud. Soon we will have a another nice flat floor to pile stuff on...

Log • ically Solar

Living seven miles away by road—or a mere mile and a half by feathered transport — LaVonne and I were able to go through the entire building process with John Benshoof when he chose to build a custom-log 4,000-square-foot home on the 40-acres of secluded mountain land he wisely bought way back in the late '70s.

It's an appealing home to take in from a distance, and it just gets better as you get closer, thanks to the expertise of Log Knowledge, a Fort Collins, Colorado company. Giant vertical logs and a massive stone chimney support the south-side roof of the heavily glazed great room, and the partially covered porch is a perfect place to relax on summer evenings. Inside, your eyes are immediately drawn to the custom log spiral staircase, leading up to John's cozy office and the small cupola above it.

Nor does John's three-level home (four, if you count the cupola) have an off-grid feel to it. The rooms are all spacious, and the kitchen contains a full complement of modern appliances, including a built-in microwave and dishwasher. Only the propane refrigerator hints at the home's measured electrical reserves. And it is on this point that John's home converges with everyone else's who has ever built miles away from the last, lonely power pole: there is only so much power to go around.

The home's 48-volt PV system is fairly robust, comprising two ground-mounted arrays of 960 watts each; an Outback charge controller; a Trace 4048 inverter; and a bank of 16 Trojan L16 batteries. When the batteries get too low, a stationary Kohler propane-fired generator kicks in automatically to charge them.

It's about as good of a system as you can get without going hog wild, but it's not perfect. "The zone pumps in the hydronic heating system are my biggest electric load in winter," John figures, so he uses the woodstove in the great room as much as possible. Its reassuring warmth cannot reach the back bedroom, however, or down into the finished basement. The answer? Add more solar modules to run the pumps. John plans on increasing the size of the array in the near future, bringing the nominal capacity up to 2,880 watts.

In the meantime, he'll kick back, take in the nature that beckons from every side, and enjoy the solitude that called to him from beyond the grid, all those years ago.

House 4,000 square feet on 3 levels; hand hewn, custom log

Heating woodstove in great room; in-floor hydronic with propane-fired boiler

Water pumped by PV system from 500-foot well into a cistern

Refrigeration propane

Solar array 1,920 watts (2,880 planned)

Wind turbine none

Inverter Trace SW4048

Batteries 16 Trojan L16s

Backup power 8.5-kilowatt, propane-fired Kohler generator, wired for automatic start

Cutting a door opening.

CHAPTER 13

WINDOWS, DOORS AND WIRING

Letting Light Into A Shrinking House

By now the superstructure is up: your exterior walls are complete and you have a roof (with big eaves) over your head. And all of a sudden your bright, sunny house has become as dark as a cave. This means, of course, that it's time to cut out the door and window openings to let in some light.

If you haven't already taken delivery of your doors and windows, they should at least be on order. Custom windows and doors will have a longer lead-time than off-the-shelf units, so it's good to order them as soon as you're sure of the dimensions. If nothing else, you should know the exact rough framing dimensions of every door and window going into the house.

CALCULATING THE OPENINGS

So how big should you cut the openings? The answer to this question is dependent on the answers to two other questions: How thick will the bucks (frames) be? And, how much space should you allow for settling?

LaVonne's Verities

RULE OF 2:
Don't be surprised
if it takes two times
longer than planned.

WINDOW AND DOOR BUCKS

To answer the first question, it's necessary to know just how you intend to trim out the windows and doors. As mentioned in the chapter on wall logs, you should know— *before* spiking down the logs—the thickness of the bucks and the depth of keyways (if any) you plan to cut into the sides of the opening.

∾ Bucks Without a Finishing Trim

Door and window bucks are often made of logs milled on two sides, heavy timbers, or simply with rough-cut dimensional lumber, 2 inches or better in thickness. With any of these bucks, a finishing trim board is not needed, since the door or window will already be amply trimmed. The depth of the bucks can range from a little less than the thickness of the logs (in which case the log ends on either side are beveled back to meet the buck), to a little deeper than the logs.

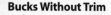
Bucks Without Trim

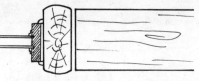
A log milled on 2 sides, or rough-sawn lumber can be used as window and door bucks.

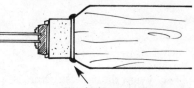
Use chinking or caulking to seal.

If you plan on using bucks without added trim, it is important that your doors and windows *not* have exterior flanges (or worse, brick molding), or you'll have to add an additional frame of dimensional lumber within the log or timber bucks, then cover the flange with a narrow trim board. Obviously, it's important to know if your doors and windows will have flanges *before* cutting the openings.

∾ Bucks With a Finishing Trim

Another option is to use standard dimensional lumber for the bucks, then cut back the logs on all sides to the width of a final trim board so that the trim boards lie flat against both the bucks and the log wall *(option 1)*. It's a lot of extra work, certainly, but it's a stylish way to finish the windows and doors. And with insulation stuffed in the spaces between the back of the trim boards and the logs, wind

Rex bevels back the logs around window and door openings before installing trim boards.

and insects will have a harder time finding a way in while the house is settling (that is, before a final seal can be made with chinking or caulking).

Two variations on this style that minimize the amount of cutting are also possible. By making the bucks from layered pieces of dimensional lumber as deep as the window (or door) jamb and as wide as the trim board, the trim board then fits snugly between the log opening and jamb *(option 2)*. Or the buck is made wider than your thickest log and the trim boards set on the surface of the logs *(option 3)*.

Flanges work well with either of the the first two options, though brick molding is still a very definite no-no.

ALLOWING FOR LOG SHRINKAGE

What about settling? If your roof has been on for a month or two (or better yet, several months), you've probably been taking periodic measurements to determine how much settling has occurred, and if the rate is constant or has been decreasing. On the other hand, if you finished the roof two days ago you will have no idea how much settling to expect. I would be much less inclined to take chances with the latter scenario than the former. With a few measurements under your belt, you at least have an idea; with no measurements you know, well…nothing.

As I've stated elsewhere, $3/4$-inch per foot is the shrinkage you should expect with green logs, all the way down to $1/8$-inch per foot as the lower limit for dry, tight fitting logs. Expect the worst—it's really no extra trouble to cut out an additional inch or two above the top buck, and it may save you a lot of work later.

But don't go hog-wild, either. Remember: you don't need to take the shrinkage for the entire wall into account, only those logs that lie within the lower and upper latitudes of your opening. In other words, if you have a 4-foot window opening in a 12-foot wall built with green logs, it may very well be that the wall will shrink 9 inches ($3/4$-inch per foot) by the time it's all said and done, but only 3 inches of that shrinkage will have occurred in the 4-foot section of wall where the window rests.

Bucks With Trim

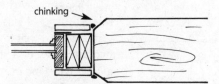

Option 1: Use one 2x buck , and flatten log to same depth; trim boards will overlap the buck and log. Log ends can be beveled for a finished look.

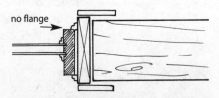

Option 2: Use double 2x bucks , and bevel the logs to match the trim board.

Option 3: Use a buck that is wider than your widest log; trim boards will set on the outside of all logs.

MARKING AND CUTTING THE OPENINGS

Now that you know how to calculate the size of the openings, all that's left is to mark and cut them out. Hopefully, you have left yourself enough room (between spikes) to position the windows so that you don't cut away more than half of either the top or the bottom log.

Begin by pounding a nail part way into one of the upper corners (preferably a nail with a small head, like a finish nail). Measure down to the bottom of the opening and make a pencil line about where you think the bottom corner should be, then use a level or a plumb bob to find the exact corner location and pound in another nail. Find the other two corners in the same way, take corner to corner measurements to make certain the opening is square, then run a level along the bottom to assure yourself that all is right with the world.

So much for the easy part.

Obviously you will want the opening to be as close to perfect as you can get it, but just how close is up to you. If you plan to use trim boards that will extend over the logs on all sides of the opening, or if you're going to chink the seam between the bucks and the logs, you may be able to get by without using a guide for the chainsaw. Otherwise, I highly recommend that you use one.

If you don't plan to use bona-fide saw guide—one that slides along the surface of a 2 x 4—then you can still use a 2 x 4 as a guide for the bar. Or you can simply mark a line all around the opening and cut it freehand. I've tried it both ways; it would seem intuitive that a person could cut straighter using a board for a guide, but it doesn't work for me. I find it much easier to follow a line than trying in vain to stay close to the edge of a board without cutting into it. I end up watching the board so intently that I don't notice if the saw is cutting perpendicular to the wall or wandering off at an angle.

To mark a line around the opening for a freehand cut, you can snap a chalk line between nails, then connect the chalk lines in the hollows with a flat-sided carpenter's pencil laid against the edge of a 2 x 4. Another—quite ingenious—method is

A window opening is cut and logs are pushed out.

described by B. Allan Mackie in *The Owner-Built Log Home*. Mackie suggests shining a bright light behind a dry line stretched between the nails, then tracing the line's shadow. A laser level also works for this purpose (see inset on page 154).

If you've got a brand-new saw chain stashed away somewhere, now is the time to use it—cutting the openings with a dull chain or a worn bar is a bad idea. And while you're at it, it won't hurt to pray to the log gods that there are no spikes in the way.

No matter how good you are with a chainsaw, there is a real possibility that the saw will kick back as you begin your cut, so be ready for it after you make sure the chain brake is in good working order.

This may sound like a no-brainer, but it's easy to overlook. Before you cut, look around the house below the openings, just to be certain the cut logs don't land on anything dear to you as they fall to the ground. Dogs, in particular, like to nap against the sides of houses. (It's one our dogs' favorite pastimes to dig nests in the soft dirt next to the foundation. Curiously, they are not dissuaded by either the noise of a chainsaw or the steady rain of sawdust.)

rex's maxims

CUTTING DOOR & WINDOW OPENINGS is like performing surgery: there's rarely a satisfying solution to a botched job.

INSTALLING THE BUCKS AND WINDOWS

I could tell you that almost everyone who builds a log house takes adequate measures to allow for settling, and those few fools who don't always end up pulling out their doors and windows and re-cutting the holes. But I'd be lying on both counts.

Many people who build with dry logs simply build window and door bucks with heavy timbers and forget about it. The house will eventually settle around the bucks, with results that run the gamut from not noticeable to comically obvious, but the doors and windows still open.

Log Knowledge used heavy bucks for all door and window openings, with a settling space above, on Benshoof's home.

Settling Options for Windows

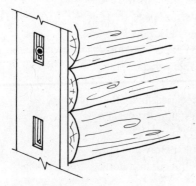

Option 1: Cut slots into the buck so bolts can slide as logs settle.

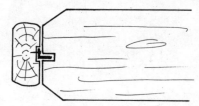

Option 2: Cut a keyway into the log, and attach an angle iron spline to the buck.

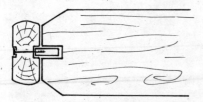

Option 3: Cut a larger keyway into the log, and attach a 2x4 spline to buck.

If you are determined to tempt fate but want to give yourself a little more cushion, leave a settling space between the header log and the top of the buck. But there is really no point in doing it this way when it is so simple to build window and door bucks that allow for unimpeded settling.

One easy method involves cutting slots in the bucks for the nails or lags screws (attached through the buck into the logs) to slide as the house settles *(option 1, at left)*. By using a router to cut a countersink slot for the heads to move without scraping against the window jamb, it's a quick, though inelegant, technique that hardly takes any extra time or effort.

The final two methods (which, I should point out, are the *only* methods accepted by the International Log Builders Association) take a little more work, but are well worth the effort if you want the peace of mind that comes with knowing you've done things "according to Hoyle." In both techniques, splines (keys) are attached vertically to the sides of the bucks, and keyways are then cut into the exposed log ends to allow for unimpeded movement as the structure slowly settles.

The splines can be made from either angle iron or wood. If angle iron is used, the edge that lies flat against the buck is recessed into the wood with a dado cut made with either a table saw or a router, and the angle iron secured with countersunk wood screws *(option 2)*. Most of the keyway in the log ends can be cut with a circular saw, and the corners finished off with a good handsaw, or a drill bit designed to perform router-type cuts.

If you choose wood splines over angle iron *(option 3)*, 2 x 4's set on edge should be used for stability, since part of the reason splines are recommended over other methods is that they eliminate any lateral wall movement in the opening. A strong spline—one that will neither bend nor break—is therefore suggested.

The keyway for a wood spline is usually cut into the log with a chainsaw and the corners finished off with a chisel. An alternate—far more tedious—method is to drill a series of holes along either side of the proposed keyway and removing the wood with a chisel.

Once the bucks are in place and square, measure your openings (height, width and the diagonals) to confirm that your delivered windows will fit properly. If you haven't ordered your windows, now is the time. Keep in mind that you may want extra-deep windows to fit within your thicker-than-average walls. I would suggest beveling the logs (with a chainsaw) around the openings before installing the windows. Finish off the logs with an orbital sander and then pop in your windows. Step back and admire the view!

Keyways are cut into the window openings at the Buckhorn Camp log home.

Settling space is evident above the windows and doors in Bob and Linda Kinglsey's hand-crafted home. *Photos: Linda Kingsley*

ADDING TRIM BOARDS

With the bucks and windows in place, fill the settling space with some type of easily compressible insulation, such as fiberglass. The trim boards can be attached to the header log or to the buck, depending on the style of bucks you have chosen.

TRIM MOVES WITH TOP LOG

If you attach a trim board to the header log, it will slide down past the buck (and the side trim) as the structure settles. Since the trim board will move with the header log, you can go ahead and install flashing and chinking over the board's top edge to repel water and bugs.

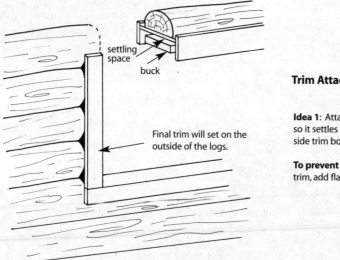

settling space

buck

Final trim will set on the outside of the logs.

Trim Attached to Top Log

Idea 1: Attach the top trim board to the top log so it settles with the logs, covering the space and side trim boards.

To prevent water trapping around the exterior trim, add flashing or chink along the top edge.

TRIM FIXED TO THE BUCKS

In this case, the top log will settle behind the top trim board which is nailed to the top buck. If you attach trim boards to the bucks, be sure not to also attach them to the log wall until you are satisfied the house is finished settling. The same goes for caulking and chinking. To stop insects and air drafts from entering the house through your sliding jambs you can stuff fiberglass insulation into the cracks with a putty knife.

Admittedly, it's a lot of work to install doors and windows properly, but not nearly as much work as installing them improperly. And once you are finished you have the satisfaction of knowing that you won't have redo it a year or two down the road.

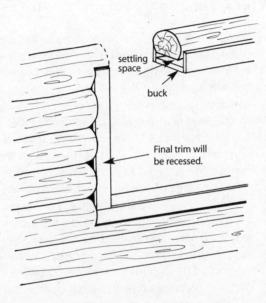

settling space

buck

Final trim will be recessed.

Trim Attached to the Bucks

Idea 2: Attach the top trim board to the buck (but not the top log). The trim board will hide the settling space.

To prevent water trapping around the exterior trim, add flashing (or chink along the top edge).

WIRING YOUR HOUSE FOR ELECTRICITY

Note: Your interior frame walls are the ideal place to run plumbing pipes/vents, and electrical wires. Your plumbers will want to have first crack at drilling holes; wiring can be run around pipes a lot easier than pipes around the wires. The next chapter on "Settling" addresses special concerns for frame walls and plumbing.

There are two ways to run wires in a log home. You can use either method if you are chinking your home, but only one of them is feasible in a chinkless, full-scribe log home. The latter method requires a lot more planning, a little more work, and final result is essentially the same.

rex's maxims

If you really want to DISCOVER YOUR OWN LATENT TALENTS, try doing something you've always known you couldn't do.

As you devise a wiring plan, take into account the fact that low voltage wiring—phone lines, stereo speaker wire, cables for satellite television and internet service, computer network cables, etc.—should not be run through the same holes as, or along side of, standard house wiring. It could result in unacceptable interference.

RUNNING WIRES THROUGH PREDRILLED HOLES

Before beginning the log work, you will need a diagram showing every wall outlet, smoke detector, ceiling fan, light switch, and light fixture, both inside and outside the house. Their locations should all be marked clearly and indelibly on the floor. Then, as the walls go up, you will drill holes—using a long, spurred, spiral bit—through each log to accommodate the wires running to and from each outlet, switch and fixture. Most of the wires are run through the floor joists and up to the height of the electrical boxes. Wires to overhead lights are more easily run through interior framed walls, but can also be run through the logs. Many builders run "fish" wires through the holes in the logs as the structure goes up,

Benshoof's home will have switches and outlets centered in a log. Wires will be pulled through predrilled vertical holes at the back of each box.

making it easier to pull wires later, but if you are careful and drill large enough holes, this step may not be necessary.

When the structure is complete, the square recesses for the switch and outlet boxes are cut into the log walls and the surfaces are flattened so the cover plates lie flush. Holes are then drilled through the back of the recesses to meet up with the holes previously drilled to run the wires.

The recesses can be cut with a chisel. You can also use a heavy-duty jig saw or a reciprocating saw with a short blade, beginning and ending the cuts at holes drilled in opposite corners with a Forstner bit. The wood inside can then be easily removed with a chisel. (The reciprocating saw is a fast way to cut the recesses, but it's a rough ride. Once your eyeballs start rolling around in their sockets you might want to go back to a chisel.)

RUNNING THE WIRES BETWEEN THE LOGS

It takes far less planning to run the wires between the logs behind the chinking. With this method, the house wires come up through the floor at the side of a door opening (where they will later be hidden by a trim board), then are stapled into the cracks between the logs before the chinking is applied. Second-story wiring can be run through framed walls or snaked up along log corners after the corner notches are opened up with a chainsaw to allow space to hide the wires. (Don't worry—chinking does a great job of hiding the wires and any unsightly chainsaw work.)

Cutting recesses for boxes is much the same as when running wires through predrilled holes, except that in this case the recesses will be nestled between two logs, rather than cut into the center of one log. Chinking will then hide any part of the box that is exposed.

The other option is to center the electrical box between two logs (either horizontal for outlets or vertical for switches) and chink up to it.

LOW VOLTAGE WIRING

Don't forget the low voltage wiring for your telephone, internet, satellite television, and sound system. Although we don't have phone land lines yet, we wired the house for them in case the phone company someday decides to run service to our home for under $18,000.

Satellite internet service require low voltage wiring, which can be run before the house is finished.

We also ran CAT-5 wires for networking our computers and for satellite TV. And since we enjoy music, we have in-ceiling speakers throughout the house and outdoor speakers on the deck. ❧

May 2000

Unsettled weather forces us indoors and we start framing the interior walls. The main floor walls are easy...everything is square, no funny angled walls or sloping ceilings. We double-plate the bottom of each wall to allow for the gypcrete that will be poured over the radiant heat tubing.

The loft walls are a bit more complicated to frame. It is only a walk-in closet and bathroom [23], but the ceiling, purlins, and roof beams are quite funky, not to mention my request for two walls at 45 degree angles. Once again, I think I'm pushing the limits with Rex on these design issues.

Outside, the soffits are a pain to do, and even more so when balancing on very tall ladders in gusty spring winds. We opt for plywood soffits instead of tongue-&-groove pine boards. The seams will be covered with our decorative purlin ends, and the boards will be stained to match the house logs. It's a nice compromise.

The day is finally here when our fort becomes a house....we can start cutting in the doors and windows. The tricky part about windows is the vertical placement. I know exactly where they will fit horizontally, but the up-and-down placement is unique to each window, except for the walls that have matching windows, side-by-side. We don't want to cut away too much of the log above or below.

It is wonderful how much light fills the house now that all the openings are cut in. A dramatic and welcome change! We buy a load of 2x6's and frame around each opening. Rex is amazed at how many windows I managed to get by him. Windows are delivered (all but one that was broken in transit) and in they go [24]...with lots of caulking to seal under the flanges. The house is looking cozier by the day. And I won't miss that rattling plastic that covered the window openings.

June 2000

Rex decides it is time to finish the exterior and the first project is to cut the wall logs ends in a random stagger [25]. I stand back at a distance and direct Rex with the chainsaw. The beaver cut on the end of each log is a nice finishing touch. Then he bevels each log where it meets the window, inside and out. This is a very tedious job of sawing and chiseling, but the effect is well worth it. These little things really add some character.

Our logs are definitely dry enough to finish. Actually, they are rather sunburnt from sitting in the sun for so long. We powerwash them, sanding any really obnoxious grey areas. Then we put on the first coat of stain/sealer. I'm so glad we chose a water-based product; cleanup is easy and it dries fast (which is good when those afternoon storms threaten).

I will always remember that morning in mid June. After working on the north side for a couple of hours, I poke my head around to the southwest and see a huge cloud of black smoke [26], which can only mean a forest fire.

The hot, dry and windy conditions are perfect for a raging fire. After two days, the firecrews start using our place as a lookout area. We stand closeby, eavesdropping on their radio conversations. The evacuation order comes just after the firemen told us that we were on our own. They will not defend our properties. I pack the truck with the computers, photos and whatever else my scrambled brain can think of. Rex cuts down any bush or tree close to the log house and the cabin where we are living. Then finally, after sleepless days and nights of watching smoke, a cold front descends a day early, bringing snow! The middle of June and it snows! Prayers have been answered. We gather together with the neighbors in a state of exhaustion and relief. The Bobcat Gulch fire, from an untended campfire, was extinguished after burning nearly 11,000 acres.

Log • ically Solar

What more could anyone want than just enough to make their life complete? It was that philosophy Glenn and Carole Brannon took with them when they retired to the Colorado high country in 1993. Where some might desire sprawling acreages, the Brannon's were overjoyed with 3.8 acres of wooded hillside. Eschewing a mansion, they chose instead a humble 1,200-square-foot, rough-hewn, square-log house. And then they set out to make it a home.

The foundation was professionally set, as was the Appalachian Log Homes shell. From that point on, it was all Glenn and Carole and an undertaking that was, truly, a labor of love. For the two years it took to complete the project, the couple lived in a diminutive log-sided structure they charitably dubbed a cabin, though it was hardly big enough for a bed and a dresser. But it was enough.

Then they developed skills they'd never before possessed.Glenn shingled the roof, Carole did stonework; Glen did carpentry, Carole did chinking; Glenn installed the modest PV system, Carole built stone steps. And, despite numerous setbacks—including Carole's broken ankle, and her battle with MS (multiple sclerosis)—they somehow made their dream come true.

It's a homey place these days; cozy and welcoming, with an old-fashioned feel. Most things run on propane, including the fridge, the water heater, the clothes dryer, the wall-mounted heater, and the stylish Heartland gas range which gives the kitchen a decidedly 19th century feel. The few large things that do require electricity—including the well pump and the clothes washer—fall into the province of the gasoline-fired generator, while the smaller items are handled by the PV system.

Consisting of 128 watts of roof-mounted PV, four L16 batteries, and an 800-watt Trace inverter, the system resides in the crawl space under the house and is only used for a few DC lights and a small satellite TV. It's not a lot, but it's just what they wanted.

"We wanted to experience a totally different life," Carole says. "Whatever hardships there may be—and they are few, really—are more than compensated for by the peace and solitude we feel up here. To live in a house we built with our own hands here in the bosom of nature is better than life in any suburban trophy home could ever be."

It's good to know when you're finally home.

House 1,200 square feet on one level; rough hewn, square logs

Heating woodstove; propane wall heater

Water pumped from 300-foot well by generator

Refrigeration propane

Solar array 64-watts

Wind turbine none

Inverter Trace TS-series 800-watt

Batteries four L16s

Backup power 5-kilowatt gasoline-fired Coleman generator

CHAPTER *14*

MORE SETTLING ISSUES

When Things That Don't Shrink Meet Things That Do

If you find yourself cringing at the thought of reading this chapter, I assure you there is no need to; by installing the doors and windows you've already triumphed over the baddest beast in the lair. This is not to say that what remains is a picnic, only that you've been tested under fire and have emerged with a ton more knowledge and experience that you started with. So let out the breath you've been holding and read on.

THE BIG PICTURE

Every house built with wood loses height over time. In the case of a frame house, it may only be a fraction of an inch; for kiln-dried milled logs, a little more. In a hand-hewn, round log house the shrinkage is harder to gauge: it may only be an inch or two, but it might be the better part of a foot. A loss in height of even a couple of inches, however, can lead to disastrous consequences if certain allowances are not made in critical areas.

Everyone knows that windows and doors should be installed in a manner that takes wall shrinkage into account, but not everything else is quite so obvious. Sewer pipes, water lines, stove pipes, chimneys, vent stacks and stairs (to name a few) must all be installed in a manner that neither impedes wall shrinkage nor experiences distortion because of it.

Fortunately, everyone who has ever built a log house with plumbing and heating and second floors has had to deal with the same problems and some very clever ways to deal with them have been devised.

FRAME WALLS

A slot has been cut in the frame wall stud, and the bolt is being sunk into Benshoof's log wall.

Settling space is evident above the double plate on this frame wall at Benshoof's home.

While you could conceivably run all the plumbing pipes through massive holes bored in the interior log walls, your spouse would probably have you committed after witnessing the temper-tantrum you'd throw the first time a leak appeared. So to play it safe, let's say your house will need at least one frame wall through which to run plumbing pipes.

What happens to that frame wall—and all the unyielding pipes going to the second story—when the log walls shrink in height? Nothing, if you go about it right. Let's begin with the wall, and worry about the pipes later.

For all practical purposes, a wall is like a big window you can't see through and should be treated accordingly. In other words, the sliding bucks you installed in keyways for the doors and windows—and the spaces you left at the top for settling—work equally as well for frame walls. The keyway should be as shallow as possible, and never more than one half of the log wall's thickness. Though the keyway alone will hold the wall in place, you can also bolt the frame wall to the log wall by running the lag bolts through slots cut into the end board that will allow for settling.

To cut the keyway, make vertical lines on the wall using the same method you used to mark the door and window openings. For a crisp, clean cut, a good circular saw can be used to cut the first $2^1/2$ inches into the log wall. After chiseling out wood between the cuts, a chainsaw can be used to deepen the keyway if necessary. By directing the saw at a slight angle inward, you will be able to avoid marring your nice beginning cut, while ensuring that you'll have plenty of space for the wall to slide in. It's important that the keyway is perfectly vertical, otherwise the log wall may push against the frame wall as it settles. (**Note**: If you want the frame wall to span the distance between two log walls, you will have to build it in two pieces, then join them after they are erected.)

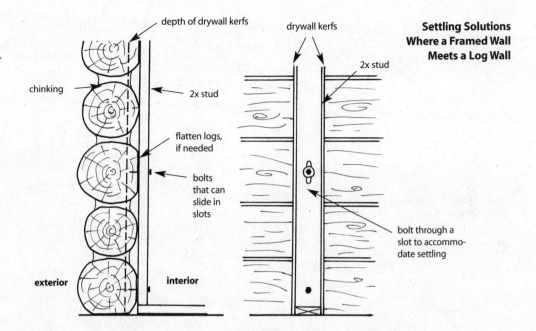

depth of drywall kerfs

drywall kerfs

**Settling Solutions
Where a Framed Wall
Meets a Log Wall**

chinking

2x stud

2x stud

flatten logs,
if needed

bolts
that can
slide in
slots

bolt through a
slot to accommo-
date settling

exterior

interior

It is common practice to also cut drywall kerfs by cutting the keyway in the log wall deep enough—and wide enough—to accommodate the wall boards (sheetrock) on either side of the frame wall. In this way, the log wall hides the rough ends of the wall board, and will slide past it as the wall settles.

On the other hand, if you are *certain* the house will finish settling by the time you get around to installing the wall board, you can cut the keyway shallow (for the stud wall only) and then scribe the wall board around the logs and chink the joints. We were able to do this on our house with no deleterious effects.

The top plate of the frame wall should be lagged through the settling space to the ceiling joists above (or boards bridging the joists if the wall falls between joists). Install the lag bolts through pre-drilled holes so that as the house settles the lags do no bind in the plate.

To hide the settling space between the top of the wall plate and the ceiling joists, attach a 1 x nailer—the same width as the wall plate *plus* the finished drywall—to the ceiling directly above the wall. (Be certain to take the thickness of the 1x board into account when calculating the settling space.) Then, after the drywall is installed and finished, attach a trim board to the 1x nailer. As the ceiling drops, the trim board will slide past the wall board.

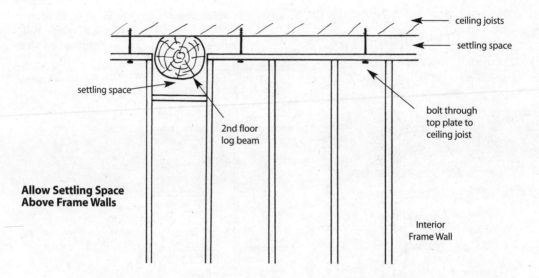

ceiling joists

settling space

settling space

2nd floor
log beam

bolt through
top plate to
ceiling joist

Interior
Frame Wall

**Allow Settling Space
Above Frame Walls**

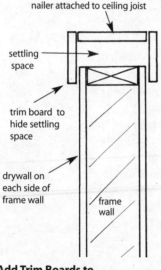

nailer attached to ceiling joist

settling
space

trim board to
hide settling
space

drywall on
each side of
frame wall

frame
wall

**Add Trim Boards to
Cover Settling Space**

STAIRS

Since stairs are one of the last structural components to be built, there is a good chance that the house will be almost settled by the time you get around to installing them, especially if the house has been an ongoing weekend project. That's good, because stairs are always tricky to build, even when the distance between floors doesn't decrease over time.

A quick and dirty temporary stair put into service while the house is still settling is the best answer, though not very satisfying if you anticipate several more years of wall shrinkage.

A straight stair (without a landing) works best in a house that is still settling. Attached (hinged) only to the upper floor and allowed to slide on the first floor, the stair angle will decrease as the house settles and the treads will tilt. With minimal wall shrinkage these changes in attitude may fall within the parameters of the venerable "slop factor." (For example: with an 8-foot-high stair built with 8 inches of rise to 9 inches of run, a 2-inch decrease in wall height would change the stair angle by a little more than a degree, and the stringer would move $1^3/4$ inches across the floor.)

By taking an educated guess at how much more the house will settle, you can then place spacers under the bottoms of the stringers and pull them out as needed. To keep from tripping on the first step, I would advise a temporary landing in front of it; one that can be shortened as the spacers are removed. The spacer technique (or a screw jack) can also be used for a spiral stair, with the big difference being that you need to be better at guessing since you won't have the same slop factor to fall back on.

Stairs with landings, or stairs built into log walls, are better left until all settling has occurred, though if only minimal shrinkage remains—and you are clever enough—you may be able to make it work.

PLUMBING PIPES AND VENTS FOR FURNACES AND HOT WATER HEATERS

Since they are not pressurized, PVC sewer and vent pipes can be fitted with a series of compression fittings that will allow the pipe sections to become shorter as the building settles. In order to restrict all movement to the compression fittings, solid blocking should be used at all horizontal offsets and at the top of the uppermost joint and the bottom of the lowest one.

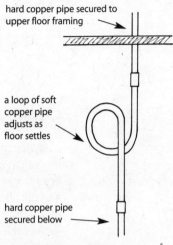

hard copper pipe secured to upper floor framing

a loop of soft copper pipe adjusts as floor settles

hard copper pipe secured below

Plumbing in a Settling House

The Benefit of Experience

Benshoof's house was built in early January by Log Knowledge, then allowed to sit through the winter and early spring before it was re-set on John's site. Naturally, I had a few questions about settling, particularly since the north-south gable was built with full (horizontal) logs at one end, vertical logs at the other, and a log truss in the middle. How did they compensate for settling of the full log gable ends, and the walls the truss was set upon, when it was obvious the vertical logs would not settle at all?

Stanley Johnson, the crew foreman, has built so many log houses that my concern hardly seemed to be an issue for him. He told me he'd cut a few inches off the bottoms of the ver-

tical posts to compensate for settling at the yard, then another inch at John's home site for additional settling yet to occur. He was confident it would be enough.

Since the house was built with dry logs and then allowed a few months to settle in a dry climate, no special precautions were made for settling around doors and windows. Instead, the crew merely spiked heavy-timber bucks to the log ends in the openings, leaving an inch or so above the headers for settling.

After building hundreds of log houses, these guys know what to expect. Had the logs been greener or had less time to settle, they certainly would have done things differently, but for this particular house it's all that was required.

All vertical copper water supply pipes running between floors should be installed with loops of soft copper below the settling space so that as the top section of pipe pushes down, the loop simply expands. As with sewer and vent pipes, the water supply pipes should be secured above and below the loops.

Any offsets in furnace or water heater vents should be completed far enough below the upper floor that they are not affected by wall settling. Also, the vents should *not* be secured to the roof flashing or any floor or wall above the first floor, so that they can slide freely through their chases as the house settles.

CHIMNEYS AND STOVE PIPES

Fireplace chimneys should be designed and built as free-standing structures, with no points of attachment to log walls, upper floors, or the roof. (Unless you are inventive enough to figure out some way to do it that takes wall shrinkage into account.) Be sure to make the roof flashing tall enough that it remains covered by the chimney counterflashing as the chimney increases in height, relative to the roof, due to settling.

In the event that you are installing a wood stove rather than a fireplace, it just might be that the stove pipe will slide through the roof opening and roof flashing unimpeded. If, however, a support box is used to provide necessary clearance for fire prevention, or to make a transition from single- or double-walled pipe to triple-walled pipe, then a telescoping section of pipe will have to be installed under the support box.

VERTICAL SUPPORT POSTS

Kingsleys crafted creative wood coverings that will wrap around the settling spaces on their posts.
Photo: Linda Kingsley

Like walls, vertical supports under floor beams or porch roofs must be able to compensate for log wall shrinkage. But since they are structural components, simply leaving a settling space at the top is unacceptable. Instead, some method should be employed to slowly lower the posts as the walls settle.

Screw jacks are commercially available for just this purpose. Permanently placed under a post, the jack is adjusted incrementally as needed. It's ugly, of course, and needs to be hidden from view, so you'll have to come up with a box or decorative cylinder that you can slide up the post, or one that has a removable panel to allow for periodic adjustments to the jack.

We tried another, riskier, method. Fairly certain that our

house was not going to settle more than 2 inches, we placed four $^1/_2$-inch spacers under each of our beam supports, then used a hydraulic jack and a post to hold up the floor beams every time we needed to remove a spacer. By the time all the spacer's were out, the house was done settling. If we'd have needed to shorten the posts even more, a chainsaw would have obliged us.

It worked for us, but our house was done settling before we got around to installing the hardwood floor or the lightweight concrete beneath it. If you even *suspect* that your house might still be settling after the finished floor is in place, it would be an expedient gesture of marital goodwill to play it safe and use the jacks.

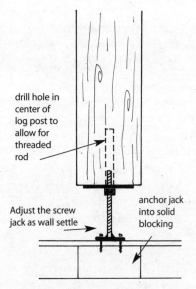

drill hole in center of log post to allow for threaded rod

Adjust the screw jack as wall settle

anchor jack into solid blocking

Screw Jack Below Structural Log Posts

KITCHEN CABINET CONSIDERATIONS

Cabinet installation on frame walls is easy, but mounting your kitchen cabinets on log walls requires special attention. Not only will the cabinets need to be shimmed to compensate for the uneven nature of the logs, you will need to think about settling. Many experts agree that the majority of settling will occur within the first three years, so if you are like us, settling won't be an issue by the time you get around to hanging the cabinets. If, however, your log walls will settle more than another $^1/_2$-inch, you may want to consider mounting your cabinets through small slots (using washers with the screws), or on sliding sleepers notched into the log wall. To avoid the tricky part of mounting on log walls altogether, frame a narrow wall in front of the log wall. The installation of back splashes is greatly simplified with this method. If you have a cabinets that wrap around a log wall to an interior frame wall, this is a good method for keeping all cabinets at the same level over time.

Our best advise is to wait as long as possible.

You'll probably run across other instances where allowances will have to be made for settling; what I've discussed here are merely the most prevalent. As a rule, don't install anything until you've thought it through and concluded that it will not be affected by wall settling. If it will be, don't worry; by now, you're savvy enough to solve the problem. ❧

Log • ically Solar

In 1998 and '99, when Greg Munsell and his wife, Carole Vesely, built their 1,800-square-foot log cabin on 63 acres near Zion National Park in southwestern Utah, they knew they'd be on their own when it came to power. But I don't think it bothered them very much; they instead saw it as an opportunity for ingenuity.

After the shell of the two-level, 8-inch milled-log home was professionally set, Greg and Carole went to work. The plumbing was easy, since Greg and Carole just happen to own the company that plumbed it. For the rest of the finish work, however, it was just the two of them—and whoever else they could lure to the place with free food and beer.

The renewable energy system is simple, clever, and unique; just the sort of thing you would expect from a couple who built their own furniture—and the cabin's spiral staircase, to boot—from wood taken from the property.

Each module of the 400-watt solar array, for instance, is mounted at a 45-degree angle on a 1-inch galvanized pipe set in a slightly larger base, such that Greg or Carole can adjust the "poor-man's sun follower" for maximum solar exposure throughout the day. Together with a Southwest Windpower Air 403, the array charges a battery bank of five inexpensive Interstate 12-volt marine-style batteries wired in parallel for 12-volt operation. And the house current is provided by a no-frills Aims 2,500-watt modified-sine-wave inverter. You can't get much simpler than that.

Water to the house comes by way of a stand-alone system: a separate 48-volt array drives a slow-but-steady DC pump in the 240-foot well. Whenever the sun is shining, water is being pumped into a cistern and gravity fed to the house.

And backup power? Well, it's unique. Using an old cook stove, a steam engine, and an automotive alternator, Greg and his son pieced together a fail-safe battery charger—it's guaranteed to work as long as there is water and firewood to power it.

Now that's thinking out of the box.

House 1,800 square feet; milled logs, contractor set, owner finished

Heating woodstove

Water pumped from well by stand-alone DC pump and PV system

Refrigeration propane

Solar array 400 watts

Wind turbine Southwest Windpower Air 403

Inverter Aims 2,500-watt modified-sine wave (RV-style)

Batteries 5 Interstate 12-volt marine type

Backup power ½-horsepower steam engine with automotive alternator

Thankfully, the art of chinking no
longer involves mortar. This old
cabin is quite drafty now.

CHAPTER *15*

CHINKING AND FINISHING

Keeping Weather In Its Place

Thirty years ago there were two standard choices for sealing and protecting logs against the ravages of nature: boiled linseed oil, with or without. Turpentine, that is. The prospects for chinking were even more dismal: mortar or meticulously cut strips of wood. Both entailed extreme outputs of labor for a woefully temporary solution.

Today, with a log home industry soaring into the billions of dollars, high-tech solutions to the age-old problem of preserving wood and chinking cracks and seams abound. This is a good thing for log home owners, since many of these new products really are as good the manufacturers claim they are. But at the same time, it's up to the homeowner to sift through the reams of promotional and technical literature to find the best products to protect their hard-won log walls against air infiltration, water, sunlight, bugs and mildew.

While it is hardly within the scope of this chapter—or the expertise of the simplicity loving woodsman writing it—to cover the pros and cons of all the various products available, I can hopefully offer a general framework upon which you can build your own mountain of knowledge before finally deciding on which products to use on your own log home.

GOOD DESIGN = GOOD PROTECTION

I have touched on these matters in other chapters, I know, but I believe it is prudent to gather them all together here and elucidate them with the same light at the same time.

The very best thing you can do for your logs is to protect them by designing (and building) a roof with big eaves. Besides keeping rain and snow away from your walls, big eaves also help shield the logs from the glaring rays of the midday summer sun. Log ends are particularly vulnerable to sunlight and moisture, and your eave design should take this into account. Purlin ends should be terminated before the fascia board, and the ends of all wall logs and floor beams should be adequately protected by the eaves.

Below the eaves, all window sills should be canted downward to repel water, as should all bucks and trim boards that stick out past the doors and windows, top and bottom. Metal flashing above doors and windows is also a good idea.

To protect the logs from splash-back from water running off the roof, or from the tons of snow that pile up next to the house in winter, all sill logs should be a bare minimum of 12 inches from the ground. A good metal flashing—again, canted downward—under the sill logs, and sealed against the weather with synthetic chinking, will protect the logs from the buildup of moisture.

Wide eaves protect the logs from the harsh elements of sunlight and moisture.

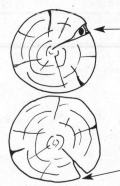

Upward-facing checks should be filled with a backer rod and then caulked.

Large checks (cracks) facing downward do not need to be chinked or caulked.

Wide, upward-facing horizontal cracks (checks) in wall logs provide places where water can pool and should be filled with a high-quality caulking material. For larger cracks, foam backer rod should be pushed into the crack first.

In general, all log surfaces should be protected from rain and snow, all joints should be designed to shed water, and any places where water can collect should be chinked or caulked.

If all of these measures are taken in due course, your log preservative will only need to work half as hard and will last twice as long. And your house will enjoy a long stress-free life.

CLEANING THE LOGS

Logs that have laid peeled in the sun and the rain too long may be stained or discolored. A 5:1 mixture of water and bleach (or any of a dozen commercially prepared solutions) applied with a garden sprayer—followed by a pressure washing—often takes care of the worst of it, though sanding and sandblasting may be needed if the staining is severe. We put four logs in our house that I had peeled months before we began the log work. If I had simply run a drawknife over them a second time, I could have saved myself—and LaVonne—a lot of work, but I didn't realize how tenacious the discoloration was until we tried to remove it. Bleach and power washing helped a little, but we still spent several hours with a sander before we were satisfied.

The logs are bleached on French's house.

There are products on the market that promise to retard staining and discoloration of peeled logs. Having never tried any of them, I can't make recommendations.

Before applying any type of preservative, your logs should be clean and dry inside and outside. Cleaning them, of course, means getting them wet. Even if they're still as pretty as the day you peeled them, they will have accumulated layers of dust and dirt that must be removed before applying a finish. A pressure washer is the best tool for the job; nothing fancy—too much pressure makes the logs look fuzzy. Water alone should remove all the dirt, though detergent can be used as long as it is thoroughly rinsed. After washing, let the logs dry completely before applying any type of finish.

FINISHES, AND FINISHING

The makers of any type of finish will recommend upper limits for the moisture content of the logs. Most of the products we looked at could not be applied if the moisture level was above 18 or 20 percent. This is roughly considered to be the transition area between green and dry logs. If you have any doubts, you should rent, borrow or buy a moisture meter. It could save you a lot of time and money.

Before sealing and chinking the logs, I highly recommend that you build some kind of scaffolding to work from. You'll still have to use ladders, but at least you will have a firm and level footing on which to place them.

I dug around in our scrap pile for leftover 2 x 4's, secured them to the rim joists, and supported them from the ground with additional 2 x 4's. I then laid 2 x 10's over the top—extra rafters left over from the roof that I had ordered for just this reason—and screwed them in place. A little shaky, and certainly not much to look at, but it worked.

One more thing: are your windows already in place? Do yourself a big favor and tape them off before you accidentally coat them with something no solvent on the planet will remove without likewise removing the finish on the window frames.

Now, what kind of finish should you use? That depends on what kind of look you want the logs to have, and what sort of environmental challenges the logs will have to face. The very best thing you can do is to talk to someone in your area who has built a few log homes; nothing beats experience. If you don't know anyone, shop around on the Internet, then talk to the local sales reps. Or better yet, call a log home supply house that deals in several different brands; they will have knowledgeable people on staff to help you make an informed decision. Be sure to get samples to try on leftover log ends before putting anything on your house. The actual product will vary in color from the printed brochures, and besides, color appears much differently when viewed on a large scale.

Two Aspects of Log Preservation

Preserve the Wood Protect against wood-destroying fungi and wood-digesting insects by using fungicides and insecticides.

Preserve the Color Prevent logs from turning black due to mildew and mold by applying a mildewicide to untreated wood. Prevent logs from greying due to ultraviolet sun rays by applying a protective material (stain/sealer).

Source: Fletcher Parsons, *Log Homes Illustrated*

I used boiled linseed oil on the log house and cabin I built in the 1980s, but I wasn't particularly happy with it. Not only did it darken the logs over time, it also gave them a "dried-out" look.

This time around, we looked at several products before deciding. In the end, we shied away from oils and opted for a water-based stain and sealant. For the outside of the house we used a three-step process, beginning with a borate-based wood preservative that protects against rot and insect infestations. (In an arid climate like Colorado's, where the air is so thin it can't hold much moisture even when there is any— which is rare—and the insects are all fairly innocuous, it was really a tossup if we needed a wood preservative or not. In the end, we decided better safe than sorry.)

We then let the logs dry for a few days before applying a single coat of an elastic, latex-based stain that protects against UV light and moisture. (Though the directions say it can be applied with a garden sprayer and then brushed-out, we quickly gave up on the sprayer and just used a roller and brush.) There was a small degree of opaqueness that remained after it dried, but it was not an unpleasing effect. Then we applied a single coat of a clear "weather repellent" that is designed to give extra protection against moisture and the sun's ultraviolet rays. Happily, we were able to use the garden sprayer—then a brush—on this operation. This top coat needs to be applied every few years, especially on south-facing walls.

rex's maxims

IF YOUR WIFE doesn't like the flimsy scaffolding you built, rebuild it.

For the interior logs we didn't need (or want) a stain or a preservative, so we simply applied two coats of a clear finish to bring out the grain in the wood (and to make the annual log dusting easier).

Sealing the interior ceiling logs.

CHINKING

Chinking a log house is one of those chores that takes time no matter how you go about it, so be prepared. On our house—a roomy structure, but certainly not big—I have calculated that if all of the chinking rows were run end to end there would be a continuous line over a mile long.

Should you chink before or after sealing the logs? That depends on what you use to seal them. Many stains can discolor chinking material so you are much better off waiting until the logs are sealed (also, it's much easier to clean drips and splatters from sealed logs). However, synthetic chinking will not adhere to certain log finishes, especially oils, so check compatibility with the chinking manufacturer before you proceed. We chinked our house after the logs were sealed inside and out since we knew the products were compatible—all were from the same manufacturer.

> ### Seal Out Bugs & Varmints
>
> If you don't like flies and mice running amuck in your in home, take extra precautions to seal all joints, cracks and openings with minimal-expansion spray foam and chinking. Tedious work, but it will save your sanity in years to come.

Since the chinking will hide the electric wires running between the cracks in the logs, you will not be able to chink the interior until the wiring is complete. You may need to chink the outside, however, *before* the wires are run—even though you will have to later touchup around outlet and light boxes. Electrical inspectors may expect a house to be completely sealed and dry before it is wired.

Before chinking is applied to joints, a foam "backer rod" should be installed. Backer rod serves the dual purpose of minimizing the amount of chinking you use, and works as a substrate against which the chinking can expand or con-

Rex applies chinking and LaVonne smoothes it, making sure it seals firmly against the logs. A light mist of denatured alcohol and water kept it workable in the dry, hot, windy weather.

tract, without pulling away from the log surface. It comes in a variety of sizes and shapes, so you shouldn't have any trouble finding what you need to fit between your logs.

Synthetic chinking comes in one-quart tubes and 5-gallon buckets. The tubes cost a bit more and take a very strong hand to apply with a manually operated caulking gun, but they entail a lot less mess. Pneumatic caulking guns or guns that attach to cordless drills are well worth the money if you go with the tubes. If you opt instead to use the buckets, consider buying a bulk-loading caulking gun or a grout bag, or rent a commercial pump—designed especially for chinking—to make it easier. Either way, leave yourself plenty of time to clean up at the end of the day.

You may feel like a fish out of water when you first try your hand at chinking, but you'll soon get the feel of it. I'd shoot chinking along an 8- to 10-foot section, then LaVonne would tool it. Her favorite tool was a small putty knife with rounded corners (I did the rounding with a file), but she also used foam brushes and occasionally a cheap little cheese knife with a bent blade. And of course, a wet rag to wipe up spills. A spray bottle filled with water and a little denatured alcohol was used to keep the material workable as she tooled it, and was especially helpful to keep the chinking from drying out

LaVonne's Verities

SOME DAY YOU WILL FINISH CHINKING, but probably not today.

when she worked in the sun and wind.

Though it hardly took LaVonne any time at all to achieve a laudable degree of proficiency at chinking, I'd be lying if I said she ever actually warmed up to the task. But she was certainly proud of her work when it was all done.

By the time you finish sealing and chinking your logs you will have covered every square inch of your walls several times. You may never want to set eyes on a paint brush or a caulking gun again. Probably you will have a hard time believing that an interminable task has really come to an end. But it has, so go to town and kick up your heels; you deserve it. ❧

Homeowner Linda Kingsley (a very talented 'chink chick') sealed all joints on the exterior log corners. *Photo: Linda Kingsley*

June 2000

June is not a month to repeat. A week after the fire, I fall off the scaffolding while trying to move a ladder. Three hours later, the HMO doctor finally looked inside my mouth and observed that I needed stitches (tears finally convinced him I wasn't as fine as my face looked!). So off to the oral surgeon I went, but by now, he is out to lunch. Eventually I'm stitched up and Rex takes me home with a 6-pack of Ensure protein drink.

Before long, I'm back at work on the house, but forbidden to climb ladders and scaffolding (at least for a few weeks or until Rex rebuilds the scaffolding with a railing).

July 2000

Outside work continues with staining and more finishing. While Rex works on the logs, I stain and seal the trim boards for the eaves, windows and doors. Many windows means you have LOTS of trim boards. Installing those fascia boards requires some tall ladders! [27] The rough-sawn trim boards are a nice contrast to the round, smooth logs.

I wash the interior log walls by hand, scrubbing with a brush to get off the dirt and grime. Then I apply the clear satin finish—it really brings out the character of the logs.

No more procrastinating. We buy a few big 5-gallon buckets of chinking, a dispensing gun and try our hand at chinking. Rex fills the gun and applies the chinking between the logs; I follow soon after with the putty knife, foam paintbrush, spray bottle and rag. The first few rows are absolutely maddening, but after awhile we get the hang of it. You really need to be in the right frame of mind. I keep threatening to write about "Zen and the art of chinking."

Our moderate-size house is getting larger by the day. Chinking goes on forever. Every time we go to town, we buy more buckets and soon it becomes a sizeable investment. I've determined that chinking is "the great equalizer;" it visually evens out any disparity in gaps between the logs.

27

CHAPTER *16*

A NEW PHILOSOPHY OF FREEDOM

Notes on Developing an Off-the-Grid Mentality

When LaVonne and I turned our backs on our old farm for the last time, we were facing a sudden and irrevocable change in lifestyle. The fact that we had just sold a 2,000 square-foot house so we could live in an amenity-free cabin with a footprint smaller than a one-car garage was the least of it. The real challenge was learning to deal with the sum of all the other changes.

Where before we had a well that pumped water at the rate of 30 gallons per minute, we now had to drive 20 miles to town once a week to fill the 200-gallon tank we'd roped into the back of a pickup. Our toilet was an outhouse, our bathtub a creek. A large cooler had replaced our spacious refrigerator (sorry, no more ice maker). We now used a wood stove for heat, a gasoline camp stove for cooking, and kerosene lanterns for light.

And when we simply *had* to have electricity, I would go solemnly into battle with a war-hardened 4,000-watt Coleman generator. If I prevailed over the surly beast, then we could run a saw or a vacuum. If I was bested, then we just had to wait until I could sneak up on the ornery brute in its sleep and yank its cord before it had a chance to suck in a carburetor-full of gas, belch flames, and flood itself.

One would think that such an abrupt "lowering" of living standards would manifest itself as individual stress, or even marital strife, but nothing of the sort occurred. Quite the opposite, in fact; more than anything, LaVonne and I embraced our new life with all the energy and ambition of a couple of kids on an extended camping trip. Having purged our lives of the leaden inertia that crystallizes in the consciousness of anyone in the habit of having an instant remedy for any earthly desire, we quickly came to appreciate every drop of water, every morsel of food, every ray of light in the midst of darkness.

THE FIRST PRECIOUS AMENITIES

We were, quite literally, starting over from scratch. Any comforts or conveniences we hoped to enjoy would have to come as a direct result of hard work and mutual cooperation, not from wringing our hands over the nature of our plight.

Living just a notch or two above primitive, we quickly prioritized our desires. (I say "desires" because we actually didn't *need* anything more than we had.) First on our wish list was hot water. And not the kind you heat on the stove in a brass pot for a cup of tea; we wanted hot water that flowed copiously from a showerhead inside a closed shower stall, within a warm room walled off from the clouds and the wind.

Toward that end, we built a small (6-foot x 16-foot) addition on the back of the cabin, just big enough to hold a tiny shower stall, a propane water heater, three water barrels, a propane refrigerator (which, as it turned out, wouldn't arrive for several months, thanks to Y2K) and everything we needed for a simple solar-electric system.

We pressurized the fresh water system with a small 12-volt RV pump, which was powered with a pair of 12-volt deep-cycle batteries; one to power the pump, the other hooked to a small solar module outside for charging. When the battery in use ran down, we switched them out.

The electrical system followed the plumbing and gas piping. Using the solar modules and power inverter we'd purchased for the log house—which, at this point, was no more than a muddy hole in the ground—we had more power than we could have ever used in that small cabin, even during a run of cloudy days of biblical proportions.

Considering that until then my most meritorious achievement as an electrician was running AC power to a few stock tank heaters for the horses, the complexity of that first bare-bones PV system seemed daunting. I read every manual front to back, one, two, three times. I put every component of the system into place and then slowly and meticulously hooked-up my wires, using a multimeter to check—and double check—every step along the way.

I will never forget the day when that first PV system came online. I had tested every connection ten times over before I finally flipped the switch to the DC disconnect and turned on the inverter. No sparks, no explosions. Just a steady hum and the soft, green glow of back-lit LCD's. After testing the AC side of the system—to see if my multimeter was as convinced as I was that we actually *were* harnessing usable power from the sun—I began trying different loads. First a small light, then an electric drill.

Impressed but still not convinced, I opted for the ultimate test: a voracious 15-amp table saw. It was the single piece of equipment that could make the burly old Coleman generator convulse with fear (of a herniated head gasket, I would imagine). I plugged it in, hit the switch (after a fleeting, jumbled moment of pensive hesitation) and watched with consummate awe as the blade spun quickly and effortlessly into motion. Though my left brain knew the whirring saw blade was merely the logical outcome of applied technology, my right brain insisted that I had just witnessed a miracle.

Regardless of which interpretation one chooses to embrace, it was in that instant when the table saw came to life that the idea of sustainable, free power from the sun was transported from the theoretical realm to the practical.

MOVING UP

By the time we were far enough along on the new log house to run wires and install the PV/wind system, I thought I knew practically everything there was to know about solar energy. It was a thoroughly absurd notion, of course; kinda like the teenager whose first distant glimpses of adulthood lead him to overlook life's myriad subtleties and draw the erroneous conclusion that life is a simple subject. (And any grownup who doesn't agree is an idiot.)

The first cracks in my thin, hard shell of ignorance came when our electrician—after not showing up for several weeks—made the grievous mistake of mouthing-off to LaVonne.

He'd have been better off poking a wildcat with a sharp stick.

With the building-boom in town, there was zero chance of finding another electrician who would be willing to drive up into the hills anytime soon. And we couldn't wait. So, (very) reluctantly, I told my wife that, given enough time—and enough books on the subject—I could finish wiring the house and install the solar and wind systems. And (I nearly choked on this part) do it all to code. I didn't have much idea what the National Electric Code was about, of course, but I was pretty sure I was soon going to find out.

On my first inspection after countless hours of work, the kindly inspector wrote me up for eighteen violations. He later called back and admitted he was wrong about two of them, leaving me with a mere sixteen breaches of code to deal with.

In an attempt to ensure that my next inspection wasn't an encore performance, I must have talked to every high-level electrical inspector in the state at one time or another. No one remembered my name, but they all knew "the guy with the wind turbine," since it was one of the sticking points in our negotiations. (Code requires all sources of electrical power to have a manual disconnect, while design requires a wind generator to be connected to a load at all times. In the end, our turbine's design won out over code.)

Happily, my wiring passed the next inspection without a hitch; for the first time in two years, we were living in an electrically correct house.

It was only then that my real education began.

LEARNING THE SYSTEM

Once we moved into the new house, we realized that—even by more than doubling our generating and storage capacities—we now possessed the means to use up energy faster than we could produce it. The well pump was the main culprit, followed by the dishwasher and the hot water circulating pumps for the propane-fired radiant-heat boiler. (The usual suspects, namely the refrigerator, range and clothes dryer, were all powered by propane.)

It quickly became clear that a means to monitor our energy usage was necessary—for peace of mind if nothing else. We checked around to see what was

TriMetric Meter
Photo courtesy of Bogart Engineering

available, then bought a TriMetric Meter from Bogart Engineering. It was a little tricky to install and calibrate but well worth the trouble. Not only can we use it to see battery voltage and rate of charge, it also keeps track of amp hours going into the batteries versus amp hours going out, providing a digital fuel gauge for the system. (The TriMetric performs lot of other useful functions, as well. It's worth its weight in gold, though it didn't cost *quite* that much.)

Once the batteries are full, the charge controllers for both the wind and solar systems back off the power delivered to the batteries. It is, therefore, most efficient to use all the energy you can while it's there for the taking. Make hay (wash clothes, run the dishwasher) while the sun shines, as the expression goes. Ideally, you don't want the batteries to become fully charged until the end of the day.

Seeing how the wind plugs into our energy equation has been as fascinating as it has been instructive. While the solar array is the real workhorse of the system, the wind is like a whimsical sprite that always seems to show up just when we need it most. More than one of our neighbors has remarked that extra solar modules would have been cheaper—watt for watt—than our wind generator and tower. And they're right. But they also completely miss the point, since the wind most often provides power at night and during stretches of cloudy weather when the solar array is idle, or nearly so. This means that we can get by with less storage capacity than any of our solar-only neighbors, since we're charging our batteries while they're depleting theirs—a fact that is particularly gratifying after three days of cloudy, windy weather.

Daily I feel more respect for our wind and solar system, and its remarkable ability to rejuvenate itself. Consequently, my attitude toward energy usage has become much more relaxed, since I know that we'll gain it all back in due course. LaVonne, too, has taken notice of my moderated vigilance over the wattage reserves. She hardly ever calls me an "Energy Nazi" anymore.

It's just a matter of learning to trust Mother Nature. ∾

Log • ically Solar

REX & LAVONNE EWING'S HOME

House 1,600 square feet on main level and loft, plus 900 square-foot basement/garage

Heating Vermont Casting woodstove is primary source; back-up system is a propane-fired boiler for in-floor hydronic heat (main floor and garage/basement)

Water pumped by PV system from 540-foot well; no cistern

Refrigeration Kenmore 19 c.f. refrigerator (with top freezer), plus a small chest freezer

Solar (PV) array 1,620 watts

Wind turbine 1,000-watt Bergey XL1 on 50-foot tower

Solar hot water 30-tube Thermomax system (evacuated tubes) with 80-gallon tank

Inverter Trace SW4024 plus 120/240-volt transformer (to run the well pump)

Charge controller Outback MX60 with MPPT

Batteries 24 Trojan L16s in 2 banks (12 batteries per bank)

Backup power 6.5-kilowatt, gasoline-fired Honda generator

CHANGING WITH THE WEATHER
～ a metaphor ～

Imagine that all of your fresh water comes from a small clear spring. You know, instinctively, that if you use the water wisely there will always be enough. Right away, you notice that when the sun shines and the wind blows, the water flows. Sometimes it gushes; other times it merely trickles. On calm nights, or when the clouds roll in so thick the wind can't blow, the flow of water stops, altogether.

All day long, every day, you fill vessels from the spring. When they overflow with water you bathe and wash and clean and drink deeply. But when darkness comes and the skies grow still, you take only what you absolutely need.

At first, it seems a capricious existence. After all, you used to live next to a bottomless river; no matter how much water you removed, the river seemed just as full. But life is vastly different now, and you can't go back to the way it was before.

You have always thought that weather was a fickle, random thing, but soon you begin to discover certain underlying patterns you have never noticed before. You see that the breeze blows one way during the day, a different way at night, and storms are almost always heralded by winds. The brightest, clearest days are those right after a storm system passes. An abrupt change in temperature means an increase in the strength of the wind. Each season, you discover, comes with a different breed of clouds and its own special wind.

Every morning you watch where the sun rises, and you make note of where it sets in the evening. You watch to see how high it climbs at midday. You come to know how much water will flow at each hour of the day, in every kind of wind, in every degree of cloudiness.

Each day that you learn something new, your fear of running out of water grows less acute, for you have come to know—almost as a matter of instinct—when your vessels will overflow and when they will run nearly dry.

After a time, as you begin to learn the rhythms of nature, your initial annoyance at being occasionally inconvenienced evolves into a feeling that approaches reverence for the ever-changing skies. The heartbeat of nature becomes the heartbeat of your house, and of your life. You become attuned to your surroundings in a way you never thought possible before. Though the weather is still unpredictable, for the first time in your life you begin to trust in constant change, for you know that the water you were denied one day will be replenished the next. And, even though you are using far less water than ever before, somehow you don't miss the excess.

Finally, on the day when you truly understand that whatever nature gives you is exactly what you need, a new unfamiliar feeling will wash over you.

Don't worry—it's called Freedom.

August 2000

While we chink, the stucco man and his son start the many-day process of applying stucco to our gable ends, around the garage doors, and below the unbuilt deck. We also schedule the plumbers to install the radiant heat tubes on the main floor.

It is a crowded job site that morning when the 6-man gypcrete crew from Denver shows up, along with the stucco team. The gypcrete is very runny mortar-looking stuff that sets up in a few hours. The guys were careful—there are very few splatters to clean off the sealed logs.

One morning Rex decides it's time to assemble the wind tower base. He welds together pipe for a base that will attach to the lattice tower; this base will be sunk in a huge concrete-filled pit, which is also reinforced with rebar. I'm confident that Rex's tower will withstand the worst of winds.

Chinking continues to the corners [28]. If I had a dime for every time I climbed up and down a ladder, I'd be rich.

The well was drilled over a year ago, but now we dig a trench for the water line to the house. The wizard of pumps, Demetri, who installed the pump last year, connects everything to the pressure tank in the house while the plumbers install the boiler and indirect water heater. It pays to have knowledgeable people doing these jobs, and we were lucky to get the best.

For a change of pace, Rex suggests we dig a trench. (Dirt work and concrete are my two least favorite things.) Under the "watchful" eye of our dog, Micky, we start the arduous task of hand-digging a trench from the wind tower to the house (110 feet), and from the solar array (only 40 feet) to the house [29]. Rocks, rocks and more ROCK. A day with a jack hammer leaves Rex numb. Why didn't we hire this out? Because it is impossible to find people to work in the mountains, I keep telling myself.

30

the ceiling inside. We find that cold weather is not bad for hanging insulation...we don't mind being bundled up, head to toe, to avoid that nasty fiberglass.

I seal the ceiling logs while Rex continues with the insulation. (Yes, I'm allowed to climb scaffolding again.)

September 2000

The stucco work is finally finished [30] and we take down the ladders, roof jacks and planks, and scaffolding. The house looks really beautiful now. I'm getting anxious to move in, but I'm guessing it will be a few more months.

Mid-September is fine weather for assembling a wind tower. Rex rounds up cousin Bob and neighbor Lane to help. I went to town, but I did climb the tower later; the view from 50 feet off the ground, on top of a mountain, is truly spectacular.

The electrician shows up (amazingly) to pull wire through the wind tower conduit and to connect the wires to the wind generator. He said he didn't mind heights, but he never showed up again.

September 24 and it snows about a foot. A great day for sledding [31] before working on

31

CHAPTER *17*

HARVESTING SOLAR AND WIND POWER

A Primer on Renewable Energy

AUTHORS' NOTE: We have prepared this section as a primer of renewable energy systems as they are commonly applied by homeowners. We've tried to pack in as much information as we could into a small space without driving our readers into the tar pits of boredom or over the precipice of despair. It wasn't easy. Needless to say, much remains to be said on the subject. And, in fact, it already has been said. For years budding off-gridders, or those straddling the fence between living off-grid and grid-tied, have been reading *Power With Nature: Alternative Energy Solutions for Homeowners,* by Rex A. Ewing, while those quite certain that a grid-tied system lurks in their future have learned all they needed to know from *Got Sun? Go Solar,* by Rex A. Ewing and Doug Pratt. So, should you find yourself enthralled with the notion of powering your home with renewable energy after reading this section, we suggest you satisfy your craving for knowledge by reading one, or both, of these books.

BASICS OF RENEWABLE ENERGY

In principle, solar and wind energy systems are not nearly so complicated as you might imagine them. There are really just a few basic components responsible for transforming sunlight and wind into usable house current. They are: the power source (solar array, or wind or micro-hydro turbine); the charge controller;

the battery bank; and the AC power inverter. That's only four things—you can count them on the fingers of one hand and still have a free thumb to do something with. What could be easier than that?

The devil, as they say, is in the details.

TYPES OF SYSTEMS

There are three basic types of RE systems to choose from, and the one you eventually end up with will be determined by several factors, including your proximity to grid power and whether or not you ever need backup power.

∾ Off-Grid Systems

When it came time to choose what kind of renewable energy (RE) system we wanted, we had it easy. With the nearest power pole at the bottom of a winding, rocky road nearly two miles away, our only logical choice was to go off grid, since the cost of running utility power to the house would have been several times the cost of the solar and wind systems we installed.

In an off-grid RE system like ours, you will have a power source that produces low-voltage direct current (DC), which is sent to the batteries via the charge controller. The batteries will store this energy at 12, 24 or 48 volts.

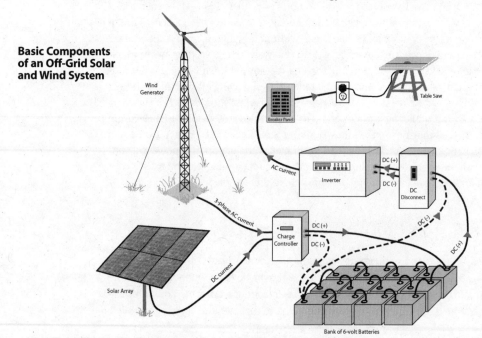

Basic Components of an Off-Grid Solar and Wind System

Wind Generator

Breaker Panel

Table Saw

AC current

Inverter

DC (+)

DC (-)

DC Disconnect

3-phase AC current

Charge Controller

DC (+)

DC (-)

DC (-)

DC (+)

Solar Array

DC current

Bank of 6-volt Batteries

Most modern homes, however, are bereft of any appliances that would have the slightest idea what to do with such unconventional electrical energy. So, unless you plan on an austere lifestyle with few modern conveniences, you'll need 120-volt AC (alternating current) to run your new log home, the type of power supplied by the power inverter.

∾ Grid-Tie with Batteries

For you, it may be different matter. If, like often happens in rural areas (at least every one we've ever lived in), you've got grid power but it's at the bottom of the utility's priority list when the grid goes south, you will probably want an RE system with a battery backup to run critical loads while you're patiently waiting for the repair crew to gravitate toward your distant corner of the county.

These systems are a bit more complicated than off-grid systems, since the inverter has to work both ways, allowing grid power to run the home and keep the batteries topped off at night or when the clouds roll in, while feeding all of your excess solar (or wind) power into the grid during sunnier times.

You will also have to wire a critical-loads sub-panel into your house system. The purpose of this is to isolate those things that absolutely have to continue running during an extended blackout, such as the refrigerator, freezer, furnace, and few lights.

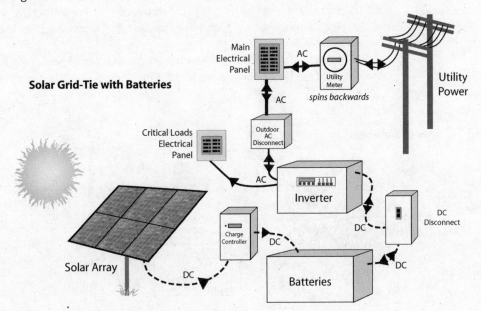

Solar Grid-Tie with Batteries

This is how it works: While the sun shines (or the wind blows) your home-grown power provides the home's electricity and keeps the batteries topped off. If there is any excess, it's fed into the power grid. This causes the meter to run backwards and earns you a credit with the power company. At night, or at times when your house loads exceed your RE output, the grid makes up the shortfall. Thus is there a constant interchange between the grid and the inverter.

But when the grid power goes down, the inverter instantly kicks in to run the above-mentioned critical loads. So long as the power is down, your house acts as an off-grid system, using RE sources to charge the batteries and run essential systems. For extended blackouts, you can even run a gas-powered generator through the inverter to charge the batteries and pick up the slack during stormy weather.

∾ Direct-Tie Systems

Battery-based systems are great during blackouts. In terms of efficiency, however, batteries exact their toll, sapping 3 to 5 percent of the system's output just to maintain a charge. So, if your grid power rarely goes down for any length of time and you live in a state that offers tantalizing incentives for solar and wind pioneers, you just might want to go with a direct-tie system that skips the batteries and the charge controller altogether.

Direct-tie systems are simplicity itself. All you have is the solar array (or direct-tie-compatible wind turbine) and the direct-tie inverter. During the day your charging sources send any extra power into the grid, then draw it back out again at night.

I should add a word of caution, however. For, while it would seem only fair that you should still be able to reap the benefits of your massive solar array dur-

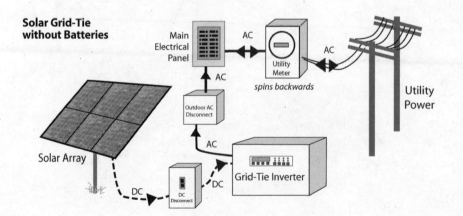

Solar Grid-Tie without Batteries

Main Electrical Panel — AC — Utility Meter *spins backwards* — AC — Utility Power

AC

Outdoor AC Disconnect

Solar Array

AC

DC — DC Disconnect — DC — Grid-Tie Inverter

ing blackouts, such is not the case; the inverter will not allow it. When the grid goes down, you're a duck in the water. Why? Well, there's this small-but-not-insignificant matter of the unwitting utility worker who will probably be laboring under the illusion that your home's power systems are as dead as the rest of grid and…well, you get the picture.

POWER SOURCES

Whichever system you ultimately install, it will only be as powerful as the solar array or wind turbine that reaps the renewable energy needed to run it. This means you'll need to do a little homework to determine how much sun and wind energy is available at your home site. Fortunately,

rex's maxims

THERE'S NEVER BEEN A PV/wind system designed by man that woman couldn't run dry.

there are means to get at least a fair idea of what you can expect before you sink a lot of money in an oversized solar array or an undersized wind turbine, as I'll explain below.

SOLAR ARRAYS

Unless you live in an exceedingly windy place (Tierra del Fuego comes to mind) or have a reliable, fast-running stream close to your new log home, the lion's share of your renewable power will come from the solar array. This is as it should be, considering that the sun is the primary source of all the energy on the planet, including the atmospheric turbulence that turns the turbine's blades, and the heat energy that lifts water vapor into the high mountains to make streams and rivers possible.

Turning light into electricity is no mean trick. It's a complicated process that uses certain energetic wavelengths of light to jostle electrons into an electrical circuit, where they can be pressed into service to power your home. (For a complete explanation of how and why this works, see the books *Power with Nature*, or *Got Sun? Go Solar*.) For all its complexity, it is a process that works quite well, as any off-gridder can tell you.

On a yearly average in the U.S., a crystalline or multi-crystalline silicon photovoltaic (PV) module will produce 50 watt hours of electrical energy per day, per square foot of surface area. This means most people can count on around five kilowatt hours of power per day for every 100 square feet of solar-array surface. (For thin-film or amorphous silicon installations, figure roughly half the efficiency, or around 25 watt hours per square foot.)

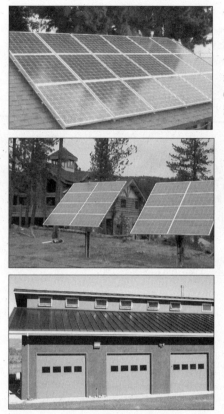

Most standard solar arrays comprise a series of individual aluminum-framed PV modules (most often rated from 120 to 190 watts each), arranged in a metal frame (or grid) mounted either on the ground or the roof. We installed a homemade ground-mounted array for the ease of installation, and the ready access for snow removal and seasonal tilt-angle adjustment. After nearly a decade to weigh the (many) pros and (few) cons of that decision, we wouldn't do it any differently, though I must admit LaVonne hates to see the array's angle steepened in winter, as it intrudes (slightly, I'd say) on her view of the southern valley.

But maybe a ground-mounted array just won't work for you? Don't worry; there's a slew of roof options.

Standard roof mounting systems include roof-integrated metal standoffs and aluminum rails designed to support an array of conventional modules on virtually any kind of roof. Or for a more aesthetically pleasing roof, you can make your array part of the roof itself. Uni-Solar's PVL-series solar laminate for metal roofs offers a 16-inch-wide, quarter-inch thick amorphous silicon "peel-and-stick" flexible panel designed to adhere—via a flypaper-like backing—directly to your standing-seam metal roof. Just peel off the back and slap it place. Carefully.

Top to bottom: roof-mounted array, 2 pole-mounted arrays, and flexible Uni-Solar PV panels on a metal roof. *Photos: Mile Hi Solar, LaVonne Ewing, and Doug Pratt*

If, like us, you prefer the look of an asphalt composition roof, you might want to take a look at Uni-Solar shingles. Just like regular shingles, these PV shingles are made 12 inches wide, 86.4 inches long, and designed for a standard 5-inch exposure. To complete the seamless integration into the roof, Uni-Solar shingles are only 0.14 inches thick—no thicker than the rest of the roof.

Going with a tile roof? Kyocera has developed the MyGen Meridian roof system to blend in

Cleaning snow off ground-mounted solar arrays is easy.

with flat concrete tile, while DRI Energy has cleverly devised a system for incorporating PV onto barrel tile. No kidding.

∾ Other Considerations

Whatever incarnation your solar array ultimately takes, the name of the game is to maximize its exposure to direct sunlight for as many hours of day as possible. Shade is not tolerable; even sunlight filtered through bare tree branches will greatly diminish the array's PV output. If you can't part with your home's south-side trees, put the array in front of them; it may make for a long (and expensive) wire run, but it's really your only option.

For roof-mounted arrays the roof pitch is important, especially for building-integrated PV where you wouldn't be able to adjust the angle of the array even if you wanted to. For year-around efficiency, the best angle for a stationary array is the home's latitude. Thus, in Colorado where we sit within a few miles of the 40th parallel, a roof pitch of 9/12 (36.86 degrees) to 11/12 (42.51 degrees) is optimal. Following this line of logic, a home in Florida would do best with a 7/12 pitch (30.25 degrees) while a home in North Dakota ought to have a 12/12 pitch roof of 45 degrees. Not everyone designs their roof with solar efficiency in mind, of course. This is fine; any loss in efficiency can regained by increasing the size of the array, which in many cases may not cost much more than a steeper roof.

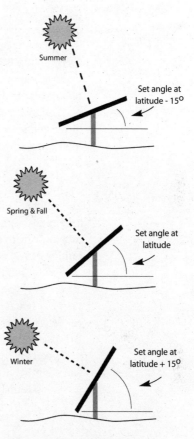

Seasonal Tilt of the Solar Array

WIND TURBINES

Our first wind turbine was a Whisper 1000, manufactured by World Power Technologies. It was a fast, two-blade machine that put out a lot of power, but it had an annoying tendency to shake loose the bolts in the tower insert and the furling bearing. To make matters worse, we discovered after a few years that we could no longer get parts for it, since the company had been sold and our model discontinued.

So, rather than continue to scab the old machine together with bubble gum and baling wire, we replaced it with a 1,000-watt Bergey XL.1. It was a good move. The Bergey is bigger, heavier, and slower—three attributes that define a well-made wind turbine. Nothing shakes loose, even in winds in excess of 100 miles per hour (a couple of which we've clocked since installing the Bergey), and it puts out more power in moderate to high winds than the old Whisper turbine did, though perhaps a bit less in light winds, since the blade diameter is 9.6 inches less than the Whisper (8.2 feet versus 9 feet).

It was inevitable that we would install a wind turbine to buttress the output of our solar array: we live at the top of hill where the wind blows more often than not; I enjoy climbing towers and admit a fascination with just about anything that turns; and it was only justice to harness, at least in part, the same force that on many days drove us to the brink of insanity while we were building our house.

❧ Is Wind Right For You?

The point is, choosing whether or not to install a wind turbine is as much a matter of personality as it is hard data concerning the practicability of reaping useful power from the wind at your site. When it's all said and done, you'll install a turbine if, and only if, the idea of a wind turbine makes you smile inside.

With that subjective observation in mind, here are the facts. For wind to work at your site, you should have an average annual wind speed of at least 10 mph. This will practically ensure you of enough wind over 10 mph (with a commensurate amount less than 10 mph) to drive a turbine successfully.

While most wind turbines will begin spinning at wind speeds of around 7 mph, you will not really see any power until the winds increase to 8 or 9 mph, and not much useful power until the winds exceed 11 or 12 mph. That's because the power of the wind increases as the cube of the wind speed, so there is over three times as much force in a 12 mph wind as there is in a breeze blowing at 8 miles per hour. (This is a handy fact to keep in mind should you ever feel the urge to calculate the force of a class 5 hurricane versus that of a wimpy little 60 mph gale.)

Both Bergey (*www.bergey.com*) and Southwest Windpower (*www.windenergy.com*) offer national and state wind maps on their web sites. These maps are painted with a rather broad brush, however, so it is doubtful that you will be able to use them to determine the exact average annual wind speed at your building site. On the other hand, they should at least be enough to tell you if you are in the ballpark or not. Then you can fall back on my tried-and-true maxim:

If the wind at your site blows often enough and hard enough to annoy you, you probably have enough wind to make good use of a wind turbine.

LaVonne's Verities

IF YOU'RE LOW ON ENERGY and need the wind to blow, serve a meal on the deck. For a gale, hang out the laundry.

It may not be rigorously scientific, but it's easier than setting up a computerized wind monitoring station at your site, and a whole lot cheaper.

❧ Finding a Site for the Tower

No matter how much wind there is at ground level, it will be blowing harder higher up. There will also be less turbulence, which means you can reap more power with less wear and tear on the machine. Generally, the height of the tower depends on the terrain, since you will—at a bare minimum—want your turbine mounted 30 feet higher than the tallest object (tree, roof peak, church steeple or castle turret) within a 300-foot radius.

And, to be on the safe side, you should erect the tower at least 15 rotor diameters from living quarters and property lines. Collapsing towers and disintegrating turbines are exceedingly rare occurrences, but Murphy ain't dead yet.

Bergey Windpower's 7.5 to 10 kW Excel turbine. *Photo: Bergey Windpower*

❧ Types of Towers

There are four basic types of towers used for residential-sized wind turbines: guyed pipe; guyed lattice; freestanding lattice (with a flared base like the Eiffel Tower); and the sleek and tapered monopole tower. Of these, the guyed pipe and guyed lattice towers are far and away the most prevalent, with the pipe tower taking top honors. That's because pipe towers are inexpensive and fairly easy to erect using a hinged base and tried-and-true rigging methods. Every turbine manufacturer I know of offers pipe tower kits (with or without the pipe) properly sized for their turbines.

Our tower is a retrofitted ham-radio guyed-lattice tower that measures 54 feet from the top of the mast to the concrete pad in which it sits embedded in three yards of reinforced concrete. It's guyed at nine different points with ¼-inch wire rope secured to concrete pads anchored in solid bedrock. It would probably take an F-5 to crumple it, and that's the way I like it.

Just about any type of tower will work for a residential-sized wind turbine, so your choice will largely boil down to three criteria: how much tower can you afford; what type of tower you want to look at every day; and whether or not you want a tower you can climb. (I scavenged ours from my Dad's old hay mill, where it was used for two-way radio communication between the mill and the hay fields. I'm glad it's lattice; besides giving me easy access to the turbine, I can climb it every time the dogs wander off and I need a lofty vantage point from which to find them. They still haven't figured out my secret.)

∾ Choosing a Turbine

Commercially built residential wind turbines are rated from around 900 watts all the way up to 10,000 watts. Smaller ones are available and thousands of people buy them, but if you're looking for serious energy production you should really opt for a bigger machine.

What does the watt rating mean, exactly? It means that the turbine you buy can be expected to produce its rated output every time it encounters a steady wind of the right (rated) speed. For most turbines, this is in the 25- to 31-mph range—rarely, in other words. Unless you live in an insanely windy place, most of the time the amperage your turbine churns out will be less than its rated output.

Four Tower Types
Guyed Pipe
Guyed Lattice
Free-standing Lattice
Tubular Monopole

A more telling statistic is the "approximate monthly kilowatt hours @ 12 mph." While still a little optimistic—as it implies a wind at sea level with no turbulence—it's a good way to compare similarly rated machines. Using this comparison we find, for instance, that the 1,000-watt Bergey XL.1 cranks out 188 kWh per month (at 12 mph), while the 1,000-watt Southwest Windpower Whisper 200 only boasts 158 kWh per month. More telling, Southwest Windpower's 900-watt Whisper 100—which is designed for areas of heavy wind and really doesn't produce well in light winds—will only produce 100 kWh per month in a 12 mph wind.

Almost every wind turbine on the market can be used in off-grid situations. These include turbines manufactured by Abundant Renewable Energy (ARE), Bergey Windpower, Proven Engineering and Southwest Windpower,.

Machines capable of working in no-battery direct-tie systems are scarcer. They include the Abundant Renewable Energy 2,500-watt ARE-110 turbine; the big 10,000-watt Bergey Excel; Proven Energy's 2,500-watt Proven 2.5; and Southwest Windpower's 1,000-watt Whisper 200. If you want something with sex appeal, take a look at Southwest Windpower's 1,800-watt Skystream 3.7. Its sweeping, scimitar-shaped blades alone are sufficient to set it apart from the others, but it also stands alone by virtue of being the only wind machine out there with a direct-tie inverter built right into the turbine. Was this a good idea? I'll withhold my personal opinion here and say only that the answer is waiting in the wind. Either way, it's certainly an interesting wind machine to look at.

rex's maxims

WIND TAKES ON A WHOLE NEW CHARACTER once you need it to power your lights.

MICRO-HYDRO POWER

The similarities between wind power and micro-hydro power are hard to miss. A micro-hydro turbine is, after all, based on the same principle as a wind turbine; the only difference is that it uses running water instead of moving air to turn the propeller; and, of course, the fact that wind is more readily available to most of us than running water is.

We are fortunate to have a creek that runs through the middle of our property; it's a constant source of enjoyment. We can easily spend a day hiking along it, jumping from rock to rock to ford it as the trail winds from one side to the other, before at we at last plop down, high and dry, to rest on a large boulder in the middle of the creek and immerse ourselves in the hypnotic sound of water cascading all around us.

But we would never be able to tap into the energy of the water that flows along its course. There's simply too little water and too little fall (drop in elevation) along the creek bed from one end of the property to the other. Besides, it's 500 vertical feet below our house.

And therein are the three things that make for a successful micro-hydro installation: a good volume of water; a good drop in altitude from where the water is diverted to where it runs through the turbine (this is known as "head"); and close proximity to the house.

Should you have a creek on your property close to your building site, you will need to make two critical measurements. First, measure the volume of water you'll be sending to the turbine by diverting that portion of the creek's flow you feel you safely can divert without endangering the integrity of the rest of the creek. The number you're looking for is cubic feet per second (cfs). One way to find it is to count how many times you can fill a 5-gallon bucket in one minute, then multiplying the result by 0.67—the number of cubic feet in a 5-gallon bucket. By then dividing this number by 60 you will arrive at the cubic feet per second.

Next, determine your gross head by measuring how many feet of drop you will have from your diversion dam to the turbine. The gross head determines the pressure at which the water will be when it arrives at the turbine. You can measure the head somewhat accurately with a GPS unit, or by taking a number of stepped measurements with the optical builders level you're going to buy to build your house.

Do you have enough flow and fall to run a micro-hydro turbine? A call to a turbine manufacturer to apply your numbers will give you a pretty good idea. Then call the county, just to make sure they'll let you do it. It might be painful, but it's better than finding out later that all your efforts were illegal.

CHARGE CONTROLLERS: TAMING THE WILD AMPS

Whatever charging sources you end up using, if your system has batteries you will have to run the output through a charge controller. It is the job of the charge controller to regulate the electrical "traffic" flowing from your renewable energy sources to your batteries, and to make sure there is no reverse flow of power, as from a charged battery bank to an idle solar array during the nighttime hours.

SOLAR CHARGE CONTROLLERS

A relatively simple 3-stage solar charge controller, such as the Xantrex C-60, will allow the amperage to flow unimpeded from the solar array to the batteries until a preset bulk voltage is reached. It then restricts the amount of incoming current in order to hold the batteries at the bulk voltage (called the absorption stage) for a preset period of time (one hour for the C-60, up to two hours for some others), after which it drops the voltage even lower, into what is called the float stage. In similar fashion, the C-60 will also regulate the battery equalization process, in which the batteries are occasionally overcharged under controlled conditions to remix the electrolyte and clean the inevitable buildup of sulfates from the batteries' plates.

OutBack's MX60 charge controller.
Photo: OutBack

A step up, both in price and sophistication, is the Maximum Power Point Tracking (MPPT) charge controller, such as OutBack Power's MX60. In addition to doing everything a standard 3-stage charge controller can do, an MPPT charge controller can tease appreciably more power from a solar array. That's because solar panels normally operate at 40 to 50 percent more voltage than their nominal rating. A 12-volt solar panel, for instance, typically puts out somewhere between 17 and 18 volts. The reason for this is simple: the charging source voltage must be higher than the battery voltage to keep the current flowing in the right direction.

Unfortunately, the power lurking in that extra voltage is lost with a standard charge controller, because neither the controller nor the battery know what to do with it. But an MPPT controller does. It uses a DC to DC converter to change the extra voltage into usable amperage.

MPPT charge controllers work best in winter, since cold panels produce more voltage than warm ones. They also outperform standard charge controllers when the batteries are heavily discharged, since this is when there will be the greatest disparity between array voltage and battery voltage.

WIND CHARGE CONTROLLERS

The charge controller you get for your wind turbine will be an entirely different animal from the solar charge controller. That's because the controller cannot simply disconnect from the wind turbine in the same way it does from a solar array, since the open, no-load circuit would allow the propeller to spin so dangerously fast that it might damage the machine.

Wind charge controllers are specific to the type of turbine you buy, so it should be included as part of the turbine package. That's because all wind turbines are a little bit different. Some send 3-phase AC to the house, others rectify the AC to DC within the turbine's nacelle. And, while one type of turbine may shut off or slow down when the batteries are full, a different model may require that excess energy be sent to a diversion load, such as a heat sink. Our Bergey XL.1, for instance, is a DC machine that can be wired either for a diversion load or to go into slow mode when the batteries are full, while our old Whisper 1000 was an AC turbine that required a heat sink. The point is, the controllers for each work in radically different ways and cannot be interchanged unless, perhaps, you have a sorcerer's gift for mixing oil with water, turning lead into gold, or making a dovetail joint fit into a saddle notch. And even then it probably wouldn't work.

BATTERIES: STORING THE SUN AND WIND

The most interesting off-grid system I ever heard of was described to me by a Frenchman. As a manufacturer of large wind turbines, he placed one of his big machines on his rural property in France and dedicated it to run a commercial electrolyzer which converted water into oxygen and pure hydrogen gas. He then stored the hydrogen gas in large propane tanks and used it to run a converted gas-powered generator that provided electricity for his home. Had he been in possession of a fuel cell stack and inverter, he could even have dispensed with the generator. The beauty of his system (the inherent inefficiencies notwithstanding) was that he was able to store his homegrown electricity in a form that did not require care or maintenance, and was not prone to losing energy from inactivity. Once the power from the turbine was converted to hydrogen gas and stored in tanks, it was safe and secure, and it would not diminish appreciatively from day to day.

The lesson here is this: energy produced by an off-grid solar and wind system is only as effective as the means you contrive for storing it. For most of us, unfortunately, that means big, heavy storage batteries and all the shortcomings batteries are heir to, including the required routine maintenance and an ongoing need to be brought back up to a full charge.

But that's really small change; for all their faults, solar storage batteries are still remarkably efficient and getting better all the time. So unless you go out of your way to find Brand X batteries, you're practically assured of years of dutiful service from your investment, with very little work on your part.

A **hydrometer** measures a battery's state of health; a **volt meter** measures its state of charge.

Batteries for renewable energy applications fall into two broad categories: those used for off-grid homes, and those used for grid-tied applications. For the former, you will want wet-cell lead acid batteries (the kind you have to add water to), while for the latter you should instead choose sealed batteries.

The reason for this dichotomy is simple: off-grid batteries are worked hard. As a result, they tend to build up sulfates on the plates—sulfates that have to be boiled off in an overcharging process called equalization, whereby the batteries are brought up to the highest voltage they can safely tolerate, and held there for one or two hours. It's a process that causes the evaporation of water from the sulfuric-acid electrolyte, and it cannot be replaced if the battery is sealed and water is lost through the safety vents.

By contrast, backup batteries in grid-tied environments are almost always maintained at a full charge and only rarely, if ever, called upon to do heavy-duty work. Theirs is a life of privilege. They can breeze through their multi-year stint in your solar and wind system without once having to endure the tortuous business of equalization. And they can live to a ripe old age without ever being given a drink of water.

Building a battery bank is something of a mathematical puzzle. This is because the nominal voltage of the battery bank has to match the voltage of the inverter: sometimes 12, but more often 24 or 48 volts DC. To reach the desired voltage you will have to buy your batteries in the proper multiples, and then wire them in series strings, a configuration whereby the positive terminal on one battery is connected to the negative terminal on the next battery. This compounds the voltage but not the amperage, so if you connect eight 6-volt batteries in series you will end up with 48 volts. To achieve more amperage, you create additional series strings and then connect them together in parallel, where the positive end of one series string is wired to the positive end of the series string next to it (and likewise for the negative ends). So, for example, if you had a bank of sixteen 6-volt batteries (a common number in

Trojan batteries, T-105 and L16H.
Photo: Trojan Battery Company

48-volt systems) you would have two series strings of eight batteries each, and the strings would be wired to one another in parallel. Simple, huh?

Not too many years ago there was not much on the market other than 6-volt batteries for renewable energy systems. It led many who might have opted for a 48-volt system to instead choose 24 volts, where 6-volt batteries can be joined in multiples of four rather than eight. But now you can find very high quality solar batteries of 2, 4, 6, 8, and 12 volts to store your wind and sunshine. Where should you look? Nothing beats the Internet. For off-grid batteries, check out the Trojan Battery Company; Surrette batteries; or HUP Solar-One batteries. These latter batteries are big and beastly—they require a forklift to set them in place—but well worth the price if you can afford (and maneuver) them.

Sealed batteries for grid-tied systems come in two basic types: Absorbed Glass Mat (AGM), in which the electrolyte is suspended within a webwork of fiberglass; and true gel-type batteries, in which the electrolyte is actually in the form of a highly acidic jelly. Gel batteries cost more than their AGM cousins, but they'll last longer and they can take a higher charge without sustaining damage. For sealed batteries, take a look at MK batteries, Concord Batteries, or Hawker Batteries.

How long will your batteries last? All batteries are rated by their manufacturers for a certain number of cycles to different depths of discharge, usually 50 percent and 20 percent. This is the expected lifetime of a battery. Depending on how you treat them and what brand you buy, you can expect solar batteries to last anywhere from 5 to 20 years. The inexpensive Trojan T-105 batteries we installed in our weekend cabin 9 years ago are still going strong, while the T-105s we put in our house succumbed to exhaustion in 5 years and were replaced with a far more robust bank of L16s. It's simply matter of what type of batteries you buy and how extensively you use them.

Wiring the Batteries for a 24-volt System

Step One: Connect each row of batteries in series (positive to negative)

Series Connections increase voltage: add voltage of each battery for total system voltage (6+6+6+6=24 volts)

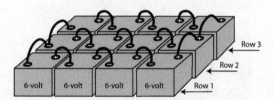

Step Two: Connect rows 1, 2 and 3 in parallel (positive to positive to positive on one side; negative to negative to negative on other side)

Parallel Connections do not increase voltage

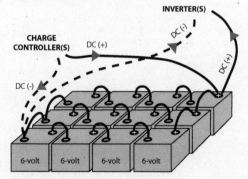

Step Three: Connect incoming current to the bank of batteries, and then run one positive and one negative connection to the inverter

INVERTERS: MAKING DC BEHAVE LIKE AC

Between the batteries and the home's wiring lies the power inverter. As the name implies, the inverter does its work by inverting the DC waveform—a flat, uninteresting stream of electrons flowing from a high potential to a low one—into an undulating AC waveform that is both rhythmic and mathematically pleasing.

There are several types of inverters on the market, and the one (or ones) you choose will depend on both the type of system you have and whether you'll be installing it in a permanent home or a small, no-frills weekend cabin.

DIRECT-TIE INVERTERS

Grid-tie PV equipment shown above includes a pair of Outback inverters, a DC box, two charge controllers, and an AC box and standard breaker boxes. The battery box is in the foreground.
Photo: Doug Pratt

Direct-tie inverters are specific to their application. They have no circuitry for charging batteries, nor any place to plug in a generator. The only thing they know how to do is to take in high-voltage DC (up to 550 volts) from a solar array or wind turbine and render it into grid-quality AC.

The AC wattage they provide is first used to power the loads in your home. Should your array or wind turbine produce any excess wattage, it will be automatically shunted into the power grid. This makes your utility meter turn backwards and should bring an instant smile to your face. (As noted in the Wind Turbine section, your wind machine will require its own direct-tie inverter, as specified by the turbine manufacturer.)

There are a number of direct-tie inverters to choose from, ranging from around 700 watts all the way up to 6,000 watts. All are designed with weatherproof enclosures, so they can be mounted on the side of your house. Sunny Boy (and Windy Boy) inverters made by SMA America are hugely popular, but others are catching up. These include: The Fronius IG-series, PV Powered, and the Xantrex GT-series.

INVERTERS FOR BATTERY-BASED SYSTEMS

If you are planning to live off grid, or grid tied with backup batteries, you will need an inverter somewhat more talented than the one-trick-pony direct-tie inverter. Specifically, it will have circuitry for charging your batteries, as well as terminals for inputting power from a gas-fired generator. It will also have to be powerful enough to supply all the electrical needs of your house if you live off grid, or that portion of the house (the critical loads) that will convert to battery power whenever the grid shuts down.

Since off-grid homes are getting bigger all the time, a single inverter is often not enough to power all the loads that may be running at any given time (particularly if a deep well pump is wired into the system and you have a special fondness for big, maniacal power tools). That's why most high-quality sine wave inverters can be stacked to deliver either twice the amperage, or twice the voltage (240 VAC, rather than 120 VAC), depending on if they are wired in parallel (double the amperage) or series (double the voltage). Will your home require dual inverters? Maybe. But considering the cost of the things, it's not a bad idea to be sure that you really need that extra inverter. Besides the additional cost, it will add another level of complexity to the system, and another continuous draw of 15 watts or so—0.36 kWh per day—on the batteries. Remember: any good inverter will be able to weather an electrical surge to more than twice the continuous-amperage threshold for a several seconds, and this is often enough to quiet down any potential overloads.

Functions of an Inverter
• Converting DC to AC
• High and low voltage shut-off
• Battery charging
• Generator and grid tie-ins
• Search functions
• Stackable (for greater voltage or amperage)
• Computer interface

∾ Sine Wave Inverters

What type of inverter should you buy? When we moved off grid in 1999, the inverters manufactured by Trace Engineering were one of very few options. Their SW series inverters produced a very clean waveform and they were absolutely dependable. We still have our original Trace SW4024 and don't feel any need to upgrade to a newer model.

Since we purchased our inverter, Trace has become Xantrex, and the old SW series has evolved into the SW Plus series inverters, offering even more surge capacity (up to four times the nominal rating) and smarter electronics for greater efficiency.

In the meantime, several of the former Trace engineers got together and formed OutBack Power Systems to go into direct competition with their old company. The inverters they put out are of exceptional quality— we have yet to hear a bad word about any of them. They are, however, a little smaller than their Xantrex counterparts (their off grid models range from 2 to 3.6 kilowatts continuous output), and for that reason they are almost always installed in a stacked configuration. The

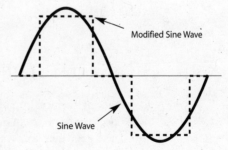

Modified Sine Wave

Sine Wave

good news is that they are made to be stacked (it's what OutBack calls modular construction), and so you should not experience any of the programming snafus that can arise with other multiple-inverter systems.

While Xantrex and OutBack both make inverters for off-grid and grid-tied systems, Beacon Power, a Maryland-based company, has begun offering 4- and 5-kilowatt inverters designed exclusively for battery-based grid-tied systems. Besides packing plenty of power, Beacon inverters can be mounted either indoors or out, along with your sealed backup batteries, in an enclosure that is sold separately from the inverter.

∾ Modified Sine Wave Inverters

In case you are building a little off-grid weekend cabin instead of a fulltime house, you might want to consider a less expensive inverter that outputs a somewhat cruder waveform than the above-mentioned sine wave inverters. Called modified-sine-wave by those who make and sell them—and modified-square-wave inverters by almost everyone else—these inverters can run most of the things you would ever use in a weekend cabin, such as coffee pots, most microwaves, power tools and most electronic equipment. With other things, like dimmer switches (rheostats) and battery chargers, you may run into problems as a result of the stepped waveform. These appliances/devices time their output from the zero-voltage point in each undulation of the current from positive to negative, but with a modified sine wave the zero-voltage point is, graphically speaking, a line that persist for a considerable fraction of each cycle. It can be hopelessly confusing for many variable-speed motors, such as some power drills and sewing machines.

Still, they're dependable, inexpensive inverters that work well within their limitations. We've had a Trace DR1524 in our cabin for years and have had no problems with it, other than with, as noted above, battery chargers and tools with rheostats.

rex's maxims

IF THE INVERTER does not seem to function properly, there's a 99% chance it's just doing what you told it to do.

SYSTEM SIZING: HOW MUCH IS ENOUGH?

One of the most important questions you will have to answer once you seriously begin to think about installing an RE system is: how big of a system do I need? It's a good question; with too many batteries in relation to your charging systems, for instance, you will have lots of energy storage but face the risk of sulfate buildup from an inability to bring your battery bank to a full charge. With too few, by contrast, you will be able to easily bring the batteries to full charge but will not have much energy saved away for a rainy day (or two). Somehow, you want to strike the perfect balance. But how?

The math is fairly straightforward. All you have to do is calculate how many kilowatt hours your home will use each day, then multiply it by the number of days you may have to go with no charging inputs. This will give you the amount of available reserve you will want to have in your batteries, which is quite a bit different than the advertised amp hour rating, since you cannot fully drain a battery without destroying it. To be on the safe side, you should never draw your batteries down below 50 percent of rated capacity.

So how much battery power do you need? To take an example, let's say your house uses 8 kilowatt hours per day, you want two day's worth of backup power, and you do not wish to draw your batteries more than halfway below capacity. In that case you will need:

$$8 \text{ kWh x 2 days} \div 0.50 \text{ untouchable reserve} =$$
$$32 \text{ kilowatt hours of total battery capacity}$$

As you can see, the calculation itself is simple. The grueling part is figuring out how much electrical energy your home will need each day. A seemingly sure-fire way to do this would be to measure the wattage of every single appliance in your home, plus the demands of the heating system, the well pump, and whatever else might conceivably tap into your hard-won energy reserves, then multiplying each value by the number of hours every individual load is used each day. By adding the results together and dividing by 1,000, you will arrive at your daily kilowatt hour usage. But that seems just a teensy bit excessive, and even if you arrive at the perfect mix (a feat attributable as much to luck as to mathematical prowess, I'd wager) there are still imponderables lurking in the days ahead, like when you add a chest freezer or maybe a big-screen TV with Dolby surround sound. Or you and your spouse discover you are doing your part to keep the world's population from dwindling to unsafe levels.

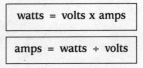

watts = volts x amps

amps = watts ÷ volts

After we had already installed our solar and wind systems, we (somewhat disingenuously, I have to admit) asked for bids from three different installers, just to see how much they would differ in their estimations of what it would take to run our house. The equipment and component lists they each provided (after plying us with innumerable questions) varied considerably—from 600 to 1,440 watts of PV, and from 1,680 to 2,300 amp hours of battery capacity.

It's simply a matter of which numbers you use and how you crunch them. But of all the dozens of off-gridders we've met over the years, we have yet to hear anyone complain that they have too much solar or wind power, or too many batteries (though on this point, at least, some did, whether they knew it or not). And therein lies the lesson: first figure what your compulsory loads will draw (well pump, refrigerator, heating system, lights, etc.) then add a comfortable cushion. This will be what you need. Then, when it comes time to purchase your system, don't buy less than you need, or more than you can afford.

And finally, make sure to leave plenty of space to add on later—chances are you'll end up using it.

MULTITUDE OF OPTIONS

One thing we've tried to stress in this section is the fact that there is really no one right way to build a renewable energy system for your home. As you read about the many homeowners in this book who have installed renewable energy systems in their log homes, you will see what we mean. Some systems are quite large, others Spartan. Some are long on solar and sparse on batteries, others just the opposite. Every system has its own peculiarities. None is perfect. And yet for all their seeming excesses or shortcomings, every system works, and those who rely on them day in and day out will tell you they are exactly where they want to be.

The best we can pin it down, it's a matter of self-reliance; probably the same reason Jim Bridger put up with bears, bugs and bad weather rather than hightailing it back to civilization. Once you get to where you want to be, you will not be dissuaded by superficial and transient reasons—you will instead embrace the uniqueness of you circumstances, while hopefully becoming just a bit more philosophical about life in the bargain.

You'll see. ∾

October 2000

Two ominous piles of drywall fill the garage. I can't believe we are going to hang 218 sheets of that heavy stuff! Renting a lift for the week to do the ceilings [32] was a back-saver. We soon figure out a system for measuring and cutting, screwing and nailing.

The garage needs to be totally encased in sheetrock since the living space is above it. That was the easy part. The main floor ceiling wasn't bad, but the loft ceiling is maddening. If the purlins were not there, it would be a snap, but each piece of drywall must be scribed and cut to fit the taper of the logs. And if the ceiling wasn't bad enough, the funky closet and bathroom walls make us pull out our hair!

We take a break to buy and install a wood stove and many, many feet of chimney pipe. Nights and mornings are getting pretty cold.

November 2000

We are still hanging drywall. Will it ever end?? The gutter company installs the gutters and downspouts, and the cabinet manufacturer delivers the pine cabinets for the kitchen and bath. We'll store them in the basement until the walls are painted.

Since we are thoroughly sick of drywall, we hire our neighbor Dave to do the taping [33]. I can fill in the nail and screw divets.

Now it is time to finish that ugly stairwell to the basement, which means attaching furring strips to the foundation walls so we can nail on the tongue-&-groove pine boards. What an improvement! It feels like we are making progress.

December 2000

Rex relocates the solar system from the cabin to the house and proceeds to learn all about wiring houses, and how the electrician ran the wires in this house before bailing out on us. I don't think Rex is happy about this.

Log • ically   Solar

Illustration by Rob Pudim

Rob Pudim and Pat Kavouras's new 3,800-square-foot log home near Nederland, Colorado, came into being as a result of a minor matter of geography. Had the existing frame house on their newly acquired acreage been a mere 50 feet farther to the south—thus affording the couple a view of the Continental Divide and the Indian Peaks Wilderness Area—Rob and Pat would now be living in it. But the old house was given a new life of sorts anyway, since they went to great pains to recycle as much of the original house as possible, including framing lumber, the original oak flooring, the stones in the fireplace, and the old 4 x 12 deck planks, which now serve as treads for the front stairway.

The logs for the main floor and attached garage were shipped in from Canada, where they had been rescued from a forest fire. Local contractor Mark Van Everen reassembled the custom-crafted logs into a tight, chinkless structure.

With the massive logs, it's an easy structure to heat in winter. A propane-fired boiler is available to heat water for the hydronic in-floor heating system, but it's rarely needed. Instead, the house is heated primarily with a Lopi Sheffield woodstove, and the sunlight which falls on the six flat-plate solar collectors mounted flush to the garage roof. "We had to run the garage at a somewhat skewed angle," Rob explains. "Otherwise, the panels would not have faced due south." The garage roof was also set at a considerable pitch to give the panels a repose perpendicular to the angle of the winter sun. The upside of this was that Rob's studio, where he spends his days designing magazine graphics and covers for mystery novels, was even bigger than originally planned.

The freeze-proof glycol that transfers heat to the solar collectors is ferried through a heat exchanger in a 1,400-gallon water tank in the mechanical room. This sizable reservoir of stored energy supplies heat for both the heating system and the couple's domestic hot water. The system's Tekmar controller is programmable, such that it's heating chores can be prioritized. It can, for instance, be told to first heat domestic water, then the master bedroom, and so on. If it's cloudy and heat is scarce, what heat remains in the system will be directed to where it's needed most.

How effective is this combination of wood and solar heat? Rob and Pat use less than 200 gallons of propane per year, a large portion of which goes for cooking. I'd say that's effective enough.

House 3,800 square feet on two levels; custom log, chinkless construction
Heating woodstove; in-floor hydronic utilizing solar hot water with a propane-fired boiler for backup
Water 55-foot well
Refrigeration electric
Solar hot water 6 flat-plate collectors
Solar array, **Wind turbine**, **Inverter**, **Batteries**, **Backup power** none

CHAPTER *18*

HEATING OF HOUSE AND WATER

Staying Warm Without Busting the Energy Bank

B y the time LaVonne and I began planning the new log house, I had logged
seven years of living in a cabin with no other heat than a woodstove.
Before and after the cabin interlude—except for the years spent in my
parents' house, which was heated with hot water circulating through baseboard
registers—I lived in dwellings with forced air (a.k.a. forced dust) heating systems.

Between the two, I far preferred the woodstove; it was quieter, easier to con-
trol, and cheaper to operate. But, after a day or two's absence in the middle of
January, it took a steely constitution to come home in the dead of night.

Though LaVonne, poor girl, missed out on the earlier cabin years—chopping
holes through the ice in the creek for bath water is one my fondest memories—
she was all too familiar with forced air heating. We were united in our loathing for
it. Owing to that fact, we were able to quickly focus our heating options when it
came time to build the house we'd been dreaming about.

Obviously, electric heat was out; the PV wind system needed to run it would
rival the cost of the house. Propane wall heaters are a good, cheap solution for
cabins but quickly lose their practicality in a larger, multi-room house. That left
us with the hot water option. Baseboard or in-floor? It was a no-brainer: definitely
in-floor.

But I'm getting ahead of myself. Before I let *all* my biases dangle in the wind,
I'd better do a little explaining.

PROPANE WALL FURNACES AND FIREPLACES

Steyn's off-grid home has four highly efficient propane fireplaces to provide heat and ambiance.

Propane-fired wall furnaces and fireplaces (also called zero clearance gas fireplaces) are small units that can be mounted on a wall. As backup heat for a cabin or small house with a woodstove, they're terrific. We have several friends who use them. The heaters save them the trouble of having to stoke the fire in the middle of the night, and keep their houses adequately warm if they're away for extended periods. When shopping for one, look at the AFUE (Annual Fuel Utilization Efficiency) rating to find a highly efficient unit.

But a propane wall unit is really a brainless animal, with little hope of ever getting any smarter. It senses how cold it is in one location, then heats that location until it decides it's warm enough. So, for a very small house or weekend cabin on a no-frills budget, a propane unit may suffice, but for a larger house you will need something more (and the county may require it).

FORCED AIR HEAT

Most houses in America—both old and new—are heated with warm forced air. The air is warmed in a furnace, then pushed through a labyrinthine system of ductwork with the aid of an electric blower—a squirrel-cage fan—into the different rooms through vents cut into the floor. It's fairly inexpensive to install, and we know people who use this system in their PV/wind homes with reasonable success. But we don't know anyone, off the grid or otherwise, who *likes* it.

Energy-wise, forced air heat is less efficient than hot water heat, requiring more propane *and* more electricity to heat a house. This is mostly due to the fact that air is thinner than water. It goes places we don't want it to go and requires more energy per unit mass to heat.

Many of the problems with forced air heat are due to poor system design. Anyone who has ever lived in a house heated with forced air knows how easy it is to throw the whole system out of kilter just by shutting a door or two. Some rooms get too hot while others get colder. Often the only way achieve any degree of equilibrium is to leave open all the doors to all the rooms—not always a satisfying solution. This problem can be alleviated, somewhat, by providing properly placed cold air return ducts, so that the air can re-circulate throughout the house without building up pressure gradients in certain areas—pushing warm air out of house in some places and drawing in cold air, in others. But as long as the entire house is run off a single, centrally located thermostat, the problem of uneven heating will persist.

Zoning is the obvious solution. By dividing the house into three or four distinct zones, each on its own thermostat, forced air heat becomes almost comfortable. Zoning comes with a price, however. Besides upping the original cost of the system by at least a couple thousand dollars, each zone requires a small motor to operate a zone damper within the duct, in addition to the main 5-amp (600-watt) blower motor located inside the furnace. It can add up to lot of wattage at the time of year you can least afford to use it.

Of course, any system that requires fans or pumps will tax your (electrical) energy budget; there's no way around it. But, if there were a system available that used less electricity and propane; a system that took up zero floor space while providing even, comfortable heat, wouldn't it make sense to use it?

HEATING WITH HOT WATER

Hot water heat has been around in one form or another much longer than propane has been available to fire the boilers that produce it. This is evidenced

---

Geothermal: Using the Earth to Heat and Cool

If you are planning to hook your new log home into the electrical grid, you really owe it to yourself to take a look at geothermal heating and cooling systems. Geothermal systems are based on the fact that the earth stays a fairly constant temperature several feet below the surface. The reason for this is that it takes so long for the ground to gain or lose heat, by the time it begins to react to one season the next season is already underway. So once you dig down 5 to 8 feet, the soil will be a fairly constant 45–50 degrees Fahrenheit in the northern latitudes, and 50–70 degrees farther south. It's a perfect place to extract heat in the winter and dump it in the summer.

The process works just like a refrigerator, which is nothing more than an electric heat pump that uses a fluid with a very low boiling point to pull heat from the inside of a box and release it into the kitchen. The difference is that a geothermal heat pump extracts heat from the earth—by running water through a network of polyethylene pipes laid out in either horizontal trenches or vertical holes—and releases it into your house in winter. For home cooling in summer the process is reversed. Although ground-source heat pumps work best with forced-air heating systems, they can also be adapted to work with radiant-floor heating systems.

According to the EPA, geothermal systems are the most energy-efficient, environmentally clean, and cost-effective space conditioning systems available. To learn more about geothermal heating and cooling, or even to find a certified installer, visit the GeoExchange web site at: *www.geoexchange.org*.

by the cast iron radiators we see in many older houses, school and government buildings. A lot of those old coal-, wood- and oil-fired systems are still in use (now mostly converted to natural gas or propane), but their day is done; evolution has taken its course. Today's hot water heating systems come in two basic incarnations: baseboard registers and in-floor radiant heat.

Of the two, in-floor radiant heat provides the most even heat throughout the house. It is also the most logical choice for a log home, for the simple fact that log walls—being round by nature—do not have flat baseboards to which you can attach the registers. (Okay; I'll concede that any enterprising home builder could find a way to make a flat, vertical surface along a log wall beset with bumps and knots, but I defy anyone to make it look like it belongs there.)

But don't despair—if you install radiant floor heat in your log home, you won't be disappointed. In fact, I believe it's the perfect way to heat a log home for reasons that will quickly become apparent.

RADIANT FLOOR HEAT

The idea of radiant floor heat is to make the entire floor one huge wall-to-wall radiator. To accomplish this, a continuous length of extremely tough (PEX) plastic tubing is snaked back and forth across the subfloor, stapled down, then embedded in a special type of lightweight (gypsum) concrete that is pumped over the floor in a soupy slurry that hardens in two or three hours.

You can have as many or as few zones as you need without installing a nightmarishly complex system of ducts. Each zone runs on its own thermostat, which controls the pump for that particular zone. We have five zones in our house: one for the garage, and another for the workshop and electrical room. On the main floor, our great room has its own zone, and the office and bathroom are on another. The pantry is unheated. A single zone in the loft heats the upstairs bathroom; the rest of the loft stays plenty warm from the heat below.

Since we heat the great room and kitchen almost exclusively with wood, we keep the thermostat there turned down to its lowest setting. And the original thermostats in the garage and shop downstairs have been replaced with 40-degree thermostats (turned to 42 degrees) because we saw no need to keep these seldom-used rooms comfortably warm, especially since the price of propane has tripled in the six years since we moved into our house.

Still—the confiscatory price of propane notwithstanding—we think radiant-floor heat is the most efficient heating system you can install because it will use less energy to heat a given space than any

LaVonne's Verities

If you ever want to take A WINTER VACATION, invest in a good heating system that won't require a house-sitter to feed the woodstove.

other type of heating system we know of. And if there were other, less expensive ways to heat the water? I'll discuss different options later in this chapter.

❧ Special Considerations for Radiant Floor Heat

An oft quoted limitation of radiant floor heat is the amount of time it takes to warm a room once the thermostat is turned up—there is no instant heat as there is with forced air. This is because no additional heat can be felt until the hot water running through the PEX tubing raises the temperature of the medium in which the tubing is embedded.

If you lived in a drafty, poorly insulated, stick-built house (of which there is no dearth in this country), this could be a real problem. But you don't. You live— or will soon, anyway—in a tight, solidly built log house possessing tremendous thermal mass. When the house is warm, the log walls soak up heat then release it as the inside air temperature cools. In effect, the walls of your house act as heat radiators just as your floor does, so you never feel the temperature swings so evident in conventional houses.

You will be limited, however, in your choices for the finished floor. Carpet is feasible, though a thick, plush carpet above a standard airy carpet pad won't work very well. You'll need a dense rubber carpet pad (not foam) to allow for the passage of heat. Considering the growing popularity of radiant floor heating, any reputable carpet distributor should know what will work.

Wood floors are far better conductors of heat than carpet, and a perennial favorite for log homes. For our great room and kitchen we installed a Kahrs engineered oak floor. It's a Swedish product that has proven to be remarkably durable, resisting even the ravages of canine claws as the dogs race across it whenever they're feeling feisty (which is all too often). The Kahrs floor "floats" above the gypsum concrete with no points of attachment. We originally thought this was a requirement of wood floors overlaying a hydronic heating system, but have since seen other floors attached to embedded sleepers in the gypcrete.

Other options include stained and sealed concrete, or tile. Not only is tile a good conductor of heat, it does not need an insulating underlayment of rubber or plastic as is required for carpeting or wood flooring.

We used tile on our bathroom floors, wood in the kitchen and great room, and carpet in the office. Every room in the house stays plenty warm even on the coldest days, but the system does have to work a little harder to heat the office.

> ### Helpful Hints When Installing Radiant Heat
>
> - Increase your ceiling height to allow for the thickness of the gypcrete.
> - Double plate the bottoms of your framed walls.
> - Make sure your floor joists can support the extra weight.

But what the heck? I enjoy the feel of a carpeted office, so—for me and the dogs at least—it's worth the small loss in efficiency.

∽ Installing Radiant Floor Heating

There are three ways to install radiant floor heating. I have already discussed the most efficient method, wherein the PEX tubing is stapled to the subfloor, then embedded in $1^1/2$ inches of gypsum concrete (or in the case of a garage or basement floor, 4 inches or more of regular concrete). Since the heating tubes are in direct contact with a considerable thermal mass, the transference of heat from the circulating water is optimized.

If you use this method—and I highly recommend that you do—there are three further considerations to bear in mind. First, you will have to allow for an extra $1^1/2$ inches of ceiling space to accommodate the thickness of the Gypcrete®. Second, any framed walls will have to be double plated on the bottom, so that you have a nailer for wallboard and baseboard. And third, you may have to beef up your floor specifications to support the extra weight. Usually, increasing the thickness of the floor joists by one size (from 8 to 10 inches, for instance) is sufficient. Your local building department will be happy to tell you what you need to do.

Gypcrete® is poured over radiant heat tubes on our main floor, and leveled to the height of 2 x 4 sleepers.

But what if you've already built the floor and discover that it is not strong enough to support the weight of the gypsum concrete? Well, short of shoring up the floor from beneath to hold the extra weight, you can always screw (or nail) a series of plywood sleepers to the subfloor, leaving just enough room between each one to push the heat tubing snugly into the groove. Setting the tubing down into a preformed, flanged aluminum sleeve will help to direct the heat upward where its needed.

The last—and positively the worst—method is to run the PEX tubing beneath the subfloor, through holes drilled in the floor joists. The tubing is stapled to the underside of the subfloor, and then covered with aluminum heat transfer plates to reflect the heat into the subfloor. Insulation should then be installed beneath the heat tubing to further prevent heat loss. The shortcomings of this system are obvious, since all the heat must pass—and therefore, disperse— through the subfloor before it can even be felt on the floor above. For folks on a strict energy budget, this may not be acceptable.

Incorporating Solar-Heated Water

An added advantage to heating your home with hot water—aside from the extra comfort and energy savings—is the fact that your heating system can be adapted to use free energy from the sun to augment its efficiency.

In a solar hot-water system, a fluid—either water or a freeze-proof glycol solution—is heated in an array of solar collectors. The collectors can be either the traditional flat-plate type, or the newer evacuated tubes (see inset on next page). As solar heat is captured by the circulating fluid, it is ferried away to a heat reservoir, usually a large tank filled with water, where the heat is given up via heat exchangers. Now cooled, the fluid is pumped back through the solar collector where it is reheated, and the cycle continues. A differential thermostat, which takes temperature readings from both the tank and the collectors, controls the pump, commanding it to run only when there is a predetermined temperature disparity between the tank and the collectors.

Solar hot water collectors (4 of 12 shown above) on Steyn's off-grid home provide hot water for the heating system and domestic hot water.

A couple of different types of systems are widely used. Either of these systems can be adapted to heat domestic hot water or to provide heat for a hot-water heating system. In colder climes, closed-loop glycol systems are common. These systems use an isolated, pressurized loop of glycol to transfer heat. Because they are filled with glycol, there is no fear of freezing in either the collectors or the pipes that carry the glycol.

Open-loop drain-back systems can also be used in cold climates. These systems use gravity to drain water back into a reservoir whenever the system is not operating. Drain-back systems require less maintenance (since the fluid, distilled water, does not degrade over time) but generally require more energy-hungry pumps to push the non-pressurized water.

The efficiency of such a solar hot-water system is dependent on many factors. The most important, the daily hours of solar radiation, is probably the least of your concerns if you're using sunlight for your electrical needs; if you have enough sun to drive your PV array, you should have enough to heat your water.

As with your PV array, the angle of the solar collectors in relation to the sun is important. Since it is highly unlikely that you will make seasonal adjustments of the hot water solar collectors, set them for winter, when you will need most of your hot water (an angle of latitude plus 15 degrees is ideal for capturing winter sunlight). If this isn't feasible, they should, at the very least, be within 15 degrees of latitude, one way or the other.

The surface area of the solar collectors is important. The bigger they are, the more water they can heat—that much is intuitive. But the solar collectors will also need to be sized for the tank through which runs the heat exchanger. If the tank is too big or the collectors too small (or too few), the water may not heat up sufficiently to do you much good. On the other hand, if the tank is too small in relation the solar heating capacity of your collectors, you will end up wasting valuable solar radiation because the water in the tank will be quickly heated to capacity during the day, but will soon lose all of its heat at night.

The best thing you can do before spending a lot of money on an improperly sized system is to seek advice from someone in your area who routinely installs solar hot water heating systems. Even if they charge you a consulting fee you'll still be money ahead in the long run.

WOODSTOVES

A fireplace is a warm romantic setting for relaxing on cold winter nights. If you plan to put one in your new home, look into fireplace inserts. These cast-iron units have large glass doors for excellent viewing, and fans and thermostatic controls for even, steady heating. But if you'd like to heat your house without noisy fans, you will be much better off with a centrally located wood-burning stove. It might not be as aesthetically pleasing as a fireplace, but it may save an argument or two over the cost of heating your home.

Our Vermont Castings wood stove (with side door and ash drawer) sits in the middle of the great room for efficient whole-house heating.

Although it's an ancient technology, burning wood for heat is still sensible and cost effective. Wood, like wind and sunshine, is a non-depleting source of power, since most firewood is standing dead or culled from overgrown forests that need to be thinned. And, with the new efficient stoves on the market, wood is a much cleaner fuel than ever before.

If someone offers you a great deal on an old, pre-1988 woodstove, you should respectfully decline the offer. Why? Because 1988 was the year that woodstoves entered the modern world. Concerned about the growing problem of air pollution and woodstoves' contribution to it, the EPA sat down with woodstove manufacturers and kindly asked (as only a government agency can) that all new woodstoves be designed to meet strict emission standards. The result was a pair of new designs that dramatically reduced emissions and greatly increased efficiency.

One of the new designs utilizes a catalytic converter, similar to the one in your pickup, that enables the stove to burn compounds within the smoke that would normally go up the flue and into the atmosphere unburned. The extra combustion means cleaner air, more heat with less wood, and a stove that can hold a fire longer than any of its predecessors.

Another EPA-approved design that accomplishes pretty much the same thing as a catalytic stove without the converter simply circulates the gases back through the stove to be burned a second time before exiting up the stove pipe. Called "secondary combustion" stoves, these stoves boast the advantage of eliminating a costly element—namely, the catalytic converter—that will have to be periodically replaced.

Which kind of stove should you buy? Though specifications vary from one manufacturer to the next, as a general rule catalytic stoves are more efficient, cleaner and more expensive than secondary combustion stoves. Our catalytic cast-iron stove is a bit of a chore to get going when it's cold, but it easily holds a fire all night long, even with fast-burning pine in the fire box. The key is to keep the stove pipe free of creosote buildup and the doors adjusted so they close tightly.

rex's maxims

IF YOU DISCOVER all the secrets of your wood stove in a single season, you have either a complex mind or a simple stove.

Will a woodstove save you money? At $2.55 per gallon, it takes $420 worth of propane to equal the heat value of one cord of pine firewood. Besides, chopping wood is much better exercise than writing out checks to the propane company.

CORN AND PELLET STOVES

Note: Corn and pellet stoves use electricity to run the auger and blower motors, making these stoves highly impractical for off-the-grid homes.

Corn stoves differ from wood stoves in that they have very small combustion chambers and do not require the expensive chimney systems needed by wood stoves; the small amount of exhaust gas is much cleaner—and cooler—than wood smoke and can be safely vented horizontally through a wall.

Pellet stoves work on the same principle as corn stoves. But instead of corn they burn pellets made from lumber mill scraps, agricultural refuse, or even waste paper and cardboard. American Energy Systems makes a multi-fuel stove that burns corn, pellets, and even cherry and olive pits. Most of these things would have been plowed under or left to rot in bygone days, but now they are considered biomass, a broad classification of environmentally friendly, plant-derived fuels that are both renewable and carbon neutral.

MASONRY STOVES

Masonry stoves have been around for hundreds of years. They were originally built as a means to conserve firewood in Northern Europe, primarily Scandinavia. The idea behind them is simple: to store as much heat energy as possible from a given amount of wood.

A Tulikivi stove made of soapstone is one style of masonry stove. Many are custom-built from local stone. *Photo: Tulikivi*

Conventional wood stoves begin to give off heat the minute the fire is lit. They heat up quickly, and if you're cold it's a nice feeling. Masonry stoves are just the opposite. They don't rely on heat-conductive properties of metal to quickly transfer heat to the room; instead, they use the thermal mass of brick and stone to soak up the heat and give it back slowly. They do this by routing the flue gases through a long series of baffles built into the structure; baffles that keep the gases moving around and giving up heat every step of the way.

Generally, owners of masonry stoves will burn a single hot fire every one to three days. Once the stove's thermal mass heats up it takes relatively little wood to keep it warm and the stove's tremendous mass acts as a constant heat radiator.

Masonry stoves should be built as close to the center of the house as possible, and will perform best in homes with lots of thermal mass—such as log homes—to soak up the constant heat. One drawback is the square footage required for this type of heater, but the benefits should easily offset the loss in room space.

WOOD-FIRED BOILERS

Wood-fired boilers have become popular in rural areas where cordwood is abundant and fuel prices are escalating. Just like gas-fired boilers, wood boilers are designed to heat water flowing through a water jacket within the combustion unit, rather than the air beyond it. Once sufficiently warmed, the water from the boiler located outside your home can augment the heat-distributing equipment within it. And they can be adapted to virtually any kind of hot-water or forced-air heating system.

To work efficiently, a boiler needs to undergo secondary combustion, where volatile gases are burned at or above 1,100 degrees Fahrenheit. This means it has to be designed right and properly sized for your home; otherwise (because it is thermostatically controlled) it will burn at too low a temperature for complete combustion to occur. This is both wasteful and polluting. In addition, it is your

Our Solar Hot Water System

When we finally got around to installing solar hot water in the fall of the 2007, we had a couple of choices to make. First, did we want to go with the clunky (and beastly) Carter-era flat-plate collectors we picked up for free, or did we want to adorn our roof with the latest in hot-water technology? Flat-plate collectors are simply glass covered metal boxes containing a network of copper tubes laid against a dark background. Evacuated tubes, by contrast, encase each individual copper tube within a double vacuum-sealed glass tube that fits into a manifold holding 20 or 30 tubes.

In the end, we chose Thermomax evacuated tubes over the old flat-plate collectors (though we still plan to use the latter for a hot tub…someday). Even though they were expensive, we picked them because they were lightweight, took up less space, and outperformed flat-plate collectors in cloudy and cold conditions.

With that decision out of the way, we then had to decide if we wanted a massive system that could heat our house, or a more conservative system that would heat 95-plus percent of our domestic hot water. While it would have been nice to have a system that would supply most of the heat for our home's hydronic heating system, we decided instead to go for just the domestic hot water. It was a matter of economics: since we live in an area where firewood is there for the taking, it didn't make a lot of sense to invest thousands of dollars in a renewable-energy heating system that replaced free fuel—there simply wouldn't be any payback on it.

Our domestic hot-water system comprises a single 30-tube manifold on the roof and an 80-gallon storage tank in the mechanical room. It will produce an abundance of hot water on all but the cloudiest days, and is not affected by cold or wind, as flat-plate collectors are. That's because the greenhouse-style heating takes place inside the innermost of two glass tubes between which exists a strong vacuum that will not allow the passage of heat back out into the atmosphere. How well do they work? On a cold day when the array is heating water to 170 degrees Fahrenheit, the tubes themselves are cool to the touch because they are not allowing any heat to escape. That's what I call efficiency.

Best of all, our new installation made us eligible for a $2,000 tax credit under the Energy Policy Act of 2005.

responsibility to feed your boiler good quality seasoned wood; if you don't, the best design in the world won't help you (regardless of what the manufacturer may claim to the contrary).

Residential wood-fired boilers range from good, to bad, to ugly. Choose wisely. If the manufacturer claims his boiler will burn green wood, run, don't walk, to next one.

HEATING DOMESTIC HOT WATER

Tankless, on-demand water heaters are an excellent option. *Photo: Controlled Energy Corporation*

Realistically speaking, you have three choices for your domestic hot water supply. The most common of these is the good old glass-lined tank with a gas burner on the bottom. They're cheap and they use no electricity, which is good, but they're all bound to fail in a few years, which is bad. You also end up heating a lot of water that's going to cool off and have to be reheated before you get around to using it, which makes it wasteful.

An indirect water heater is another option. These units are heated with water from the home heating system, by way of a heat exchanger. On the plus side, they last far longer than conventional hot water heaters and, though the initial cost is greater, they will probably save you money over the long haul. On the minus side, they have the same problem of leaking heat while in standby mode, and they also require an electric pump to run water through the heat exchanger.

Tankless on-demand water heaters are your third, final, and probably best choice. These units heat water in a compact gas-fired burner as you use it. Formerly suited to nothing grander than a weekend cabin, on-demand heaters have gained a lot of sophistication and well-earned respect in recent years. Although the larger models (5-plus gallons per minute) are expensive, they last practically forever and can pay for themselves in a few short years on the energy savings alone.

If you decide to supplement your water-heating system with solar hot water, you should plan for floor space to accommodate a solar water tank (available in various sizes). And, while solar hot water can be used together with virtually any type of tank heater, only certain models of on-demand heaters have the capability to use solar-heated water.

Whichever way you go, check for federal and state incentives for installation of energy-efficient water heaters (*www.dsireusa.org*). ❧

December 2000

While Rex finishes the stairwell to the garage, Dave tiles the bathroom and pantry floor, and I try my hand at texturing the walls. I want an earthy, hand-troweled look. Silly me, I think, after many, many days of texturing massive amounts of drywall.

The holidays are approaching, but we will be spending another season in the little cabin. I was so hoping to be in the new house by now, but the cabin is cozy. Rex, however, is getting tired of chopping wood to heat both places.

My only wish for Christmas is to soak in a tub. With the floor finished in the bathroom, I paint those walls first. The plumber will come up soon to install the toilet, sink and clawfoot

tub. The rest of the house is still a disastrous construction zone, but I'll get my Christmas wish after all.

It's mid-December when Rex starts the challenging log stair to the loft [34]. A large post, set in the corner of the L-shape stair, will support a landing and two log stringers. The hard part is calculating the exact rise and position of the each log tread, so all steps will be identical. Once this is calculated and re-calculated, each log tread is then scribed to fit snugly against the log wall. It will truly be a beautiful masterpiece.

While Rex crafts the stair, I paint and paint and paint. The interior doors arrive and are stacked in a corner until the painting is done. I'm not one for a plain wall, so I sponge on other colors for a textured, warm look. After our last house, I will never have stark white walls again: when the ground is white with snow and the sky is white with cloud, nothing is more depressing than white ceilings and white walls. A neutral palette of creams and beiges complements the honey-colored log walls quite nicely.

January 2001

The log stair is finished after nearly 4 weeks of work, so now I can start staining it with a tough Varathane finish on the treads. Then it's time to chink (again)...around all the purlins, stair logs, floor beams, you name it. It just never seems to end.

Log • ically Solar

In 1969, when Ken and Glady Cudworth began building their 1,370-square foot custom-milled log home near the town of Como, Colorado, solar panels were found only on earth-orbiting satellites and landing craft for moon explorations. Living four miles from the nearest power line, they instead got their electricity from a small pull-start generator which they used throughout the entire building process.

A lot has changed between then and now. In the early 1980s, Ken, Glady, and their three teenage sons dug a basement below the existing house with no more than picks, shovels and elbow grease. And in 1990, when the couple both retired (Glady from nursing, and Ken from the Bureau of Reclamation, where he'd worked as an engineer on water-reclamation projects) and moved full-time to their 20-acre high-country retreat, they added a garage and widened the house by 12 feet (don't ask how).

Like the house, the Cudworth's electrical system has evolved over the years. Their first "quiet" electricity came in 1985, when Ken bought a few deep-cycle batteries which he and Glady used to run a some lights, a radio, and a small TV. Then, in 1988, when Ken finally grew tired of hauling the

batteries to town every few weeks for recharging, they bought a dozen small Arco solar modules and a Heart modified-sine-wave inverter. After 28 years, they were finally producing their own electricity.

Since then, the Heart inverter has been replaced with a Trace SW4024 sine-wave inverter; two Siemens solar modules have been added to the array, bringing it up to 716 watts; and the battery bank has been upgraded to eight Trojan L16s.

And here it stays, for now at least. With propane and wood for heating, and two propane refrigerators, a propane kitchen range and propane clothes dryer, they really don't need any more electricity than the 3 or 4 kilowatt hours their system produces every day.

And that's just the way Ken and Glady Cudworth like it.

House 1,370 square feet plus basement; custom-milled logs; owner-built
Heating wood and propane
Water pumped by PV system from 110-foot well
Refrigeration propane
Solar array 716 watts
Wind turbine none
Inverter Trace SW4024
Batteries 8 Trojan L16s
Backup power 12-kilowatt, propane-fired Generac generator, wired for automatic start (rarely used).

Photo: Ken Jessen

CHAPTER *19*

PUMPING WATER

Getting It from the Ground to Your House,
Without Overtaxing the Renewable Energy System

Water is your property's most valuable asset. Electricity you can make; propane can be brought in by truck. But if your land doesn't have sufficient potable water, your life will revolve, to a large extent, around the transportation and storage of this life-giving elixir.

In some places, water is abundant; in others it's a crap shoot. Our neighbor to the west got a good well (3 gallons per minute) at 340 feet, while our neighbor to the east got a trickle (5 gallons per *hour*) at 700 feet. We had no idea what to expect, but after watching the driller sink a hole 480 feet through impermeable rock with no water in sight, any optimism we earlier felt quickly dissolved. Then, like magic, the morphology of the rock changed and water appeared. Lots of it. By the time the drill bit reached 540 feet, we had a well producing 5 gallons per minute. We let out the breath we'd been holding for several days and uncorked a fine Merlot.

Our problems were far from over, of course. Being off the grid and therefore on a strict energy diet, we still had to figure out the best way to get the water from the bottom of the well to the house. But at least we were dealing with definable parameters. After what we'd just been through, it seemed like a manageable concern.

Just the same, we carefully weighed the options—numerous and varied as they were—before deciding what we'd do.

SHOULD YOU INSTALL A CISTERN?

Before deciding on a pump, you will need to decide if you are going to store water in a cistern and then pressurize the house water with a much smaller pump, or simply forget the cistern idea and pressurize the house directly from the well pump. There are three primary reasons people use cisterns: low producing wells; not enough energy to run the well pump; and water for fire protection.

Low Producing Wells — People who have wells with very low recharge rates use cisterns to provide a buffer between what the well can store within its casing and the amount of water they might need to use within a short period of time. As an example, let's say that you have a well with a paltry 5 gallons per *hour* recharge rate. In one day, it will provide 120 gallons of water. Not much, but enough for two people aware of the limitations. But if the well casing only holds 70 or 80 gallons, that's all that can be used in a short period of time. However, by pumping the entire contents of the well casing into a 1,000 or 1,500 gallon cistern every time the well is fully recharged, you will be assured of always having enough water, even though the well is a poor one. A really deluxe setup uses a float system within the cistern (similar to the one in a standard toilet) to automatically shut off the well pump and turn it back on (and also start a generator, if needed). A sensor within the well can shut down the pump when the water level falls too low.

Not Enough Energy To Run the Well Pump — There seems to be almost a paranoia about running an AC deep-well pump with a PV/wind system. This is partly because many people don't want to commit that much precious wattage to running a high amperage pump, and partly because they don't want to push the limitations of their inverters. Whether their fears are well-founded or not, most people on PV/wind systems with deep-well pumps choose to pump their water into a cistern with a fossil-fuel-fired generator, or a stand-alone, direct solar-powered DC submersible pump. They then pressurize their house water line with a small (AC or DC) pump. I'll be the first to admit that these people are right on both counts: it *does* take a fair bit of energy to run a deep-well submersible pump from the batteries, but not all *that* much; and it does tax the inverter at times, though in our case never enough to threaten the integrity of the system. We knew we were asking a lot from our PV/wind system by using it to pump water from 540 feet down with an 11 amp, 240-volt pump, but we had to try it even though many people told us they doubted it would work. The reason we did it is simple enough: by automatically pressurizing the house water with a deep well pump, it's one less thing to think about, meaning that we never have

Reasons for a Cistern

- Low producing wells
- Not enough energy to run the deep well-pump
- Water for fire protection

to worry that we'll be soaped-up in the shower some morning only to discover that one of us (namely me) forgot to fill the cistern. Besides, we don't even like to listen to our neighbors' generator run every night from a half mile across the canyon; we like to listen to our own even less.

But don't despair; as you will soon discover, a good DC pumping system can bypass all of the above concerns, though it will open yet another can of worms. (Is there no end to the worms in this business?)

Water for Fire Protection — Fire is always on everyone's mind around here. Having been on the fringe of a massive fire in 2000, and within a mile of four lesser lightning-started fires a year later, we think about fire a lot. The local volunteer fire department recommends that everyone have at least 2,500 gallons of water stored for fire protection. A big cistern can accommodate a large part of that amount. Since we don't have a cistern, we put in a 1,500-gallon agricultural tank outside the house, then built a pair of ponds to hold an additional 1,400 gallons. We figure after the sheriff forces us to evacuate (if he can find us), the firefighters will have a much easier time finding a pond and a big, conspicuous, above-ground green tank than they will an indoor or below-ground cistern.

WELL PUMPS

There are two broad categories of submersible well pumps: AC and DC. Both have their strong and weak points, and neither can be used successfully in every application. In most instances, I agree with Demetri, the venerated pump installer that services most of the wells in these hills, when he says that you should never ask a DC pump to do what an AC pump can do better. But I'm getting ahead of myself.

DC WELL PUMPS

DC-operated well pumps can withstand a range of voltage that would quickly destroy an AC pump. Because of this, they are used primarily in stand-alone systems. This means that you can wire them to their own solar array or wind generator and forget about them. They will pump water whenever the sun shines or the wind blows. They are designed to work with whatever power is available to them (within limits, of course), so long as it's enough to start the pump turning. With the addition of a charge controller, the

rex's maxims

A GOOD WELL with a trouble-free delivery system is more comfort than a healthy bank account... water will get you through times of no money better than money will get you through times of no water.

pump can be wired into a float switch that shuts off the power when the cistern is full, and starts it again when the water drops below a preset level.

Admittedly, it's an attractive idea. With a big enough cistern, you'll never have to worry about having enough water, even during a cabin-fever-inducing run of non-productive weather. And, by having the pump hooked to its own power supply, you won't have to draw from your household energy savings—or drag out the generator—to shower or wash the dishes.

Well-pump technology is getting better every day. Top of the line pumps, such as the Grundfos SQ flex series, are amazingly versatile. These pumps can lift water up to 650 feet and operate over a wide range of voltages (30 to 300 volts DC and 90 to 240 volts AC volts). They have built-in protection against dry-run, over and under-voltage, mechanical overload and over-temperature. If the pump is wired directly into the AC side of your home's solar system it will not slam the inverter on startup, as other pumps do. And if you want to use one of these pumps in a stand-alone install-it-and-forget-about-it system—a configuration I find most satisfying—it can be run from a single PV module and a pump controller, with no need for batteries or inverters.

It's certainly worth looking into.

AC WELL PUMPS

In the race to supply your water, DC pumps are the tortoises: they plod along slowly and ceaselessly. AC pumps, by contrast, are the hares—on steroids. They're lean and mean and tough. They eat a lot, but they produce even more. They can pump from virtually any depth the well driller can find water, and you can expect them to last for many, many years without service or replacement.

Since AC pumps move such a high volume of water (our 1.5 hp pump delivers 6 gallons per minute, even at 540 feet) the total *amount* of energy they use is surprisingly small. We figure that about 200 watts of our solar capacity is dedicated to powering our well pump. The problem is, an AC pump needs so much power *all at one time*. Specifically, we're talking about the surge amperage the pump demands in the split second when it goes from "off" to "on," which may be as much as three times higher than its rated amps.

For us, as I've said many times in these pages, it's not really a problem. But it may be for others. Our brand of well pump operates nicely within the rated capacities of our Trace SW4024 inverter and 240-volt transformer, as long as we're mindful of other loads that might be operating at the same time. To be running the clothes washer, a stereo, and a couple of computers the instant the pump kicks-in does not present any difficulty. But if we were also running a microwave and toaster, we might be pushing the system toward the edge. And throwing a table saw into the equation would certainly cast it into the abyss. Voilà! Our own personal blackout. (But really; how much stuff do you need to run at one time, anyway?)

A larger inverter, or two stacked inverters, would alleviate the problem and if you go with a watt-gobbling AC well pump, your PV/ wind equipment supplier will almost certainly try to convince you to buy two inverters. The choice is yours. I'll be the first to admit that a lot of families have trouble trying to run a large well pump with a single inverter, but in all likelihood the problem lies more with the pump than the inverter.

This is because all AC well pumps are not created equal; some require more power to start than others. Your pump installer should be made aware of the limitations of your inverter(s), and should be able to sell you a pump that falls within the parameters set by the inverter manufacturer.

Specifically, you will want a pump that requires a separate starting box outside the well (inside the mechanical room), rather than a pump that has the starting circuitry built into the motor casing. A simple relay-type starting box will work better with an inverter than an electronic one.

Also, if you use a 240-volt transformer to supply power to the well pump, it is less work for the inverter if you place the transformer between the pressure switch and the starting box, rather than between the inverter and the pressure switch.

Explain these things to your pump installer. He or she should know exactly what your concerns are and how to remedy any potential problems. If not, there are always other installers down the road.

> **Rainwater Collection**
> Rainwater from your roof can provide an amazing amount of water: a $1/2$" of rain falling on a 1,200 square-foot roof is over 370 gallons of water.

DECISIONS, DECISIONS

It's not easy to weigh the pros and cons of all the different ways people have conceived to deliver water from the earth under your feet to the sink in your kitchen. Just when you think you have it all figured out, some intractable fact lurking in the shadows jumps out and trips you. Happens to me all the time.

Odd as it may seem, the best remedy for too many facts is more facts. Talk to people on every side of the issue, AC and DC. Talk to your neighbors. Talk to your well driller and your pump installer. Call the inverter manufacturer. Tell them all what your particular circumstances are.

Then follow your instincts. ∾

Log • ically  Solar

Heating a home in Arizona, even at 5,000 feet of altitude, is not nearly so problematic as cooling it. So when Roger and Kathryn Wirth decided to build a log home on 47 acres outside of Kingman, one of their primary concerns was to design a house that could stay reasonably cool throughout the long hot summer—without air conditioning. This is because their home site is five miles from utility power and it would've been a practical impossibility to meet an air conditioning system's severe energy demands with only an off-grid electrical system.

To keep cool naturally, Roger and Kathryn built their Expedition square-log home over an earth-cooled walkout basement, and included a covered porch that wraps around three sides of the house and keeps the harsh desert sun away from the walls. It's an idea that works; they only need to use their swamp cooler a couple of days a year, which is good, considering how much house they have to cool. Their home boasts three bedrooms and two baths on the 2,400-square-foot main and loft levels, and another bedroom and bath in the fully finished 1,400-square foot basement.

Still, it can get cold in the high desert, so the Wirths installed three fireplaces and a Vermont Castings woodstove. And, for those really chilly nights, a propane-fired forced-air heating system kicks in to pick up the slack.

As pleasing as the house itself has been, the renewable energy system has, until recently, fallen short of their expectations. The original system included a 400-watt Southwest Windpower turbine, a 1,240-watt array of Uni-solar modules mounted on the roof of the detached garage, a pair of Trace SW4024 inverters, and a bank of 24 Rolls L16-style batteries. The weak link in this impres-sive energy chain was the solar array—it was simply too small to charge the batteries and, at the same time, drive a well pump and otherwise power a large home with two electric refrigerators. Nor does it help that the pair of inverters together consume 0.72 kWh per day just to keep themselves in operation.

In 2006, following a fair bit of deliberation (Roger and Kathryn are both lawyers, after all) the couple finally decided to more than double the solar output by adding 1,600 watts of Sanyo modules on a pole-mounted array that makes for easy snow removal and seasonal adjustment. "It has made all the difference in the world," Roger later told me. "Previously we seldom topped out the batteries, but now we do pretty much every day."

It was a pricey addition—$11,000, including installation—but worth every penny. That's because Arizona sunsets are far more beautiful when, at the end of the day, you have the satisfied feeling of knowing that the glowing red orb on the western horizon has given you enough energy that day to get you safely through the star-studded, desert night.

House 2,400 square feet on main level and loft, 1,400 square-foot basement; square-logs
Heating woodstove, 3 fireplaces, propane-fired forced air
Water pumped by PV system from 273-foot well
Refrigeration two electric refrigerators
Solar array 2,840 watts
Wind turbine Southwest Windpower Air-403
Inverter 2 Trace SW4024
Batteries 24 Rolls Surrette S460
Backup power 12-kilowatt, propane-fired Cumins generator, wired for automatic start

February 2001

We need a railing around the loft opening and the stair, but since we are both pretty tired of peeling logs, sanding and staining, Rex suggests that we incorporate copper tubing with the log spindles [35]. It is a wonderful marriage of wood and metal. I patina the copper to give it that aged, dark look before we assemble copper spindles in between every log spindle.

We add tongue-&-groove boards to the lower half of the framed walls upstairs, finish trimming the windows and add some mop boards...a sizeable job! Interior doors are next, and then two coats of clear finish for everything.

A common misconception of those who are building a house for the first time is that once the drywall is hung, you'll be moving in soon. I guess that'd be true if you could sub-out all the finishing details, but it's taking us forever. That dim light, however, at the end of the tunnel is getting brighter every day!

March 2001

With radiant floor heat, we choose to float our hardwood floor above it so it can expand and contract as it warms and cools. After much research and shopping, we choose an engineered floor from Sweden—Kahrs is the brand. An exotic wood is my first choice, but the price is too steep. We'll settle for a red oak with a super tough finish (for the dogs, you know).

First we make sure the great-room floor is level and fill any spots that are not. The flooring assembles easily, and the best part of this job is that the boards are all stained and finished...no need to do anything else except install matching stair nosing and trim boards where it meets the tile and carpet. To cover the edges around the log walls (which are very irregular) and still allow for expansion, we chink. It looks better than I thought it would when Rex first suggested it.

I try my hand at tiling the odd-shaped hearth for the wood stove [36]. Rex then trims it with small log poles. Another project to check off the list!

March 2001 continued

The cabinets are tricky to hang on the irregular log walls. We use lots of shims to get them just perfect. The island is customized with tongue-&-groove boards on three sides and log posts on each corner. Then we set the countertops, hang the microwave over the stove, and tile a backsplash [37]. A few closet rods to put up, and we can hang clothes. We hook up the front-loading washer and gas dryer. Now I don't need to drag all the wash to a laundromat, 45 minutes away!! These conveniences really make a woman happy!

37

I take a deep breath before attempting to tile the shower walls and bathroom countertop. I'm happy to report that it turned out well. Now I can call the plumber to hook up the final fixtures.

Rex hangs the light fixtures, and wires all of the outlets and switches, after many hours of trying to figure out how the ex-electrician ran the wires for our 3-way and 4-way switches.

March 26: the county inspector gave us the okay to move in with a temporary certificate of occupancy. Only 3 more inspections to go (wildfire, electrical final and then the FINAL).

We are ready to clear out that storage unit in town. And wouldn't you know it, the day we move the piano, couch, bed, and tons of other stuff, it starts snowing a few miles out of town. It snows and snows. We barely make it up the mountain with our trailer, but that's a story in itself. The mountain really has a way of testing anyone who wishes to live here.

April 2001

April is a month for sleeping and unpacking, and thoroughly enjoying our obsession of the past 3 years. The spaciousness and conveniences most people take for granted (like indoor toilets) are appreciated daily.

The high point of April: the state electrical inspector finally says the wind and solar systems (and all of the AC wiring) are up to code, and we can really live here.

CHAPTER 20

FINISH WORK:
MAKING YOUR HOUSE A HOME

Running the Final Mile, in Style

Anyone who has ever built a home can tell you: the finish work can be the most tedious, but also a rewarding part, of the project. Unlike the structural work, when at the end of the day you can look at what you've done and feel a sense of accomplishment, with finish work it seems that all you see is what you *haven't* done. That's because finish work is more exacting and therefore more time consuming. It is a fact that you can frame, sheath and shingle a roof in a fraction of the time it takes to insulate it, hang, tape and texture the drywall, then paint the ceiling. That's just the way it is. The good part is, when you're done, you're done.

It is not the intent of this chapter to teach you skills you do not already possess. That would be folly. Entire books have been written on many of the subjects touched on here. But there are numerous considerations unique to log homes, and I would be remiss if I didn't take the time to point them out in the course of this whirlwind tour of the work that remains to be done.

HANGING AND FINISHING DRYWALL—
WITHOUT LOSING YOUR MIND

I've never considered hanging and finishing drywall to be my idea of a good time, so here are a few tricks for hanging, texturing and painting drywall that may save you a lot of time and aggravation, a possible domestic spat over the mounting cost of ruined wall board, and may even make your house look better in the process.

FITTING DRYWALL BETWEEN PURLINS

LaVonne and I spent a lot of time butchering wallboard to fit between the purlins in the loft ceiling until we hit upon the right technique. Since the purlins curved inward toward the rafters, it was impossible to get a tight fit of drywall between them. Any sheet that would fit between the wide parts of the purlins was too narrow to hide the gaps between the edge of the sheet and the purlin once it was in place.

After insulating, Rex screws the ceiling drywall to the rafters. The center seam of drywall is visible near his elbow.

Then we realized we were making our lives miserable trying to do too much at once. Wouldn't an extra joint in the middle be preferable to large gaps at the edges? We changed our tactics: we began by cutting a full sheet of drywall lengthwise down the middle. Then I chalked a line on the rafters, midway between two purlins, and measured the distance from the chalk line to the purlin at 8 or 10 inch intervals. LaVonne plotted these measurements on the cut edge of each half sheet and then connected the dots. We cut off the excess, and had a perfect fit when we pushed the cut edge into the purlin and laid the long tapered edge against the chalk line. Repeating the process on the other side of the line gave us a tight fit at both purlins and an easy-to-finish tapered joint in the middle. (By design, our purlins are less than 4 feet apart; less than the width of a sheet of drywall.)

SCRIBING DRYWALL INTO A LOG WALL

If you've ever hung drywall before, you know that you should avoid butting a cut edge against a factory edge, if at all possible. But it isn't easy to make the factory edge break on a stud if you have to scribe a cut edge to fit against a log wall (that is, a log wall *without* a kerf to hide the edge of the wall board). Here's how to do it:

Measure the distance between the deepest crack on your log wall (between two logs) to the center of the stud where the drywall will be seamed. Cut the sheet at this length and place the cut edge next to the log wall, so the tapered factory edge is near the stud. Now scribe along the log wall, tracing the pattern of the logs onto your drywall. Cut along the scribe line carefully. (A small jigsaw works much better for curvy cuts than a drywall handsaw, and is less likely to accidentally break off the weaker parts of the curve. To make it really easy, try a RotoZip®.)

LaVonne scribes drywall to fit around the log wall.

APPLYING TEXTURE BY HAND

Once the drywall is taped and sanded, it's ready for texture. You could rent a texture machine or use textured paint, but for a finish to truly accentuate the majesty of the logs, try doing it by hand.

This is a job better left to one person, preferably the artist in the family. For our texture compound, we used off-the-shelf joint compound, silica sand to give it a gritty look and feel, and a little water. LaVonne applied it with a mason's finishing trowel, slapping random-sized globs against the wall (in a random fashion) and then smoothed it out with quick, slashing motions. She developed her technique inside a basement closet, then polished her skills in the electrical room. By the time she got to the areas anyone would actually see, she was admiringly proficient.

The result was even better than we'd hoped for: eye-catching in a subtle way. No two places on the walls or ceilings are the same, yet they all blend together into a cohesive whole. (And I'm beginning to sound like an art critic, so I'll move on to something else.)

ACCENTS WITH PAINT

The idea of covering her beautiful texture with a single, uniform color of paint was an insult to LaVonne's sensibilities. So, after applying a primer coat and one coat of off-white paint, she went back with a sponge (a real sponge, like from the bottom of the ocean) and lightly (and, again, randomly) daubed on splotches of paint of a slightly different color. For the first go-round she used a light tan, then a light gray tint for the *pièce de résistance*.

She picked her shades well. The best way I can describe the effect is to say that you "feel" the contrasts, without actually being

LaVonne's Verities

If you are still HAPPILY MARRIED when you are ready to move into your home, you've married the right one.

consciously aware of them. And yet it's as plain as day to anyone who knows what to look for. Good job, hon!

WAINSCOTING

The closet and bathroom walls in the loft have a wainscoting of tongue & groove pine boards, and vertical log posts on the corners.

Even the most original of drywall finishes can get a bit monotonous if it's not broken up with other elements. The same goes for logs. So, to enhance the richness of the interior, we installed wainscoting in a few key locations: the stairwell leading to the basement, two interior walls of the office, the long wall outside the upstairs closet and bathroom, and around the kitchen island. We found a supply of 1 x 4 tongue & groove, beetle-killed pine (with swirls of blue, grey and brown) at a local sawmill. It's a nice accent.

INTERIOR DOORS, KITCHEN CABINETS AND COUNTERTOPS

By this point you have almost certainly come to the realization that what looks good in a frame house in town is not what you had in mind for your log home in the country. This is especially true of doors. LaVonne found a local door company that special ordered tongue & groove pine doors for the main floor and loft. They also ordered wrought iron door handles to complete the effect. Everyone asks us if we made the doors ourselves, which is exactly the look we wanted.

What holds true for doors is equally true for kitchen cabinets. Off-the-shelf cabinets in a log home are about as discordant as plastic seat covers in a Porsche. We got bids from several custom cabinet makers. Surprisingly, the only company willing to built the cabinets exactly as we wanted them (tongue & groove knotty pine, to match the interior doors) also came in with the best price.

Getting the kitchen cabinets to fit against a log wall is not nearly as difficult as you may think, though it will require a certain amount of time and patience. You'll find yourself chiseling in some places, and shimming in others. The nice part is, you won't have to worry about finding wall studs to sink your screws into. (See *Chapter 14: More Settling Issues* when hanging cabinets on log walls that are still settling.)

We just couldn't put Formica countertops over our beautiful knotty-pine cabinets. Nor did we want to pay for granite or marble. Tile was an attractive option, but we didn't want to deal with cleaning grout lines over the years. We needed something simple and solid that didn't draw attention to itself. After a great deal of searching, we found a composite material called Fireslate; a dense, manufactured stone that seems to be impervious to anything that might happen to get spilled on it—after LaVonne sealed it a few times with Tung oil. (When I'm in the kitchen, a lot of stuff gets spilled.) The solid, gray-black color emanates strength and adds richness to the other elements of the house.

A CUSTOM LOG STAIR

I knew from the outset of our home-building project that the time would come when I would have to build a log stair. In my customary self-delusional manner, I told myself it would be easy, fun, and rewarding. I was right on one count: I love the stair, and therein lies my reward. But it certainly wasn't easy, and to say that it was "fun" is stretching things a bit.

Had it been a straight stair with a log stringer on either side it might have been more fun and easy than it actually was. But this stair wraps around a corner, with a landing at the midpoint. And rather than using a stringer against the wall, I notched each step into the wall for a cleaner, lighter look.

The treads were all cut from a single 13-inch log. I first cut it in half lengthwise with a chainsaw, then cut up the halves into twelve 4-foot sections. That left me with one extra tread for a single mistake (which I obligingly made).

Using a table saw, I removed the sharp edges from each tread and made them all a uniform width. I then used a hand-held power planer to smooth and level the surface of each tread, finishing with a belt sander and, finally, an orbital sander. After marking out the placement of each stair against the log wall (and checking and rechecking my measure-

Our finished stair to the loft.

ments) I built the landing with doweled and glued 2 x 6 planks over a 2 x 4 frame. Then I scribed and notched the treads into the log wall, securing each one with a pair of lag bolts angled into the wall through countersunk holes (which I later filled with dowels).

Rather than trying to guess at the length, I let all the treads run wild toward the inside of the room, and supported them with makeshift 2 x 4 stringers until they were all in place. I was then able to chalk lines and cut all the tread ends even, using a handsaw. After that, it was a fairly simple matter to push the log stringer against the cut ends, mark and chisel out the notches, then set the stringers into place and bolt them to the treads.

Then came the magic moment when, at last, I was able to remove the extension ladder that had provided access to the loft for over a year. That much, at least, was fun.

The Magic Number

For reasons no one fully understands, stairs with a combined tread width and riser height of $17^1/_2$ inches are the most comfortable. The Uniform Building Code sets the minimum tread width at 9 inches, and the maximum riser height at 8 inches. This adds up to 17, and is the steepest stair you can build and still meet code. If you've got the room, add another half inch to the tread width. If you've got lots of room, a $10^1/_2$ inch tread with a 7 inch rise makes a very easy stair.

THE DECK: HOW TO SAVE A TREE— AND A LOT OF WORK

When LaVonne told me she wanted to look at "designer" decking for our big wrap-around deck, I though she was spewing blasphemy. Didn't she know log homes required solid wood decking? Apparently not. Certain she would abandon her silly notion once she saw how ugly the stuff was, I decided to humor her. We shopped around one morning to see what was available. I didn't like any of it. But she saw possibilities I didn't and finally settled on a product called ChoiceDek Plus, by Weyerhaeuser.

I had to admit it was a crafty idea, making a weather-proof decking material out of oak chips and old plastic bags and milk jugs, but I still wasn't sold. Then she reminded me of the yearly ritual

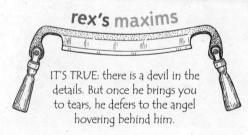

rex's maxims

IT'S TRUE: there is a devil in the details. But once he brings you to tears, he defers to the angel hovering behind him.

we'd established at our house at the farm: move all the furniture off the deck, barricade the stair to keep the dogs away, hose the deck down and let it dry, then spray $200 worth of sealant on the planks in two coats. My thinking clouded by far-from-fond memories, I finally gave in.

Much to my surprise, it turned out to be a self-serving act of capitulation. Not only was the decking a joy to lay down (no twists or curves), it took fewer screws because it never warps. Best of all, it *looks* good. After a couple of rainstorms and a little sunshine, it mellowed to a uniform weathered-wood shade of gray that contrasts nicely with the stained log walls, deck supports and railings. And since it never has to be stained or sealed, we'll make up the extra cost in a few years just by doing nothing.

We've completed the decking on the west side, and continue working on the south side. We stagger the cut ends to break on different joists.

LaVonne had other reasons. With a coy smile, she told me she likes it because it matches the chinking. As usual, she's right.

RAILINGS FOR STAIRS, DECKS AND LOFT

When you first see a deck or look up at a loft, the one thing that catches your eye is the railing. To a lesser degree, this is even true of handcrafted log stairs. So, if you've built something you really want to draw attention to, finish it off with a stout handcrafted railing.

What is a deck, after all, but a floor with gaps between the boards? It's plain and boring and it needs some help: a railing and support structure that belongs with your log home. We opted for heavy log supports and hand-peeled poles for the spindles and handrails.

We used leftover 9-inch logs—resting on concrete piers—to support our deck, and peeled corral poles for the railing. Since the Uniform Building Code now requires all railings to be built so that a 4-inch sphere cannot pass through it at any point, we decided that the railing would look too heavy if we were to use all wood spindles. (Besides, we were beginning to get a little tired of logs.) Instead, we ran two sections of $3/4$-inch copper tubing between each handmade pole spindle. It's a nice balance.

Usually, log railings are built in sections and then installed between the support posts, using mortise and tenon joints. It's a nice way to build a railing but a ton of work if it ever has to be replaced. With that in mind, we decided to position the support posts toward the edge of the deck and build the railing along the inside of it. It looks good and it provides a continuous handrail along the entire distance.

We built the railings for the loft and the stairs using the same motif of two parts copper to one part wood. LaVonne put an aged patina finish on all the interior copper spindles before assembly. Although Mother Nature will obligingly put her own patina on the exterior copper spindles, you'll avoid discoloration of the wood on the bottom rail if you do it yourself and then coat the spindles with a clear lacquer. It's also a good idea to drill a small ($^1/4$-inch) hole at the bottom of each mortise to allow rainwater to drain.

The log and copper spindles are ready to be fit into the top railings.

LOG ACCENTS

We found so many other uses for logs, poles and tree branches inside the house that I couldn't possibly list them all. Log uprights, with a quarter section removed lengthwise, work great for finishing off drywall corners. Similarly cut poles make a nice frame for a hearth. Half-poles (cut lengthwise on a table saw) worked splendidly to help trim the upstairs windows.

The most fun of all was in finding the free-form pieces to finish off the stair handrails and the horizontal section connecting the log columns supporting the deck stair. We spent many hours wandering through the woods near our house, bringing home every oddly-curved branch that appeared to have some promise.

Our searching eventually paid off. The stair handrails all terminate into eye-catching examples of naturally sculpted forest art, and the beautifully twisted and gnarled branch that greets you at the bottom of the deck stairs looks as though it grew in place.

Let your imagination roam free. Don't be stuck thinking "straight" when "curved" might add an extra pleasing dimension. You'll amaze yourself with your own cleverness long before you've peeled the last log, pole or branch. Just remember: there is no reason to settle for the ordinary when the extraordinary takes just a little extra reach.

A twisted branch finishes the stair rail.

MANY USES FOR TILE

Mosaic tile on the bathroom floor.

Besides being a good conductor of heat for in-floor heating systems, tile is an attractive floor covering, offering a pleasing contrast to a home that also has carpeting and wood flooring. Its surge in popularity in recent years is good news for the home builder, because there is practically no end to the colors, styles and patterns you can use to make a one-of-a-kind floor. But flooring is just the beginning of tile's many uses. We tiled the shower stall and bathroom countertop, plus the backsplash on the kitchen countertops. For our hearth, we first screwed a heat-resistant tile backer-board to $^3/_4$-inch plywood, then covered it with 12-inch tiles in a diagonal pattern. I used 3-inch logs (poles, in other words) with a quarter-section removed to form a border which covered the edges of the tiles.

While the basement door itself—an off-the-shelf steel door made to withstand the elements blowing in from the north—is certainly nothing to brag about, the natural stonework surrounding it is. To help the one blend into the other, we needed a bold transition between the stonework and the door. Our neighbor, Lane Dukart, provided it for us. The handcrafted architectural tiles he made boast a rich three-dimensional leaf pattern, blending into a headpiece with the Latin phase *Montani Semper Liberi* (People of the Mountain are Always Free) prominent in bas-relief.

Custom architectural tile by Lane Dukart surrounds our walk-in garage door (and dog door).

STONEWORK

The idea of doing our own stonework on the foundation walls on the north and east side of the garage was nothing we warmed up to overnight (or even over a year), but the bids we got—ranging from $15 to $20 per square foot (labor only; you supply the stone, please)—were enough to get us in a stone mason's frame of mind.

The brick ledge to support the stone was the first order of business. To make it, I first cut away the 2-inch foam insulation (that had served as the form for the concrete wall) at ground level in a 4-inch high strip. I then pounded short pieces of rebar into predrilled holes (filled with construction adhesive) in the foundation, spaced roughly one foot apart. A simple form— 6 inches by 4 inches—was filled with concrete to become the ledge.

That was the easy part.

All the stone—lichen-covered granite or "moss rock"—came from the hillside on the south side of our house. LaVonne had spent many hours the year before gathering the stone into piles, which she marked with blue flags. It was my job to hump it all up the hill. But even after all of her piles of stone were depleted, we still had only half as much as we needed. "It's good exercise," I kept telling myself, as I roamed farther and farther down the hill in search of flat, interesting rocks. (It might have been "exercise," but at the time the word "torture" kept gnawing its way through my overheated brain.)

The metal mesh is mortared for the next rock.

The rock is securely fastened with temporary wire ties, then the mortar between rocks is tooled smooth.

After the stone was all gathered, it was time to prepare the wall. We used lightweight expanded-steel mesh as a surface to grab the mortar, and to affix wires to hold the stone while the mortar hardened. Deck screws worked well to secure the mesh to the rim joist (which was first covered with felt paper), and to the plastic spacer ties in our concrete foundation forms.

At this point, we were inexplicably encouraged that all that remained to be done was to attach several tons of rock and mortar to the wall. It was late October when we began and the sun had long since lost interest in the north side of anything, including our wall. Cold yet motivated, we pushed on.

Any skilled stonemason would probably get a chuckle out of our methods, but since none of them, as far as we could determine, has ever written a book describing a better way to go about it, I'll explain what we did.

First, I'd lay the rock against the wall and mark around it with a felt marker. I'd then hook long pieces of wire into the mesh near the line, to later hold the stone. While LaVonne mortared inside the stone's outline on the wall, I mortared the backs of the stones. (We found the "Type S Mortar Mix" made by Quickcrete to contain a workable mixture of sand, Portland cement, and lime.)

I then pushed the stone against the wall, tapped it with a rubber mallet, and secured it with the wires I'd earlier attached to the mesh. (After the mortar was set, it was a simple matter to clip the wires flush with the mortar, using wire nips.) LaVonne used a small, $1/2$-inch trowel to smooth the joints between the stones, then cleaned off any excess with a sponge. We moved laterally whenever we could, to avoid placing too much vertical weight in one place on any given day.

It took us the better part of 3 weeks to cover 350 square feet of wall, but it was worth it. It may not be the best stone work we've ever seen, but it's better than most. And our total investment in materials and tools was under $200.

AND FINALLY.....

The myriad details of finishing a home are the very things that *make* your house a home. And the more you do yourself, the more the house becomes *your* home. When it's all said and done, it is the little things that you'll notice; the beveled glass panel above the bathroom door, or the small stained glass window on the stair landing that reflects rainbow hues on the handcrafted stair treads. Every time you step out of the shower, you'll see the decorative mosaic tile pattern in the floor.

It's the little things that warm your heart, and bring a smile to your face. And it's the little things that remind you that, at long last, you are through.

With that, LaVonne and I bid you adieu. May your new home be as grand as your dreams! ~

A stained glass window, created by LaVonne's mother, Glee Grau, adds wonderful color to our stair landing.

Photo: Mike Fox

May 2001

The deck construction begins in earnest. Since we really dislike staining redwood or cedar every other year, we choose a composite decking made of oak and plastic. The weathered gray color complements the tan/grey chinking. Visiting family members, from Costa Rica and North Dakota, are

put to work—framing up the joists, pouring concrete piers, screwing down the decking, building the stairs and putting up the log posts for the railing. Once again we use the copper pipe/log spindle design. The crowning touch is a natural archway made with a very twisted, multi-branched tree limb [38].

Summer 2001

Flag day, June 14th, is a great day to celebrate. After 19 inspections, we have the final signature from the last inspector. Yea!

I declare absolutely no more building for many months. We hang the hummingbird feeder and lounge in the hammock, keeping a wary eye out for wildfires. It's time now for long hikes, and maybe we'll even see a movie in town.

September 2001

The last two 50-foot logs have been gnawing away at my crazy husband all summer. Finally he can't take it any more, and declares that we will have a rope swing "like none other" in the

meadow below the house. I withhold any really serious comments, but he can sense my skepticism. Ummm. This will be interesting.

We drag the remaining two logs with chains hooked to the pickup and get them in their horizontal position. Hey, more logs to peel and stain. What a deal! Rex bolts the contraption together. I'm still skeptical.

Deep holes are dug in the meadow, and the log ends are treated so they won't rot. Erection day is conveniently scheduled while I'm in town. Neighbor Lane, whose sense of adventure matches Rex's, agrees to help. Well, the first attempt didn't go so well, but the 2nd try, with more guy wires firmly anchored to the tractor, works. Concrete is poured in the holes

around the logs, and four piers anchored in bedrock hold the four guy wires. Soon a platform is built. And between you and me, it's the biggest blast. I should never have doubted my husband's sense of fun. It is quite a ride to swing on a 40-foot rope over a meadow that drops away! [39]

That's me!

October 2001

The weather is turning, so we'd better get going on the last big project—stonework. It's freezing this October day when we hang the metal mesh on the foam walls. We've never done this before, but I keep saying, "It can't be that hard."

The biggest moss rocks go on the bottom row and, like a puzzle, we build up from there. Day after day we mortar and set rocks [40]. Someday I'll count the hundreds of rocks we set after 3 weeks of physically exhausting work. I have a new appreciation for anyone who does this, or any of the other trades, for a living. Rex will tell you I was not a happy camper at the end of every day, but I'm very proud we did it ourselves. The rough, dark, irregular stonework is the perfect compliment to the round, golden logs and light-colored stucco.

It is what I had pictured in my mind so many months and years ago. I am home, at last.

August 2002

Looking back over the past few years, I can easily recall the thousands of hours of work we put into our home (and believe me, it redefined my idea of 'work'), but the rewards far outweigh the sore muscles. Of course we take pride in our home; it is more than we hoped it would be. But more than just a happy home, we are rewarded by the nature that surrounds us, and provides for us. Being self-sufficient is a powerful, yet humbling feeling. Never again will we take for granted the conveniences of running water from the tap, the brightness of a light bulb, the ease of cooking and laundry... just to name a few.

Nature becomes very real when you live in the midst of it, and depend on it. We have a new appreciation for the winds that carry the hawks, the rising and setting of the sun, the changing of seasons, and every drop of rain that falls.

Life is as it should be.

ACKNOWLEDGMENTS
∼ thanks! ∼

No book is entirely the work of its authors, especially one that covers as much ground as this one. We have relied throughout on the kind assistance of people who know far more about particular disciplines than we ever will. In this sense, the adage, "it's not what you know, but who you know," rings loud and clear. To the book's credit, we have been blessed by knowing a large number of very capable people. Here are a few of them who have helped us in various ways.

For reading the manuscript and finding ways to make it better: Dave Masaitis, the most exacting home builder we've every known; Joe Bolte, who's helped me with every house, garage, cabin, barn, outhouse, doghouse and loafing shed I've built since 1980; Doug Pratt, former technical editor of Real Goods' *Sourcebook* and my co-author of *Got Sun? Go Solar*; Rex Bosworth, who builds homes in Montana with really big logs and makes really good drawknives; Gary Schroeder, president of Schroeder Log Home Supply; David Petroy from RMS Electric; and Steve Iwanicki, a friend who shares our love for nature.

For having the good judgment to be building their log homes at the same time we were writing this book: Josh French, John Benshoof, and Gregg and Donna Kernes.

For all the cool crane rides, so we could get bird's eye photos of John Benshoof's house as it was being erected, a special thanks to "Light Touch" Roland Younghein, owner of Rocky Mountain Boom.

For providing photos and valuable information: all the fine companies whose products are mentioned in these pages, even though they didn't try to buy us off with freebies.

We'd also like to thank our friends Mike Fox and Colorado history author Ken Jessen, whose photos, as always, are first-rate.

Nor can we forget everyone who helped with our home: neighbors, friends, family and subcontractors (at least the ones who finished the job).

And last, but certainly not least, we'd like to acknowledge two important family members: Inspector Micky, who dutifully monitored construction progress each morning, while Newt the Regulator made our work site safe by keeping the velociraptors and saber-toothed tigers at bay. They only asked for yummy dog food, a walk in the woods, and a few pats on the head each day for payment.

APPENDIX A — COSTS TO CONSIDER

Financing Fees
Engineering Fees
Land & Survey Fees
Building Plans & Permits

Site Prep
road work
clear building site
excavation

Foundation
footings/piers
walls
concrete flatwork
waterproof & backfill

Floors & Support
steel beams & posts
lumber (rim joists, floor joists,
    subflooring)
supplies (joist hangers, nails,
    bolts, screws, glue)
gypcrete

Logs & Delivery
logs or log kit
kit erection (crane, labor)
special log tools
supplies (spikes, drill bits)
chinking, backer rod, caulking

Roof System
special trusses
ridge beam, other logs
rafters
sheathing
roof vents, flashing
roof covering (shingles, tile,
    metal roof, etc.)
insulation, vapor barrier

subfascia, fascia
soffits
supplies (nails, hurricane clips)

Windows / Doors
windows
exterior doors
framing lumber
flashing, trim
supplies (caulking, screws)
skylights, light tubes

Exterior Finish
stonework, stucco, cedar sid-
    ing
drainage
decks/porches (decking mate-
    rial, railing, posts, joists,
    joist hangers, deck screws)
exterior stain/sealer
gutters & downspouts

Plumbing
labor (if subcontracted)
piping (water, gas/propane,
    vents)
kitchen sink, disposal
bathroom sinks, toilets, tub,
    shower
laundry hookups / vents
utility sink
fixtures
water heater
water softener
sump pump

Septic System
perc test
tank & piping
leach field
hookup

Water Well
drilling & casing
well pump
piping to house
pressure tank
cistern
hookup

Grid Utilities (if needed)
hookup fees for water, gas,
    sewer, phone, electricity

Electrical
permit fees
labor (if subcontracted)
house wiring
solar electric system
    solar modules & frame
    inverter(s)
    charge controller(s)
    DC disconnect(s)
    120-240 transformer
    meter
wind system
    turbine & charge controller
    tower, base & guy wires
    batteries & cables
    battery box, venting
exterior wiring (from solar
    and wind systems)
low voltage wiring
supplies (outlet boxes, cover
    plates, etc.)
fixtures (interior & exterior)
compact fluorescent light
    bulbs
lightning protection

continued

Heating Systems

solar hot water system (solar
  collectors, storage tank,
  piping, supplies)
main heating system & relat-
  ed materials (piping, ductwork, etc.)
auxiliary heat: fireplace, woodstove, masonry stove,
  corn/pellet stove, propane
  heater
hearth, chimney
fans: ceiling, bathroom,
  kitchen

Interior Finish

framed walls (lumber, drywall
  & tape)
ceiling (T&G or drywall)
insulation
wainscoting
paint & primer
trim boards
stain
interior doors & handles
kitchen cabinets
countertops, cabinets
bathroom vanities
closet rods, shelves

flooring materials, installation

Stairs & Railings
  interior & exterior

Appliances
stove, microwave
refrigerator, freezer
dishwasher
laundry: washer & dryer

Garage Doors & Openers
Landscaping

NOTES FOR OFF-GRID HOMES

Use compact fluorescent light bulbs...they add up to big energy savings. For example: if 6 bulbs are on for 5 hours a day; 60-watt incandescent bulbs will use 1,800 watt hours per day; 13-watt compact fluorescent bulbs will use only 390 watt hours.

Low-usage, high energy appliances (hair dryers, microwaves, coffer makers, etc.) are not much of a problem since they draw very little power when averaged out over time. You can also choose not to use them if you're low on power.

Invest in a new **refrigerator and/or freezer**. You'll be amazed at how much more energy-effi-cient they are. The typical new fridge now uses 80 percent less energy than models from the late 1980s and early 1990s. Do your research on *www.energystar.gov* before buying and always read those yellow tags!

If you want to cook when the grid is down, and you don't have battery backup, buy an **oven** with spark ignition instead of the typical glow bar. Glow bars use 300-400 watts ALL the time your oven is on. Peerless-Premier is one brand that is ideal for off-grid homes.

To conserve energy and water when washing clothes, a **front-loading clothes washer** is a must, as is a gas-fired clothes dryer. Better yet, use a clothesline or indoor rack for drying.

Instant (on-demand) water heaters, either gas or electric models, use 20 to 40 percent less energy because they only work when someone turns on the hot water faucet. They also last 30 to 40 years, reducing landfill and resource waste.

A **solar hot water** system uses NO energy (that you'll ever get a bill for). Combined with an instant water heater you've got the lowest-cost, and most ecologically responsible way to heat domestic hot water.

One watt delivered for one hour = **one watt-hour** | 1,000 watt-hours = one **kWh**
amps x volts = watts (*2 amps x 120 volts = 240 watts*)

APPENDIX B — RESOURCES

The information listed below will give you a good start in the right direction. The internet is an excellent tool for finding new information and resources in this ever-changing business of building and energy.

LOG HOME INFORMATION

Manufacturers of Chinking & Finishes
Perma-Chink Systems, Inc. www.permachink.com
Sashco www.sashco.com
Weatherall Company, Inc. www.weatherall.com

Suppliers: Log Tools/ Supplies/Chinking/Finishes
Bailey's, Inc. www.baileysonline.com
Bosworth Tools www.bosworthtools.com
Log Home Center & Supply
www.loghomecenter.com
Log Home Resource Center
www.loghomeresources.com
Log Home Store, Inc. www.aloghomestore.com
Schroeder Log Home Supply www.loghelp.com

Log Home Plans
Log home magazines an excellent source for ideas, in addition to these books:
Best Log Home Plans, Robbin Obomsawin
Log House Plans, B. Allan Mackie
Small Log Homes, Robbin Obomsawin
The Log Home Plan Book, Cindy Thiede with Heather Mehra-Pedersen

Log Home Building Schools
International Log Builders Association
www.logassociation.org/directory/schools.php
Lasko School of Log Building
www.laskoschooloflogbuilding.com
LogHomeLinks.com
www.loghomelinks.com/build.htm

Log Home Shows
Log Home & Timber Frame Expo
www.logexpo.com
The Log & Timber Home Shows & Seminars
www.thelogandtimberhomeshow.com

ORGANIZATIONS

American Solar Energy Society www.ases.org
International Log Builders Association
www.logassociation.org
Log Homes Council www.loghomes.org

REFERENCE WEBSITES

Database of State Incentives for Renewable and Efficiency www.dsireusa.org
Energy Star® www.energystar.gov
Find Solar www.findsolar.com
U.S. Solar Radiation Resource Maps
http://rredc.nrel.gov/solar/old_data/nsrdb/redbook/atlas
Wind Energy Maps/Tables
http://rredc.nrel.gov/wind/pubs/atlas/maps
http://rredc.nrel.gov/wind/pubs/atlas/tables

MAGAZINES

BackHome Magazine
www.backhomemagazine.com
Country's Best Log Homes
www.loghomesnetwork.com
Home Power
www.homepower.com
Log Home Living
www.loghome.com/loghomeliving
Log Homes Illustrated
www.loghomesnetwork.com
Mother Earth News
www.motherearthnews.com
Mountain Living
www.logandtimberstyle.com/mountain/index.html
Solar Today
www.solartoday.org

APPENDIX C — GENERAL BIBLIOGRAPHY

Aldrich, Chilson D., with Harry Drabik. *The Real Log Cabin*. Minneapolis, MN: Nodin Press, 1994.

Burch, Monte. *Complete Guide to Building Log Homes*. NY: Sterling Publishing Company, 1990.

Feirer, John L., and Gilbert R. Hutchings. *Carpentry and Building Construction, 3rd Ed.* Encino, CA: Glencoe Publishing Company, 1986.

Gipe, Paul. *Wind Power for Home and Business*. Post Mills, VT: Chelsea Green Publishing, 1993.

Glover, Thomas J. *Pocket Ref*. Littleton, CO: Sequoia Publishing, 2001.

Gundersen, P. Erik. *The Handy Physics Answer Book*. Detroit, MI: Visible Ink Press, a division of Gale Research, 1999.

Mackie, B. Allan. *The Owner-Built Log House*. Ontario, Canada: Firefly Books Ltd, 2001.

Mackie, B. Allan, and others. *Log Span Tables*. Canada: International Log Builders Association, 2000.

Muir, Doris, and Paul Osborne. *The Energy Economics and Thermal Performance of Log Houses*. Gardenvale, Quebec, Canada: Muir Publishing Company Ltd, 1983.

Phelps, Hermann. *The Craft of Log Building*. Ottawa, Ontario: Lee Valley Tools Ltd, 1982.

Stewart, John W. *How To Make your Own Solar Electricity*. Blue Ridge Summit, PA: Tab Books Inc., 1979.

Threthewey, Richard, with Don Best. *This Old House Heating, Ventilation and Air Conditioning*. New York: Little, Brown & Company, 1994.

Tiepner-Thiede, Cindy, and Arthur Thiede. *The Log Home Book*. Salt Lake City, Utah: Gibbs Smith, Publisher, 1993.

The Solar Electric House. Worthington, MA: New England Solar Electric Inc., 1998.

U.S. Department of Energy. *Home Wind Power*. Charlotte, Vermont: Garden Way Publishing, 1981.

APPENDIX D — SUGGESTED READING

We also recommend the following books:

Power With Nature: Alternative Energy Solutions for Homeowners, Rex A. Ewing

Got Sun? Go Solar: Get Free Renewable Energy to Power Your Grid-Tied Home, Rex A. Ewing and Doug Pratt

The Independent Home, Michael Potts

Log Homes Made Easy: Contracting and Building Your Own Log Home, Jim Cooper

The Passive Solar House, James Kachadorian

INDEX

Italic numbers refer to photos/illustrations